# Leonardo da Vinci

1452–1519

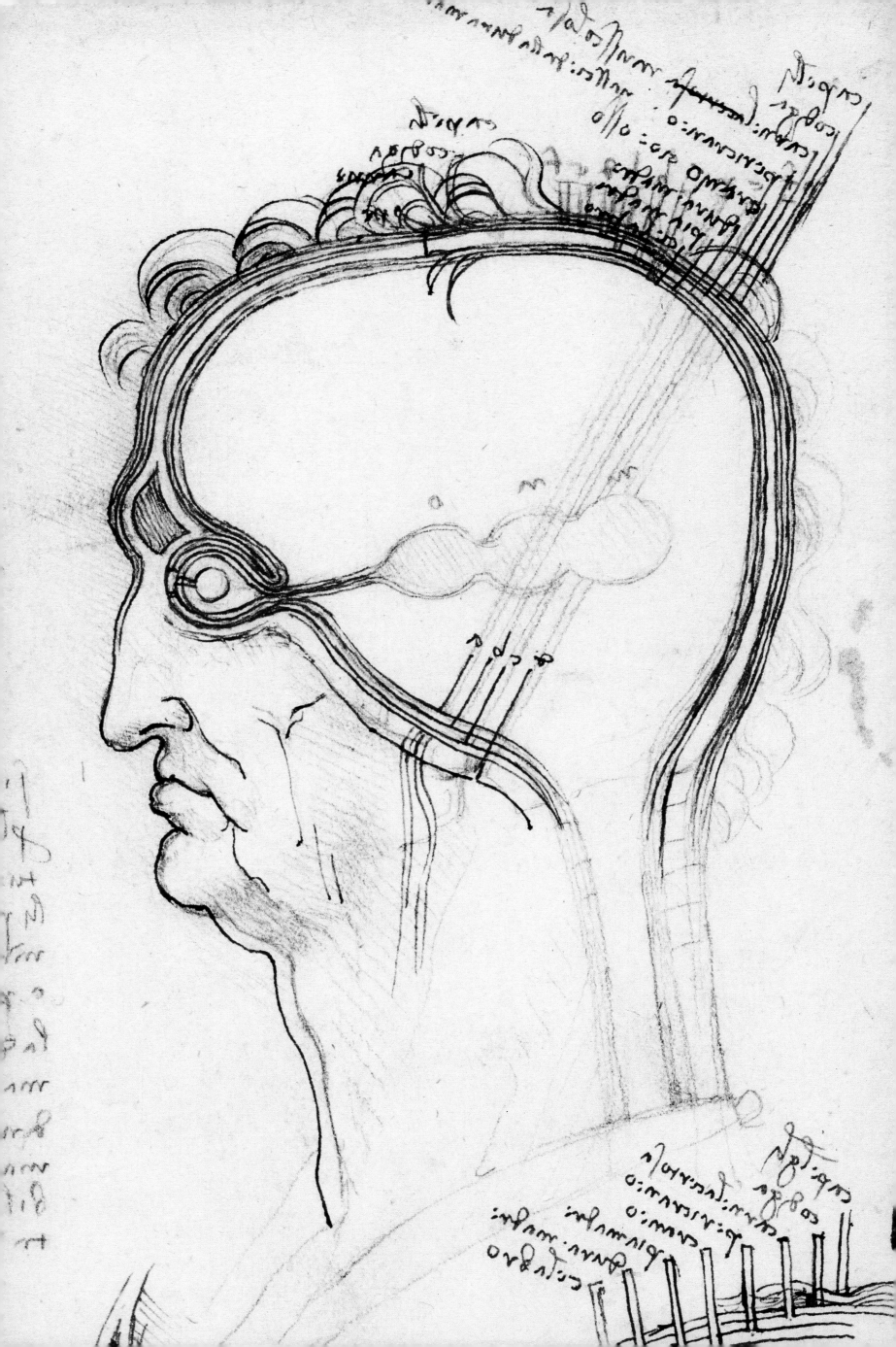

Frank Zöllner

# Leonardo da Vinci

## 1452–1519

Sketches and Drawings

**TASCHEN**

KÖLN  LONDON  LOS ANGELES  MADRID  PARIS  TOKYO

# Contents

   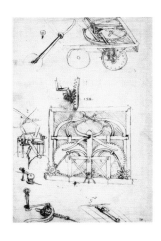 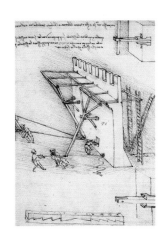

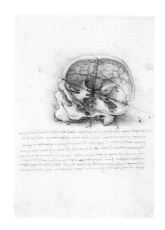

BIBLIOGRAPHY

# Perfecting the art of drawing

It is clear from even a brief glance at the illustrations in this volume that Leonardo da Vinci's drawings are characterized by enormous variety in terms of technique, formal vocabulary and subject matter. His work ranges in scope from the mostly early studies executed in metalpoint on prepared paper (Cat. 103) to the impulsive chalk drawings of his mature years, from the animated figure studies, which he sketched with a pen and a brush, to his extraordinarily disciplined pen-and-ink studies in the fields of anatomy (Cat. 148) and technology (Cat. 321). Leonardo seems to have been the first to make systematic use of red chalk and over the course of his career would develop a distinctive range of graphic techniques, such as hatching, which follows the form, through which he invoked rounded volumes with particular plasticity (Cat. 211).

The significance of Leonardo's variety of technique for the process of artistic invention can be seen, for example, in his preliminary studies for the *Last Supper*. Thus he develops the overall arrangement of the figures and their poses in a traditional pen drawing (Cat. 11), but opts for the two softer media of black and red chalk in his studies of heads for individual Apostles (Cat. 12–15), allowing him to render their facial expressions in greater and more differentiated detail. Indeed, the potential of red chalk to achieve certain effects is something that seems to have interested Leonardo from an early stage; he experimented with this medium in particular in his technical studies relating to the Sforza Monument (Cat. 39, 40) and returned to it again after 1500 (Cat. 20, 25–27, 60, 72, 73, 75).

There may be a connection between Leonardo's growing use of red chalk (here represented by some 45 drawings) and his diminishing use of traditional metalpoint (of which some 35 examples are included here), which appears hardly at all in his surviving œuvre after 1500. A clear increase can also be identified in his use of black chalk (represented here in some 110 drawings), a medium that Leonardo employed far less in the years before 1500 (Cat. 76, 148, 154, 216) than in the two decades afterwards and that often appears in conjunction with pen, the technique Leonardo deployed most frequently of all. In his choice of red and black chalk, Leonardo acknowledged his interest in the creation of soft transitions between light and shade; chalk permitted more suggestive tonal values, an effect that could be heightened

yet further in the case of finer-grained, red chalk drawings executed on paper coated with a reddish preparation (Cat. 13, 14, 20, 25–27). There are parallels, furthermore, between the possibilities offered by chalk drawing and those inherent in oil painting, a technique that Leonardo took to new levels. Here, too, the artist aimed at smooth transitions between areas of light and dark. The red chalk drawing similarly represented a medium within which he could explore these effects.

Although the young Leonardo underwent an artist's apprenticeship, and although his talents in particular as a painter contributed to his early fame, only a fraction of his surviving drawings relate to projects for paintings, sculptures or buildings. By far the largest part of his graphic work is devoted to problems that are related to his activities as an artist either only indirectly (as in the case of physiognomy, anatomy, mechanical engineering, light and shade, for example) or not at all (as in the case of cartography, military engineering, flight and flying machines). It seems that Leonardo did not always find it easy to draw lines between his various fields of interest. Several of his drawings make it clear that he was often working on quite different problems at the same time. This emerges from a large sheet from his mature years (320 x 446 mm; Cat. 105), on which a number of geometric studies are joined by drawings of the human figure and sketches of plants, clouds and horses. Although examples of such sheets (cf. Cat. 11, 16, 71, 286) make up only a small proportion of Leonardo's surviving graphic œuvre as a whole, there is plenty of evidence that others of the same kind have since fallen victim to the scissors. Amongst the drawings of so-called character heads, for example, we find a large number of fragments not much bigger than a postage stamp; the sheets from which these tiny sketches were once cut would probably have looked very similar to Cat. 105, on which we also find the bust of an old man in profile.

Many of these small fragments undoubtedly bear witness to early and sometimes misguided attempts by later generations to put Leonardo's surviving works into some kind of order. When, for example, Pompeo Leoni (*c.* 1533–1608) got hold of several manuscripts and a large number of drawings by Leonardo in the 1580s, he proceeded to demonstrate just how far-reaching such incursions could be. Leoni namely glued the loose sheets into two very large al-

bums, devoting one to studies relating to engineering and machinery and the other to Leonardo's artistic drawings and anatomical studies. The album dedicated to engineering has since become known as the Codex Atlanticus, while the second contained the drawings today housed in the Royal Library in Windsor Castle. Since countless numbers of Leonardo's original sheets of drawings contained both artistic and technical studies, Leoni repeatedly resorted to scissors in order to ensure the consistency of his system. This means that several fragments in the Windsor Leoni volume actually belong in the Codex Atlanticus, which is today housed in the Pinacoteca Ambrosiana in Milan.

Even if Leoni's drastic measures all but defy comprehension today, the desire to introduce order into Leonardo's graphic œuvre remains understandable. The difficulties this presents, and the fact that Leonardo himself was fully aware of the disorganized state of his papers, emerges from a note that the almost 60-year-old artist wrote at the start of one of his manuscripts: "Begun at Florence, in the house of Piero di Braccio Martelli, on the 22nd day of March 1508. And this is to be a collection without order, taken from many papers which I have copied here, hoping to arrange them later each in its place, according to the subjects of which they may treat [...]" (RLW § 4). This New Year's resolution of 1508 (in Florence, the new year began at the start of spring) echoes the impression that can easily be given by the originally largely unordered mass of drawings. It is not surprising, therefore, that the task of presenting Leonardo's legacy has caused many a headache over the years. His œuvre is largely a sketch, a plan, a concept. Tipping the scales opposite a dozen or so original paintings are thousands of sketches of varying degrees of elaboration and notes for the most part recorded in mirror-writing.

Leonardo's habit of using mirror-writing in his notebooks and manuscripts, in other words of writing from right to left, for centuries cast a particular air of secrecy over his legacy. He was regularly suspected of having deliberately veiled his writings so as to prevent unauthorized access to his ideas and inventions. While the sense of mystery with which this surrounded his work may have served to heighten its fascination, Leonardo's reasons for choosing mirror-writing seem to have been chiefly practical in nature: he was left-handed, and if he wrote in the normal fashion from left to right he risked smudging the wet ink with his hand. Leonardo evidently made no secret of his reversed method of writing, since the early sources (Vasari, 1568, IV, p. 35) regularly mention that his notes are best read with a mirror.

Thanks to characteristics such as his mirror-writing, but not least also due to the sheer volume of his surviving drawings, Leonardo has bequeathed to us a body of work that follows the opposite pattern to the œuvre of most of his contemporaries. Whereas artists such as Ghirlandaio, Botticelli and Perugino are known to us in dozens of paintings but just a few drawings, the opposite is true of Leonardo, by whom we have a huge number of works on paper and just a handful of paintings. This cannot be explained simply by the fact that Leonardo left his drawings and manuscripts to Francesco Melzi, a conscientious pupil who fervently protected the works he had inherited against loss or destruction. Equally decisive is the fact that Leonardo produced very little as a painter, but an extraordinary amount as a draughtsman. In view of the wealth and variety of his drawings, it might appear necessary and sensible to organize Leonardo's sketches and notes chronologically. In the case of a small selection of drawings, this solution might even be feasible, but a serious attempt to impose such a chronological order upon Leonardo's entire graphic œuvre would soon come to a dead end. How do you date single sheets such as Cat. 105 discussed above, for example, which combine a number of sketches that appear to have been executed over an extended time span? In response to this problem, art historians have sought to extrapolate, from the style of Leonardo's drawing and writing, criteria by which his works can be dated. The success of this method is limited, however, since the chronological framework that can be built up from drawings dated by Leonardo himself (Cat. 104, 149, 229, 240, 336), from sketches datable with reference to external events (Cat. 71, 282), from studies that arose in connection with documented projects (cf. Ch. 1–2) and from dated manuscripts is still full of gaps when it comes to dating other drawings. Dating works of art on the basis of stylistic criteria is always a matter of interpretation, moreover, and often gives rise to controversy. The situation is further complicated by the fact that Leonardo is known to have experimented with and developed certain subjects and motifs over lengthy periods of time. An obvious example is the

background group of battling horsemen in the *Adoration of the Magi* (1481/82), which subsequently forms the basis of the central group in the *Battle of Anghiari* (1504–1506), but this same practice can be found in most spheres of Leonardo's art and science. Hence earlier attempts to order Leonardo's graphic œuvre into a rigid chronology led to a distorted view of his working method. In view of this fact, many of the dates given here should be understood simply as starting-points for further discussion.

The most sensible option thus still appears to be to present Leonardo's graphic œuvre not in chronological order but in terms of subject matter. In the present volume, this has been kept as specific as possible. Rather than generalized categories such as "Art" and "Science" or "Microcosm" and "Macrocosm", the headings chosen are those that Leonardo himself identified as specific areas of his research. This method follows on from the work of Arthur E. Popham, who in 1946 set the standard with his *Drawings of Leonardo da Vinci*, bringing together some 300 black-and-white illustrations and a detailed commentary. With its considerably larger number of reproductions, however, most of them in colour, and with its more differentiated distribution of the drawings into 16 groups, the present catalogue allows us to take a more precise look at Leonardo's spheres of interest and working methods. In contrast to Popham's selection, moreover, greater attention has been devoted to Leonardo's manuscripts, within which the lion's share of his drawings appear. This has been proved all the more necessary by the rediscovery of the Codices Madrid I and II in 1965 (Cat. 38–40, 259, 302–321). Also included are studies from Leonardo's manuscripts that convey an impression of the series into which Leonardo himself organized his drawings (Cat. 164–184, 270–280, 302–321). Even in the case of the very large number of drawings reproduced here, it has of course been necessary to be selective. One victim of this selection process, which was based not least on aesthetic arguments, have been diagrammatic illustrations, which are difficult to understand without a knowledge of Leonardo's accompanying writings.

The short essays prefacing each chapter introduce the subject area and its position within Leonardo's œuvre and shed light on the artist's method via detailed analyses of individual sheets. They thereby start from the premise that Leonardo's graphic legacy

not only represents an expression of his artistic talent, but also bears witness to his intensive study of almost all the phenomena of the visible world. Characteristic of this study was not simply Leonardo's polemic attitude towards the body of knowledge represented by established authorities (RLW § 12, 1159; Ms. I, fol. 102 [Fumagalli, 1952, p. 43]; Cat. 172), but also his desire to perfect his own abilities as a draughtsman and thus to assert the primacy of the image (MK 25). For the image was, for Leonardo, the dominant medium of all communication.

*Johannes Nathan/Frank Zöllner*

**Literature:** Meder, 1919; Popp, 1927; Berenson, 1938; Popham, 1946 (1994); Pedretti, 1957; Clark/Pedretti, 1968; Ames-Lewis, 1981, 1990; Ames-Lewis/Wright, 1983; Edgerton, 1985; Kemp, 1989; *Il disegno*, 1992; Nathan, 1995; Bambach, 1999.

# 1 Drawings and sketches for surviving or documented paintings

One of the first drawings in this catalogue, a study for the raised arm of the angel in the *Annunciation* attributed to Leonardo in the Uffizi, is seemingly unspectacular (Cat. 3). But the sheet, which measures a modest 78 x 92 mm, embodies several features typical of Leonardo's graphic work. The small drawing is in fact the only surviving study for the *Annunciation*. This in itself makes it characteristic of Leonardo's œuvre, for although the master undoubtedly executed dozens of preliminary drawings for each of his paintings, there are several pictures – including, for example, the *Mona Lisa* – for which not a single study has survived. When examining Leonardo's drawings, therefore, we must constantly remind ourselves of the enormous percentage of works that have been lost. Even those sheets that are still extant have not all come down to us in their original form. Thus the study for the *Annunciation*, like many other drawings, has been trimmed, as evident from the fragment of a red chalk sketch still visible in the upper right-hand corner – probably part of a study of a head. The small pen drawing was probably cut out of a larger sheet by a later collector, or may even have been snipped out by the artist himself, perhaps because he thought it particularly worth remembering or keeping. One of the purposes of this drawing is namely to portray the angel's sleeve in a manner that expresses the motion of the arm beneath.

Leonardo's interest in this artistic problem manifested itself in other drawings (see below) and in many details within his paintings, and equally, too, in his theoretical writings on how to depict the movements of the human body and the accompanying human emotions: "The good painter has to paint two principal things, that is to say, man and the intention of his mind. The first is easy and the second difficult, because the latter has to be represented through gestures and movements of the limbs" (MK 388).

As in so many other passages within his treatise on painting, Leonardo here seeks to convey fundamental insights into the creative process – an aim that also underlies his artistic production. Thus Leonardo's drawings, even more than his paintings, shed light on his thought processes as an artist. Amongst his thousands of extant studies, only a relatively small number of drawings serve the evolution of a planned painting or sculpture; instead, Leonardo devoted by far the largest part of his graphic œuvre to investigating the fundamentals of artistic design and to evolving formal solutions that did not necessarily have a direct practical application. Even in sheets that can be assigned to a specific project or work, we often find him processing ideas to which he would return again at a later date.

Thus the close interaction between the human figures in a *Study for the Benois Madonna* (Cat. 4), for example, anticipates the sketches for the *Virgin and Child with St Anne* (Cat. 16, 18, 19), while a study of three men in animated discussion, executed in relation to the *Adoration of the Magi* (Cat. 1), shows a theme that would also be granted importance in the *Last Supper* (Cat. 11). As already suggested, the small study of an arm at the start of this catalogue similarly focuses upon a detail that – in different forms – would claim the artist's attention again and again (Cat. 21). Hence it is possible that Leonardo himself cut the study out of an originally larger sheet. We know for a fact that the artist was not careless with his drawings, but collected them and bequeathed a large number of them to his most faithful pupil, Francesco Melzi.

One of the reasons why Leonardo collected and kept his drawings can perhaps be deduced from a drawing for the first version of the *Virgin of the Rocks*. The *Study for the Head of a Girl* (Cat. 7) could hardly come closer to the corresponding head of the angel in the final painting, and its plasticity and the precision with which the young woman fixes the viewer with her gaze suggest that Leonardo was here drawing from a real-life model. Those who take the trouble to view the study in a mirror, however, will be struck by its astonishing resemblance to the *Portrait of Cecilia Gallerani*, the mistress of Leonardo's later patron, Ludovico Sforza. Although Cecilia's gaze and shoulders follow a different direction to the drawing, the comparison suggests that, when Leonardo came to create the portrait of 1489/90, he remembered his work on the *Virgin of the Rocks* (from 1483) and opted to re-use the facial type he had employed earlier. Just as Ludovico Sforza was guided by a certain ideal of beauty in choosing his mistresses, so Leonardo oriented himself towards the same ideal in formulating the *Virgin of the Rocks* and the *Portrait of Cecilia Gallerani*. Leonardo's drawing reveals his ability to solve an initially very specific task in such a way that the result can serve as a prototype for other applications.

In view of Leonardo's ability to develop an ideal type and use it more than once, it is understandable why sketches of details or studies for individual figures (and especially for idealized figures) are far harder to assign to a specific painting than drawings containing a number of figures, which often portray an entire compositional sequence or isolated excerpts from such a sequence. This is true of the rapidly sketched figure studies (Cat. 2) that can be related to the *Adoration of the Magi* (1481/82) and in which Leonardo experiments, for example, with the grouping of expressively gesturing figures (esp. Cat. 1). A pen drawing of the *Last Supper* (Cat. 11), probably

*Altogether, his genius was so wonderfully inspired by the grace of God, his powers of expression were so powerfully fed by a willing memory and intellect, and his writing conveyed his ideas so precisely, that his arguments and reasonings confounded the most formidable critics.*

GIORGIO VASARI, 1568

▶ 1 **Figural Studies for the Adoration of the Magi (Joseph and Two Shepherds and Sketches for a Christ Child),** c. 1481
*Pen and ink over metalpoint on purple prepared paper,*
*173 x 111 mm*
*Hamburg, Hamburger Kunsthalle,*
*Inv. 21488*

executed more than ten years later, shows Leonardo making use once again of his earlier compositional studies from the period of the *Adoration of the Magi*. Leonardo here follows the same procedure of dividing up a populated composition into sub-groups – a system he employs even in the wall-painting itself, which essentially comprises a central figure and two flanking groups of figures in action. Leonardo's interest in creating focal points of action with just a few figures is even more pronounced in his studies for the *Virgin and Child with St Anne* (Cat. 16–19), the *Battle of Anghiari* and the *Leda* (Cat. 28–30).

Particularly noteworthy with regard to Leonardo's compositional method is the sheet relating to the *Virgin and Child with St Anne* in the British Museum (Cat. 16). The main study is a tangled confusion of strokes virtually unique in pre-modern graphic art. In an underdrawing exploring countless alternatives in black chalk, Leonardo tried to fix the most convincing solution in pen and ink and with a brush. The final composition was then transferred through the paper onto the other side (Cat. 17), it would seem by laying the sheet face-up on a dye-coated support and then using a stylus to trace over the relevant outlines of the drawing on the front. The pressure of the stylus caused the black dye on the support to imprint itself onto the back of the sheet.

The intensity of Leonardo's work on this drawing, with its apparently impenetrable layers of strokes, recalls his advice on how to stimulate the mind to new inventions, which in turn takes up a theme found in classical literature (Philostratus, *Life of Apollodorus of Tyana*): "I shall not refrain from including among these precepts a new aid to contemplation, which, although seemingly trivial and almost ridiculous, is none the less of great utility in arousing the mind to various inventions. And this is, if you look at any

walls soiled with a variety of stains, or stones with variegated patterns […], you will therein be able to see a resemblance to various landscapes graced with mountains, rivers, rocks, trees, plains, great valleys and hills in many combinations. Or again you will be able to see various battles and figures darting about, strange-looking faces and costumes, and an endless number of things that you can distil into finely rendered forms. And what happens with regard to such walls and variegated stones is just as with the sound of bells, in whose peal you will find any name or word you care to imagine" (MK 572). Leonardo thereby adds a cautionary note: "First make sure, however, that you have fundamentally mastered the depiction of the parts of the things that you would like to set down" (TPL 66).

Ernst H. Gombrich rightly linked these recommendations with Leonardo's studies for the *Virgin and Child with St Anne*, but he wrongly saw in them a complete break with the draughtsmanship of the past. For the "parts" that Leonardo mentions towards the end are nothing other than the building-blocks of all composition – parts of the body, faces, figures and figural groups. These form the basic vocabulary of drawing, without mastery of which no artist can orient himself within the chaos of a stained wall or variegated rock. Just as for his teachers, therefore, the technical skills honed through a draughtsman's training played an eminently important role for Leonardo, too. He was able to lend these skills a whole new dimension, however, by applying them to a compositional method of increased sophistication. He refined his method to such a degree that, with just a few strokes of the pen, he was able to convert another study for the *Virgin and Child with St Anne* – for a long time unrecognized as such by art historians – into a study for a *Leda* (Cat. 28, left). The intensive efforts

devoted to mastering the basic vocabulary of drawing here suddenly open the door to a new freedom in the handling of the subject.

*Johannes Nathan*

**Literature:** Heydenreich, 1933; Popham, 1946 (1994); Gombrich, 1966, 1986; Pedretti, 1983a; Nathan, 1992, 1995; Wiemers, 1996.

◄ **2 Figural Studies for the**
*Adoration of the Magi, c.* 1481
*Pen and ink over metalpoint on*
*prepared paper, 213 x 152 mm*
*Bayonne, Musée Bonnat, Inv. 658*

*Out of the secret places of a unique temperament he [Leonardo] brought strange blossoms and fruits hitherto unknown; and for him, the novel impression conveyed, the exquisite effect woven, counted as an end in itself – a perfect end.*

WALTER PATER, 1893

3

4

5

**3 Drapery Study for the Arm of an Annunciation Angel,** *c.* 1472–1475
*Pen and ink, 78 x 92 mm*
*Oxford, Governing Body,*
*Christ Church, Inv. JBS 16*

**4 Studies of a Virgin and Child (right, a Study for the Benois Madonna),** *c.* 1478–1480
*Pen and ink, 198 x 150 mm*
*London, British Museum,*
*Inv. 1860-6-16-100r*

**5 Perspective Study for the Background of the** *Adoration of the Magi,* 1481
*Pen, ink, traces of metalpoint and white, 165 x 290 mm*
*Florence, Galleria degli Uffizi,*
*Gabinetto dei Disegni e delle*
*Stampe, Inv. 436E recto*

**6 Composition Sketch for the** *Adoration of the Magi,* 1481
*Pen and ink over metalpoint,*
*285 x 215 mm*
*Paris, Musée du Louvre,*
*Cabinet des Dessins, R. F. 1978*

6

7

8

**7 Study for the Head of
a Girl, _c._ 1483**
_Silverpoint on brownish prepared
paper, 182 x 159 mm
Turin, Biblioteca Reale,
Inv. 15572r_

**8 Study of a Hand, _c._ 1483**
_Black chalk heightened with white
on dark grey prepared paper,
153 x 220 mm
Windsor Castle, Royal Library
(RL 12520r)_

9

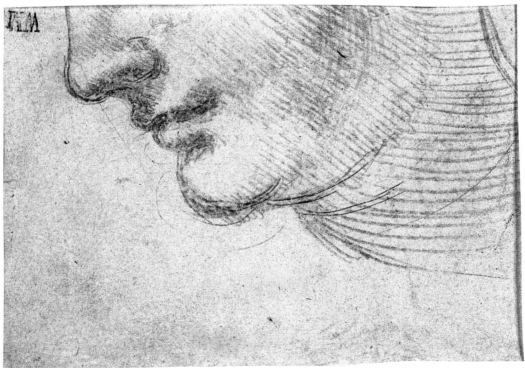

10

**9 Study of the Head of
a Woman,** *c.* **1490**
*Silverpoint on greenish prepared
paper, 180 x 168 mm
Paris, Musée du Louvre,
Cabinet des Dessins*

**10 Study of the Head of
a Woman,** *c.* **1490**
*Metalpoint, 68 x 89 mm
Frankfurt am Main, Städelsches
Kunstinstitut am Main, Graphi-
sche Sammlung, Inv. 6954v*

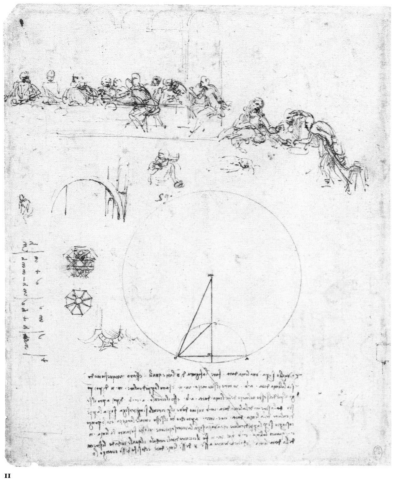

11

12

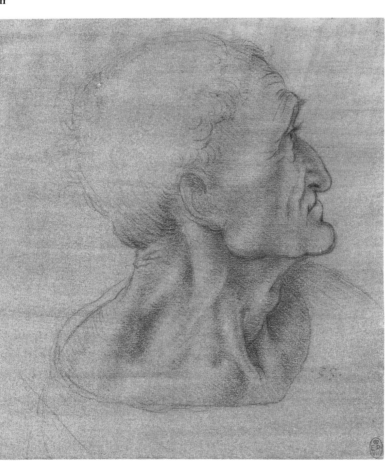

13

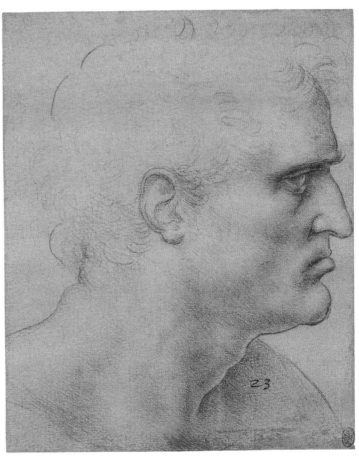

14

**11 Preliminary Sketch for the *Last Supper*, *c.* 1495**
*Pen and ink, 260 x 210 mm*
*Windsor Castle, Royal Library*
*(RL 12542r)*

**12 Study for the *Last Supper* (St Philip), *c.* 1495**
*Black chalk, 190 x 150 mm*
*Windsor Castle, Royal Library*
*(RL 12551r)*

**13 Study for the *Last Supper* (Judas), *c.* 1495**
*Red chalk on reddish prepared paper, 180 x 150 mm*
*Windsor Castle, Royal Library*
*(RL 12547r)*

**14 Study for the *Last Supper* (St Bartholomew), *c.* 1495**
*Red chalk on reddish prepared paper, 193 x 148 mm*
*Windsor Castle, Royal Library*
*(RL 12548r)*

**15 Study for the *Last Supper* (St James the Elder) and Architectural Sketches, *c.* 1495**
*Red chalk, pen and ink, 252 x 172 mm*
*Windsor Castle, Royal Library*
*(RL 12552r)*

15

16

17

18

19

**16** Study for the *Virgin and Child with St Anne*, c. 1501 (?) (recto of Cat. 17)
*Pen and ink over black chalk, 260 x 197 mm*
*London, British Museum, Inv. 1875-6-12-17r*

**17** Study for the *Virgin and Child with St Anne* and Drawing of a Head in Profile, c. 1501–1510 (?) (verso of Cat. 16)
*Pen and ink over black chalk, 260 x 197 mm*
*London, British Museum, Inv. 1875-6-12-17v*

**18** Study for the *Virgin and Child with St Anne*, c. 1501–1510 (?)
*Pen and ink over black chalk, 120 x 100 mm*
*Paris, Musée du Louvre, Cabinet des Dessins, R. F. 460*

**19** Study for the *Virgin and Child with St Anne*, c. 1501–1510 (?)
*Pen and ink over black chalk, 121 x 100 mm*
*Venice, Gallerie dell'Accademia, Inv. 230*

**20** Studies for the Infant Christ, c. 1501–1510 (?)
*Red chalk and white heightening on reddish prepared paper, 285 x 198 mm*
*Venice, Gallerie dell'Accademia, Inv. 257*

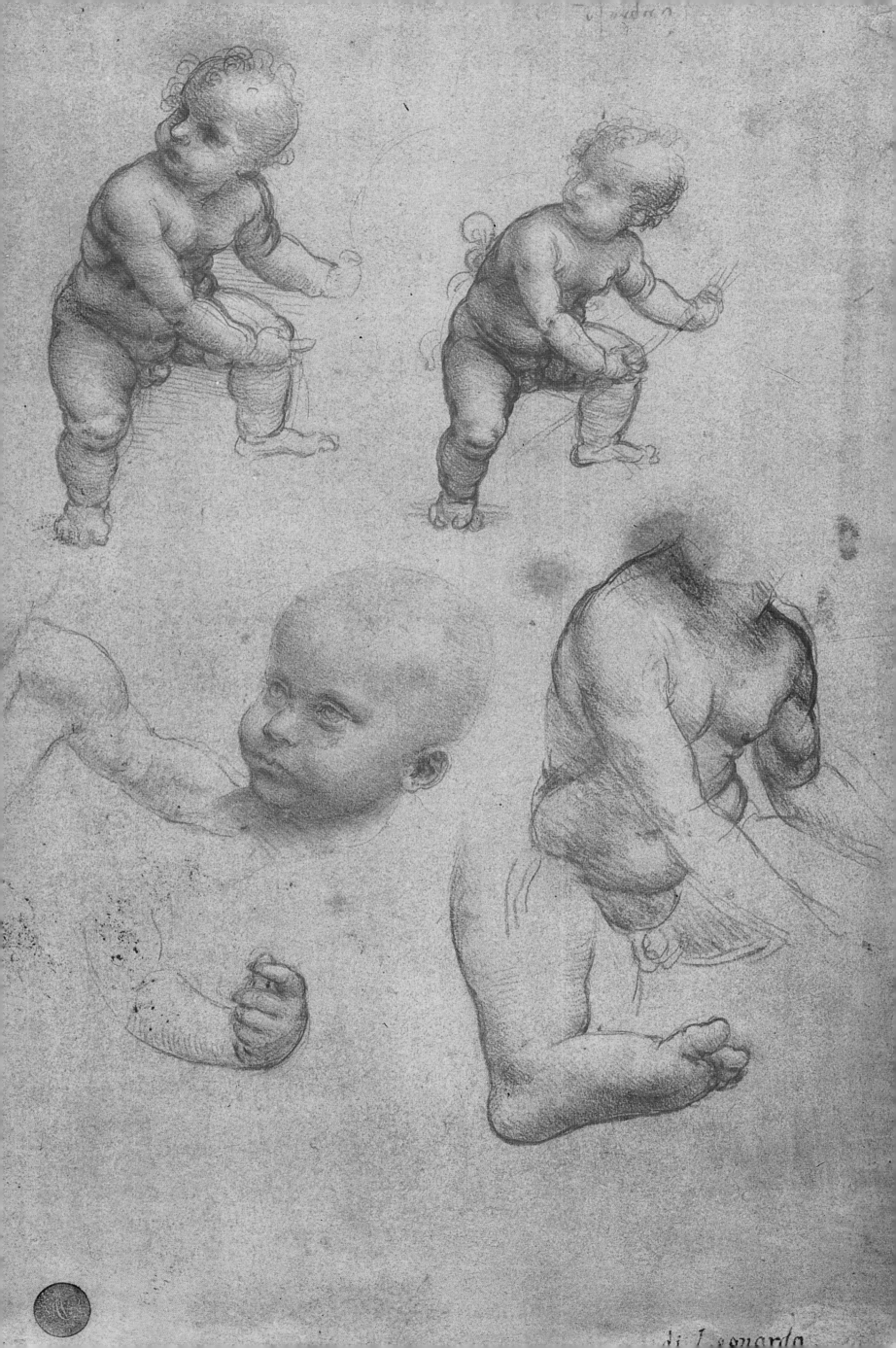

21

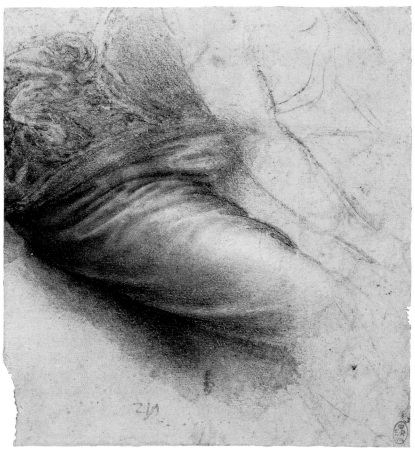

22

23

21 **Study for the Drapery
of the Virgin's Right Arm,**
*c.* **1501–1510 (?)**
*Pen and black chalk, heightened
with white, on reddish prepared
paper, 86 x 170 mm
Windsor Castle, Royal Library
(RL 12532r)*

22 **Drapery Study for the
Virgin,** *c.* **1510/11 (?)**
*Black chalk and white heightening
on yellowish prepared paper,
164 x 145 mm
Windsor Castle, Royal Library
(RL 12530r)*

23 **Drapery Study for
St Anne,** *c.* **1510/11 (?)**
*Black chalk and white heightening
on dark grey prepared paper,
175 x 140 mm
Windsor Castle, Royal Library
(RL 12526r)*

24

25

26

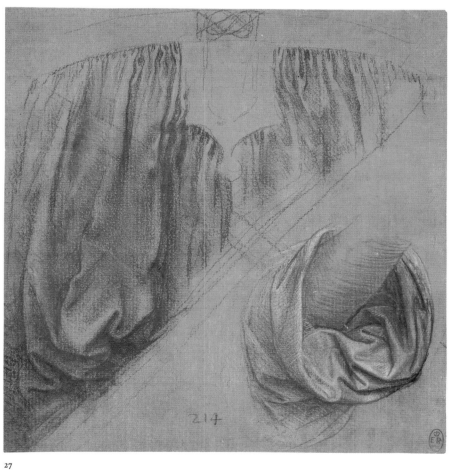

27

**24 Drapery Study for
St Anne,** *c.* 1510/11 (?)
*Black chalk and white on saffron-
coloured prepared paper,
167 x 147 mm
Windsor Castle, Royal Library
(RL 12527)*

**25 Study of a Bust of
a Woman, 1501**
*Red chalk and white on pink
prepared paper, 221 x 159 mm
Windsor Castle, Royal Library
(RL 12514r)*

**26 Drapery Study for a Left
Arm,** *c.* 1504
*Red chalk and white on reddish
prepared paper, 220 x 139 mm
Windsor Castle, Royal Library
(RL 12524r)*

**27 Drapery Studies with
Belt Buckle,** *c.* 1504
*Red chalk on reddish prepared
paper, 164 x 158 mm
Windsor Castle, Royal Library
(RL 12525r)*

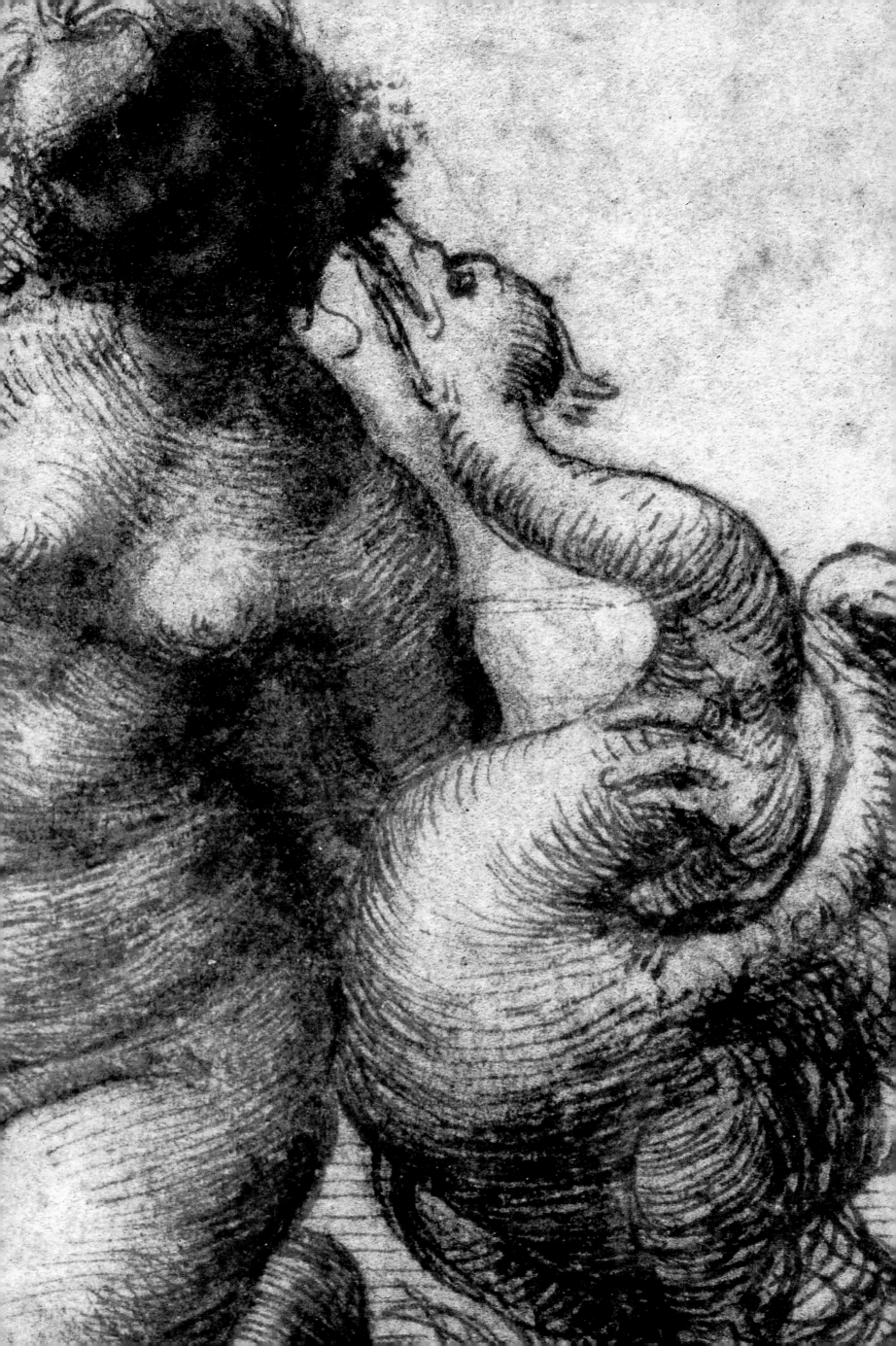

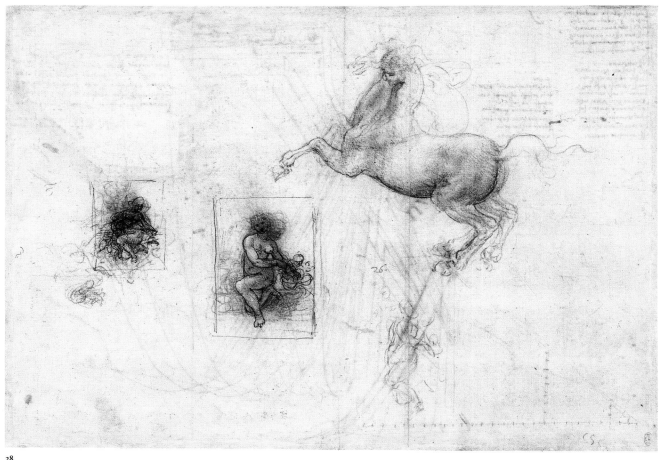

28

29

30

**28 Sketch for a *Leda and the Swan* and Study of a Horse,** *c.* 1504 (?)
*Pen, ink and black chalk,*
*287 x 405 mm*
*Windsor Castle, Royal Library*
*(RL 12337r)*

**29 Study for a Kneeling *Leda and the Swan,*** *c.* 1505–1510
*Pen and ink over black chalk,*
*125 x 110 mm*
*Rotterdam, Museum Boijmans*
*van Beuningen, Inv. 446*

**30 Study for a Kneeling *Leda and the Swan,*** *c.* 1505–1510
*Pen and ink over black chalk,*
*160 x 139 mm*
*Chatsworth, Devonshire*
*Collection, Inv. 717*

31

32

33

**31 Head of Leda,** *c.* **1505–1510**
*Pen and ink, 92 x 112 mm*
*Windsor Castle, Royal Library*
*(RL 12515r)*

**32 Head of Leda,** *c.* **1505–1510**
*Pen and ink over black chalk on*
*brownish prepared paper,*
*93 x 104 mm*
*Windsor Castle, Royal Library*
*(RL 12517r)*

**33 Head of Leda,** *c.* **1505–1510**
*Pen and ink over black chalk on*
*brownish prepared paper,*
*177 x 147 mm*
*Windsor Castle, Royal Library*
*(RL 12518r)*

**34 Head of Leda,** *c.* **1505–1510**
*Pen and ink over black chalk,*
*200 x 162 mm*
*Windsor Castle, Royal Library*
*(RL 12516r)*

34

# 2 Studies for equestrian monuments and horses

As can be seen from the preliminary studies for the *Adoration of the Magi* (esp. Cat. 5, *c.* 1481), Leonardo was keenly interested in the representation of horses right from the start of his career. Horses enjoyed a special status in the society of the Italian Renaissance and consequently formed an essential part of an artist's repertoire. The zeal with which Leonardo studied the movements and anatomy of the horse is nevertheless unparalleled. This may be connected with the fact that horses played an important role in warfare in the Renaissance, and that Leonardo was particularly interested in exploring subjects such as conflict, combat and battle. He frequently portrays horses in moments of aggression. Thus the background of the *Adoration of the Magi* reveals a fierce battle between horsemen, and the same motif appears again in two studies for a dragon fight (Cat. 54). In compositional sketches for battle scenes, too, horses invariably play a central role (Cat. 60).

Leonardo's enthusiasm for his subject emerges almost more clearly still from a description he wrote of a fictitious battle, which culminates in the following passage: "And you will see a river with horses galloping in it, churning up the water into a tumult of waves, foam and spray, in the air and between the legs and bodies of the horses" (TPL ad 148). This description, like Leonardo's pictures of horses, raises the question as to the interplay within the artist's work between observation and invention. Just as none will doubt that this description of a battle scene is a work of the imagination, so too we can be sure that an ensemble as perfectly constructed as the *Battle of Anghiari* was born not of Leonardo's observation of a real skirmish but of his compositional sensibilities.

Leonardo's ability to create works such as the *Battle of Anghiari* was also founded on his detailed studies of the natural world. Testaments to these studies include his sketches of grazing animals and a series of further sheets of horse studies (Cat. 50–53). Upon looking through the drawings brought together in the present section, however, it quickly becomes apparent that by no means all of Leonardo's horse studies can have been drawn from life. This is true not just of the artist's designs for equestrian monuments, all of which show horse and rider in highly complex poses (see below). On practical grounds, his drawings of horses rearing and galloping, too, can have been achieved only by combining individual elements into a plausible whole.

This process can be demonstrated in the case of the study of a *Rider on a Rearing Horse* (Cat. 56). The most important details of the horse and his rider, who is turning to look behind him, are already in place. Only the horse's back legs are still the subject of experiment and are sketched in two positions, albeit each time in the same pose. Leonardo has thereby started off in silverpoint and then laid down

his preferred solution with pen and ink. The principle of this method makes it clear that this drawing cannot be a study of an animal in motion – even if the repeated outlines of the horse's legs prompt "cinematographic" associations in the mind of the modern viewer. Rather, the unaltered pose of the legs shows that Leonardo is chiefly concerned with their position in relationship to the overall figure, in other words with the proportions of the whole. Leonardo's exhaustive investigation into the effect of different positions is thereby made possible only by his supreme mastery of detail, as demonstrated in particular by the leg furthest from us, sketched in twice in virtually identical fashion but in two different places. The effort which Leonardo devoted to acquiring this same mastery of detail is in turn revealed by a glance at other sheets (cf. esp. Cat. 57).

Leonardo's practice as a draughtsman thus involved not just the recording of observations on a sheet of paper; equally, if not more so, it extended to the consideration of their pictorial effect. This is also true of studies such as that of a wildly rearing horse (Cat. 57), in which he experiments with a number of leg and head positions – research that would reach a provisional conclusion in another drawing. For what this second study was intended it is hard to say, since it resembles none of Leonardo's surviving compositions. Nevertheless, it encapsulates the essence of a rearing horse: the animal's neck and head are twisted round as if towards the viewer and are thereby lent a plasticity beyond the two-dimensional. The evident emphasis upon the contours in this – probably late – drawing illustrates once again that this plasticity is the fruit of many rigorous corrections.

Leonardo's method is seen at its most impressive in studies conceived in connection with his unfinished equestrian monuments. Some of his work on the first monument to Francesco Sforza (1401–1466) is documented in a series of technical drawings relating to the casting process (Cat. 38–41). Two designs in particular (Cat. 36 and 37) can be clearly associated with this project. They do not show the planned sculpture in its final form, however (the rearing horse seen here would later evolve into a walking horse, not least for reasons of stability). On the contrary: in particular Cat. 37, a very free sketch, could have preceded the actual preliminary work on the monument by a number of years. Leonardo in fact offered to undertake the project in a letter of introduction that he wrote to Ludovico Sforza long before work actually started on the monument. The above-mentioned study might thus show him giving early thought to the commission.

Another group of drawings (Cat. 42–46) appears to relate to the monument for Giangiacomo Trivulzio (1441–1518), but clearly draw upon ideas generated during the first project. It seems that here, too, Leo-

nardo initially envisaged a horse rearing up over a fallen soldier, before opting once again for a walking horse. Even though he was able to draw upon a broad range of designs developed for the earlier Sforza monument, Leonardo proceeded to execute new drawings for the Trivulzio monument with the greatest care. This is evidenced in particular by two sheets, both featuring drawings on their recto and verso (Cat. 43). Noteworthy is the fact that Leonardo has copied the outlines of the upper studies from one side of the sheet to the other, apparently by holding the paper up to the light. While this doubtless allowed him to work his way gradually towards a definitive compositional solution, there may be another reason why Leonardo adopted this somewhat elaborate procedure: by tracing his drawing though the sheet onto the back, he obtained his original design in mirror image. That Leonardo was thereby ultimately aiming to assess its pictorial effect is also implied by his recommendation that the artist should use a mirror when working: "I say that when you are painting you ought to have by you a flat mirror in which you should often look at your work. The work will appear to you in reverse and will seem to be by the hand of another master and thereby you will better judge its faults" (MK 527).

The fact that Leonardo identifies the merciless process of eliminating faults as one of the preconditions of artistic perfection points to his intelligence and openness. In particular Leonardo's studies of horses illustrate how pictorial effect is extensively indebted to such processes.

*Johannes Nathan*

**Literature:** Bush, 1978; Pedretti/Roberts, 1984; Popham, 1946 (1994); Nathan, 1995; *Leonardo da Vinci's Sforza Monument Jorse,* 1995.

36

37

**36  Study for the Sforza Monument,** *c. 1488/89*
*Metalpoint on blue prepared paper, 116 x 103 mm*
*Windsor Castle, Royal Library (RL 12357)*

**37  Study for the Sforza Monument,** *c. 1488/89*
*Metalpoint on blue prepared paper, 148 x 185 mm*
*Windsor Castle, Royal Library (RL 12358r)*

**38  Sketch of the Casting Pit for the Sforza Horse seen from above (top) and the side (bottom),** *c. 1493*
*Pen and ink, 210 x 144 mm*
*Madrid, Biblioteca Nacional, Codex Madrid II (MS 8936), fol. 149r*

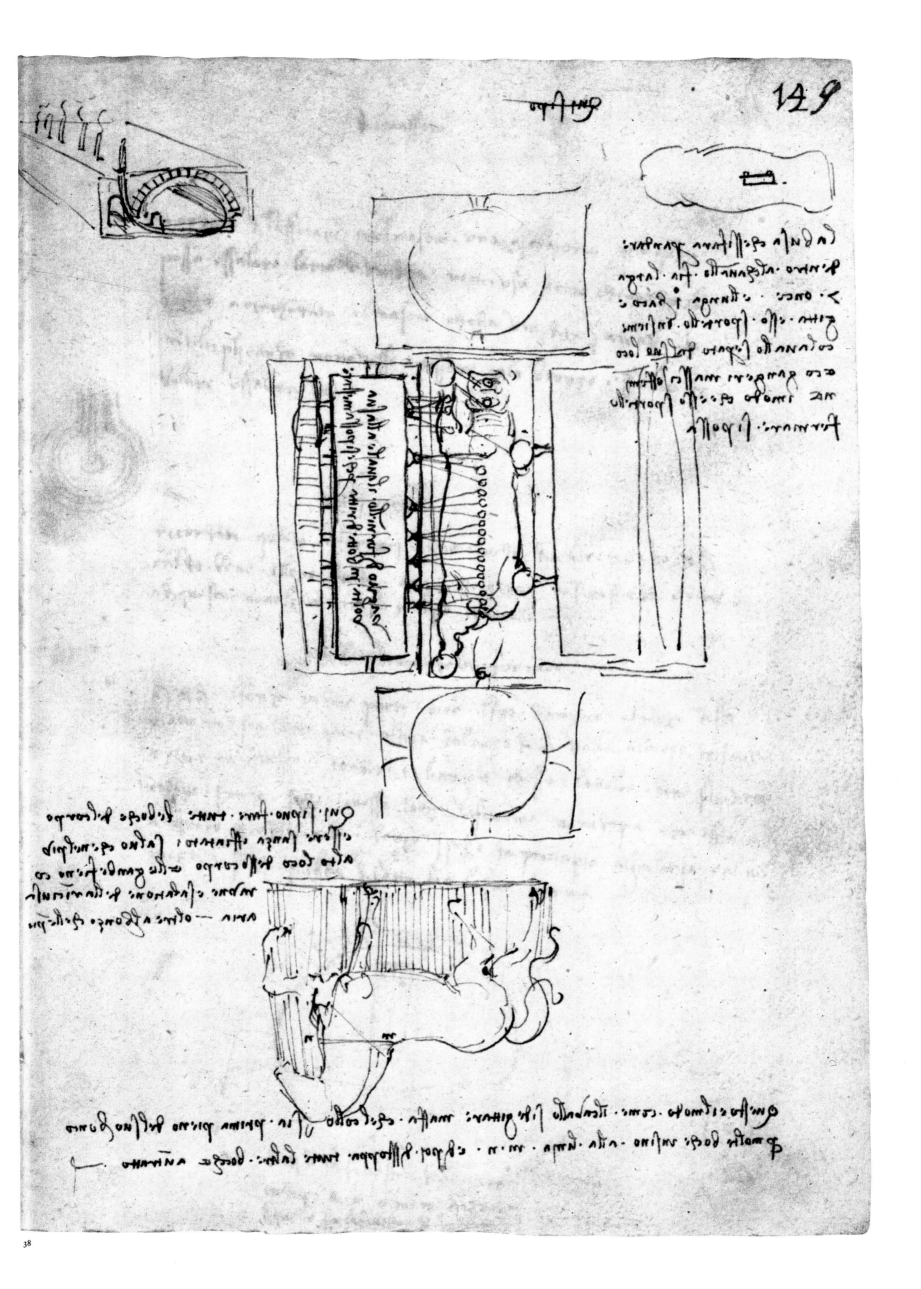

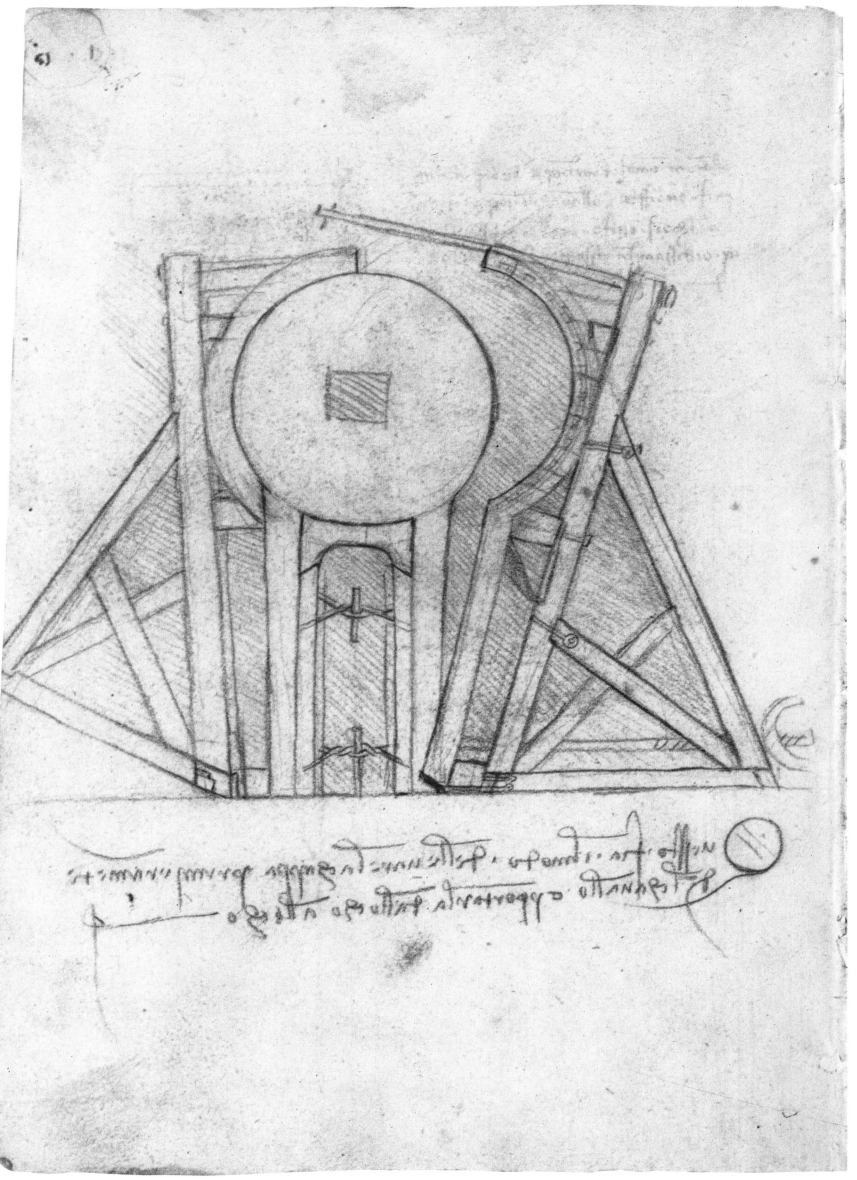

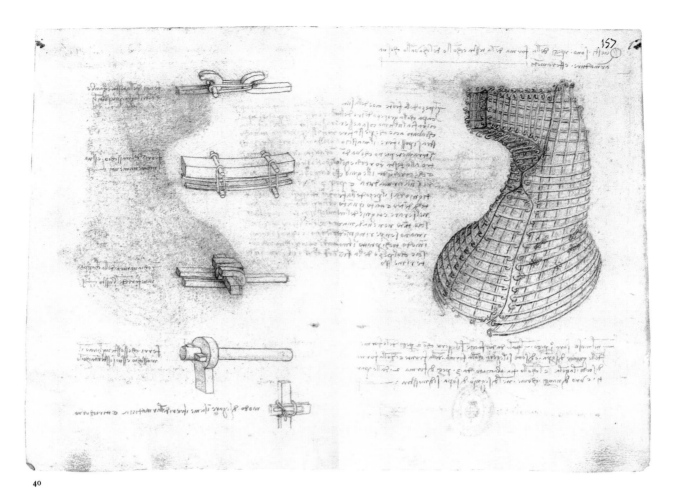

40

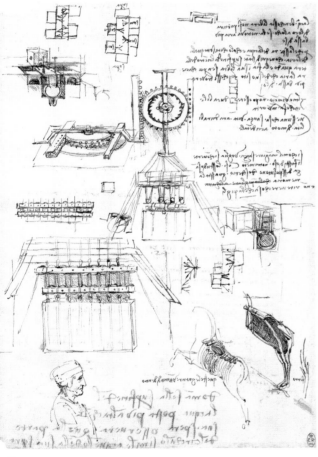

41

42

**39  Study of the Wooden Framework with Casting Mould for the Sforza Horse,**
*c.* **1491–1493**
*Red chalk, 210 x 146 mm*
*Madrid, Biblioteca Nacional,*
*Codex Madrid II (MS 8936),*
*fol. 155v*

**40  Drawing of the Ironwork Casting Mould for the Head of the Sforza Horse,**
*c.* **1491–1493**
*Red chalk, 210 x 290 mm*
*Madrid, Biblioteca Nacional,*
*Codex Madrid II (MS 8936),*
*ff. 156v–157r*

**41  Studies relating to the Casting of the Sforza Monument,** *c.* **1491–1493**
*Pen and ink, 278 x 191 mm*
*Windsor Castle, Royal Library*
*(RL 12349r)*

**42  Studies for the Trivulzio Monument,** *c.* **1508–1511**
*Pen and ink, 280 x 198 mm*
*Windsor Castle, Royal Library*
*(RL 12355r)*

44

45

46

◄ **43  Studies for the Trivulzio Monument**, *c. 1508–1511*
*Pen and ink over black chalk,*
*203 x 143 mm*
*Windsor Castle, Royal Library*
*(RL 12344r)*

**44  Study for the Trivulzio Monument**, *c. 1508–1511*
*Black chalk, 201 x 124 mm*
*Windsor Castle, Royal Library*
*(RL 12354r)*

**45  Studies for the Trivulzio Monument**, *c. 1508–1511*
*Black chalk, 267 x 161 mm*
*Windsor Castle, Royal Library*
*(RL 12359r)*

**46  Study for the Trivulzio Monument**, *c. 1508–1511*
*Pen and ink over black chalk,*
*153 x 144 mm*
*Windsor Castle, Royal Library*
*(RL 12343r)*

► **47  Horse Studies,**
*c. 1493/94 (?)*
*Metalpoint on blue prepared paper,*
*212 x 160 mm*
*Windsor Castle, Royal Library*
*(RL 12321r)*

47

48

49

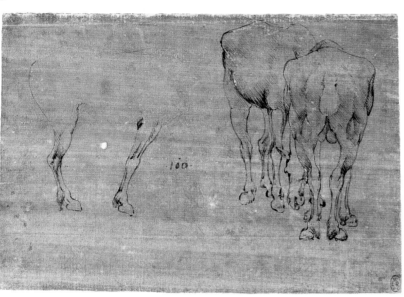

50

51

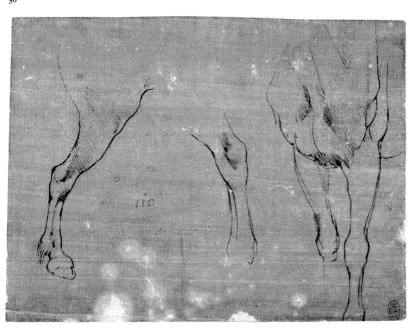

52

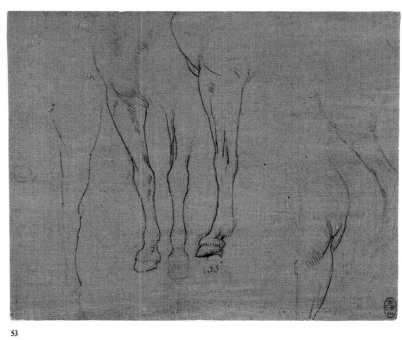

53

**48 Horse Studies,** *c.* **1480**
*Metalpoint, 114 x 196 mm*
*Windsor Castle, Royal Library*
*(RL 12315r)*

**49 Horse Studies,** *c.* **1480**
*Metalpoint, pen and ink on orange*
*prepared paper, 117 x 194 mm*
*Windsor Castle, Royal Library*
*(RL 12325r)*

**50 Horse Studies and Study**
**of a Mule,** *c.* **1478**
*Metalpoint, 143 x 199 mm*
*Windsor Castle, Royal Library*
*(RL 12308r)*

**51 Horse Studies,** *c.* **1479**
*Pen and ink and black chalk*
*on orange prepared paper,*
*134 x 188 mm*
*Windsor Castle, Royal Library*
*(RL 12306r)*

**52 Horse Studies,** *c.* **1479**
*Pen and ink over metalpoint,*
*127 x 158 mm*
*Windsor Castle, Royal Library*
*(RL 12307r)*

**53 Horse Studies,** *c.* **1480**
*Pen and ink over metalpoint,*
*132 x 159 mm*
*Windsor Castle, Royal Library*
*(RL 12305r)*

54

55

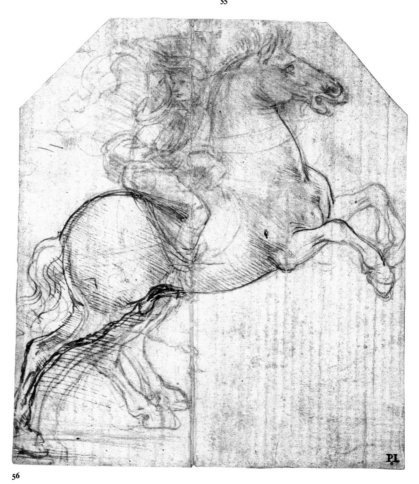

56

**54** Leonardo (?)
**Two Horsemen fighting a Dragon and Horse Studies**
*Pen and brush on paper,*
*190 x 119 mm*
*Paris, Musée du Louvre, Cabinet*
*des Dessins, Inv. 781 recto,*
*Collection Edmond de Rothschild*

**55 Horse Studies,** *c.* **1505**
*Pen and ink, 210 x 283 mm*
*Windsor Castle, Royal Library*
*(RL 12328v)*

**56 Rider on a Rearing Horse,** *c.* **1482 (?)**
*Pen and ink over metalpoint,*
*141 x 119 mm*
*Cambridge, The Fitzwilliam*
*Museum, P.D. 44-1999*

**57 Horse Studies,** *c.* **1505**
*Pen and ink and red chalk,*
*153 x 142 mm*
*Windsor Castle, Royal Library*
*(RL 12336r)*

58

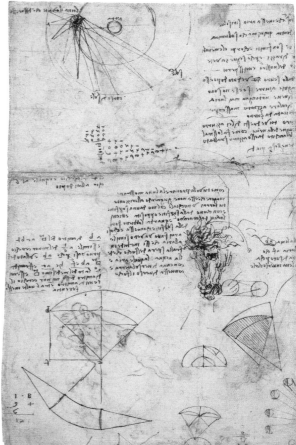

59

60

**58  Horse Studies,** *c. 1503–1505*
*Pen and ink, 170 x 140 mm*
*Windsor Castle, Royal Library*
*(RL 12330r)*

**59  Study of a Horse's Head
and Various Studies relating
to the Solar System,**
*c. 1503/04 and 1506–1508*
*Pen and ink, 308 x 196 mm*
*Windsor Castle, Royal Library*
*(RL 12326v)*

**60  Study of a Battle
with Horsemen and Foot
Soldiers,** *c. 1511*
*Red and black chalk on reddish
prepared paper, 148 x 207 mm*
*Windsor Castle, Royal Library*
*(RL 12332r)*

**61  Sheet of Studies of
Horses, a Cat and Fight
with a Dragon,** *c. 1508*
*Pen and ink over black chalk,
298 x 212 mm*
*Windsor Castle, Royal Library*
*(RL 12331r)*

# 3 Drawings of human figures, animals and monsters

Indicative of Leonardo's posthumous image is the fact that the question of his training as an artist has attracted scant interest up till now. For according to conventional thinking, a "genius" needs no schooling. But as our examination of his horse studies in the previous chapter has shown, Leonardo both scrutinized and strove to improve his work all through his life. Even in his very last sketches of the animal he had been studying from his youth onwards, he can be seen correcting his drawing in an effort to achieve ever greater accuracy. He was thus well aware of the importance of constant practice, a method of learning that seems to have accompanied him to the very end of his life.

The decisive significance of constant practice emerges from an important sheet from Leonardo's early career (recto, Cat. 65; verso, Cat. 97), one of the few to have survived the passage of time relatively unscathed. Its unusual format (405 x 290 mm) and the condition of its edges show that it has been trimmed significantly less than most of Leonardo's drawings. The clearly visible vertical fold (just like the horizontal one) probably originally marked the centre of the sheet, indicating that at some point in time a good third of the right-hand side – a strip about 180 mm wide – must have been cut off. Since the original ratio of the height to the width would have corresponded to the golden section (approx. 1:1.41), as was already the convention in Leonardo's day, the sheet must also have lost another 10 cm or so in width (405 x 1.41 = 571). It would thus originally have measured approx. 405 x 570 mm, a format at that time commonly produced by paper manufacturers. This simple calculation shows the wrong that could be done to a drawing from this era – for a vari- .ety of reasons. Firstly, paper was still an expensive material. Since Leonardo probably folded the sheet himself, it seems likely that it was already trimmed when he got it; otherwise he would hardly have used

it for a loose form of free sketching, but would have reserved it for a more important presentation drawing. The sheet may have been cut down the second time by a later owner, perhaps Pompeo Leoni (cf. Introduction). The fact that the sheet subsequently survived relatively intact is probably due to the large study of a Madonna that occupies almost the entire front side and which would be virtually impossible to cut up into smaller pieces. Were it not for the Madonna, however, the numerous studies of heads in profile that also appear on the sheet would have been easy targets for the scissors, as wielded so often and without scruple in other cases (cf. e.g. Cat. 96, 98, 101).

It is precisely because the profile studies have survived on this sheet as an ensemble that they are able to shed important light on Leonardo's training as a draughtsman, for they show how intensively he practised sketching certain subjects. Thus the idealized profile of a young person appears no less than 17 times on the recto and verso, in places one straight after another. After the large study of the Madonna had been drawn, studies of heads in profile were scattered, like a series of *études*, across those parts of the sheet still blank. Leonardo was sketching not from a model, in other words, but by heart, so to speak. Like a musician practising an instrument, Leonardo is here rehearsing a profile drawing that flowed particularly smoothly from his left hand. We have namely only to visualize the process in our head or indeed pick up a pencil ourselves to appreciate that, for a left-handed artist, it is easier to draw a profile facing towards the right, because the hand moves more naturally around the outlines (for right-handed artists, the reverse is true). Heads in profile looking to the right are correspondingly in the majority in Leonardo's graphic œuvre.

Not all of the profile heads on the present sheet are equally successful. Although the best of them show

that Leonardo had already largely assimilated his subject, a number of sketches are clearly weaker. One such is the study in the bottom left-hand corner – and this despite the fact that Leonardo must have been familiar with this particular motif since the early days of his apprenticeship. Leonardo is here attempting the motif of an idealized human face, one at that time fairly common and also employed by Leonardo's teacher, Andrea del Verrocchio. Leonardo's training was evidently based on the same principles as that of his contemporaries. It was thereby founded upon copying: only in this way could a fledgling artist of the Early Renaissance equip himself for his own independent career. This same practice had already been recommended by Cennino Cennini (active around 1400) in his *Libro d'Arte* or *Craftsman's handbook*, in which he writes in his rather florid style: "... exert yourself and take delight in copying always the best things – crafted by the hand of great masters – that you can find" (Ch. 27). Elsewhere (Ch. 13) he asks: "Do you know what you will achieve if you practice drawing with a pen? It will enable you, trained and skilful, to draw a great deal in your head."

The principle of copying and repetition can be seen in a large number of Leonardo's drawings in a very wide range of techniques, but it is perhaps no coincidence that the studies on the two sides of the sheet reproduced here as Cat. 65 and 97 were executed with a pen, just as Cennini recommended. If these parallels between Leonardo's sketches and the advice of a colleague living almost one hundred years earlier might seem to some a mere matter of chance, others may be persuaded differently by the following passage from Leonardo's own writings: "How to learn well by heart: When you wish to be able to make use of something committed to memory adopt this method, which is that when you have drawn the same thing so many times that it seems you have it by

*It seems to me that a painter shows not inconsiderable grace when he paints his figures well. If he does not possess this grace by nature he can acquire it by this incidental method of studying: make an effort to collect the good features from many beautiful faces, but let their beauty be confirmed rather by public renown than by your own judgement. [...] Therefore select your examples of beauty as I have said and commit them to memory.*

LEONARDO DA VINCI, MK 530

► 62 **Studies for a** *Madonna with a Cat, c.* **1478–1480**
*Pen and ink over black chalk,*
*274 x 190 mm*
*London, British Museum,*
*Inv. 1860-6-16-98*

heart try to do it without the exemplar. Have your exemplar traced on to a thin flat plane of glass. Place this on top of the drawing you have done without the exemplar, and note carefully where the tracing does not match up with your drawing, and in those places where you have made a mistake, resolve not to repeat the error. In fact, go back to the exemplar and draw over and over it the erroneous part till you have it firmly in your memory" (MK 534).

The notion that relentless practice might of all things be a vehicle of the imagination is foreign to us. Once we accept that Leonardo committed many of his motifs to visual memory, however, we find ourselves looking at many of the sheets in this chapter through new eyes. In particular his Madonna studies (Cat. 62–67) bear witness to Leonardo's extraordinary ability to arrive at ever new combinations, an ability barely conceivable without an in-depth knowledge of the pictorial vocabulary – and indeed independent of whether or not Leonardo drew his inspiration from a real-life mother and child. His method can be seen perhaps most exquisitely in a sheet featuring, on its right-hand edge, a familiar study of a head in profile to the right (Cat. 62). The unusual profile view of the Virgin on the opposite side of the sheet serves to illustrate how an idea could be sparked and how Leonardo was able, thanks to his extraordinary mastery of his repertoire, to develop unconventional compositional solutions – here, Mary in profile. A closer look at all these sheets also quickly reveals which details Leonardo found easier to draw, and which posed him more problems.

Superbly captured in each case is the child (a motif of which Andrea del Verrocchio also had a masterly command, as evidenced by one of his few surviving drawings, in the Louvre [Inv. 2 R.F.]). Overall, a similarly high degree of technical mastery can also be seen in the case of the Madonna. The cat is drawn with somewhat less confidence, in places rendered in

very typical poses but in others appearing rather clumsily drawn. In comparison with the human figure or the horse, the motif of the cat is one that occupies a subsidiary place within Leonardo's œuvre. It is typical of Leonardo that his artistic inventiveness becomes its richest where his technical confidence is at its highest – in this series of drawings, in the child. This compositional type reaches its ultimate form in the *Study for the Virgin and Child with St Anne* in the Louvre (cf. Ch. 1, Cat. 18), where it is only his confident mastery of the motifs that enables Leonardo to orient himself within the confusion of strokes.

If Leonardo's ability to draw from memory was thus an encouragement to inventiveness, it also explains the constant metamorphosis that his motifs undergo in the drawing process. Leonardo's drawings, unlike those of other artists of the Early Renaissance, leave it frequently unclear whether a study has been executed with a view to a specific project, or whether it is "simply" an exercise undertaken out of sheer pleasure in experimentation and with no specific objective in mind. It is as the latter that we may view the sketches for a *Madonna with a Cat* (Cat. 62 and 63) – in Christian iconography an extremely unusual motif, which Leonardo never actually translated into a painting, but the exploration of which nevertheless provided him with valuable ideas for other Virgin and Child compositions. His studies of human communication and interaction also reveal similarities with details from the *Adoration of the Magi* and the *Last Supper*, even though no direct link with these projects can be proved. In another group of sheets of small figures in action, probably dating from later on in his career, Leonardo again appears to be drawing upon his earlier series of figure studies.

Despite the apparently breathtaking speed with which Leonardo scatters his figures in various poses across the sheet, there is system behind the variation

in the motifs. In a similar fashion to the profile studies discussed above (Cat. 65 and 97), Leonardo's sketches thus gradually crystallize into a set of preferred views and poses. In the case of the male nude, for example, this is the standing figure with legs slightly apart and arms slightly raised (Cat. 73–75), a pose that finds its way even into Leonardo's anatomical drawings (Cat. 152, 153).

It seems as if standard poses and types of this kind formed the baseline in the process of artistic exploration. It is worth taking another look at Cat. 122. At the bottom of the sheet two lions' heads are drawn opposite the head of a dragon. As in the case of a number of the human heads in profile on this sheet – for example where the profile of a child is set beside the head of an old man – the combination could hardly be more effective. Like the motif of the profile view, the principle of contrast thereby also emerges as a constant within Leonardo's œuvre, one in which the combination of motifs serves a purpose in itself (cf. Ch. 5).

*Johannes Nathan*

**Literature:** Gombrich, 1976; Ames-Lewis, 1981 (pp. 91–100); *Leonardo & Venezia*, 1992; Nathan, 1995, 2002.

◄ **63 Sketches of a Child with a Cat**, *c.* 1478–1480
*Pen and ink, 206 x 143 mm*
*London, British Museum,*
*Inv. 1857-1-10-1v*

*[Leonardo] explained that men of genius sometimes accomplish most when they work the least; for, he added, they are thinking out inventions and forming in their minds the perfect ideas which they subsequently express and reproduce with their hands.*

GIORGIO VASARI, 1568

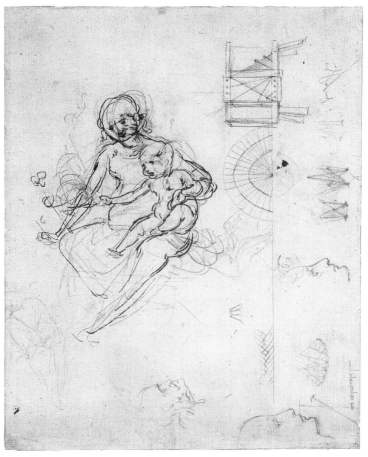

64

65

66

67

**64 Studies for a Virgin and Child and of Heads in Profile and Machines,** *c.* **1478–1480**
*Pen and ink over metalpoint on a reddish prepared surface, 198 x 150 mm*
*London, British Museum, Inv. 1860-6-16-100v*

**65 Study of a Virgin and Child with the Infant St John, and of Heads in Profile and other Figures,** *c.* **1478–1480**
(recto of Cat. 97)
*Pen and ink, 405 x 290 mm*
*Windsor Castle, Royal Library (RL 12276r)*

**66 Sheet of Studies of Female Heads,** *c.* **1478–1480**
*Silverpoint on reddish prepared paper, 232 x 190 mm*
*Windsor Castle, Royal Library (RL 12513r)*

**67 Studies of a Virgin worshipping the Christ Child,** *c.* **1482–1485**
*Pen and ink over preliminary pencil drawing, 195 x 162 mm*
*New York, The Metropolitan Museum of Art, Rogers Fund, 1917 (17.142.1)*

68

69

70

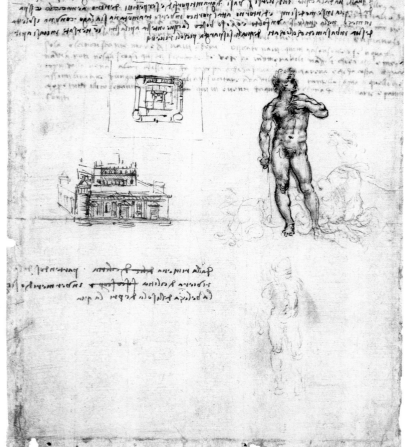

71

72

**68  Head and Shoulders of
a Christ Figure,** *c.* **1490–1495**
*Metalpoint on grey prepared paper,*
*116 x 91 mm*
*Venice, Gallerie dell'Accademia,*
*Inv. 231*

**69  Study for a St Sebastian,**
*c.* **1480/81**
*Pen and ink over metalpoint on*
*prepared paper, 174 x 64 mm*
*Hamburg, Hamburger Kunsthalle*

**70  Study of a Naked Man
with a Staff (St John?),**
*c.* **1476–1480 (?)**
*Metalpoint with white heightening*
*on bluish prepared paper,*
*187 x 122 mm*
*Windsor Castle, Royal Library*
*(RL 12572r)*

**71  Drawing after
Michelangelo's *David* and
Architectural Sketches,**
*c.* **1504**
*Pen and ink and black chalk,*
*270 x 201 mm*
*Windsor Castle, Royal Library*
*(RL 12591r)*

**72  Hercules and the Nemean
Lion,** *c.* **1504–1508**
*Black chalk, 180 x 190 mm*
*Turin, Biblioteca Reale,*
*Inv. 15630*

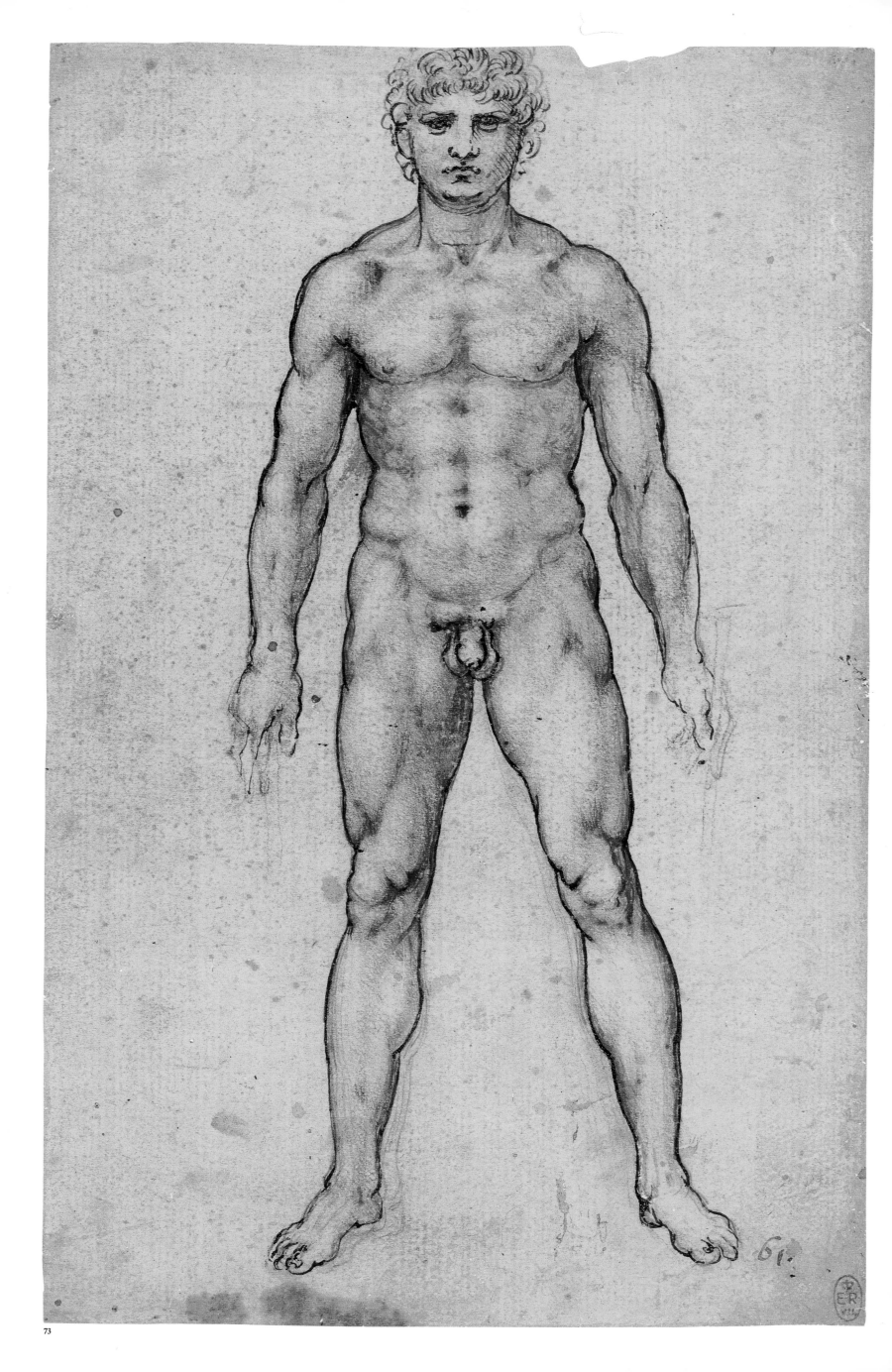

73

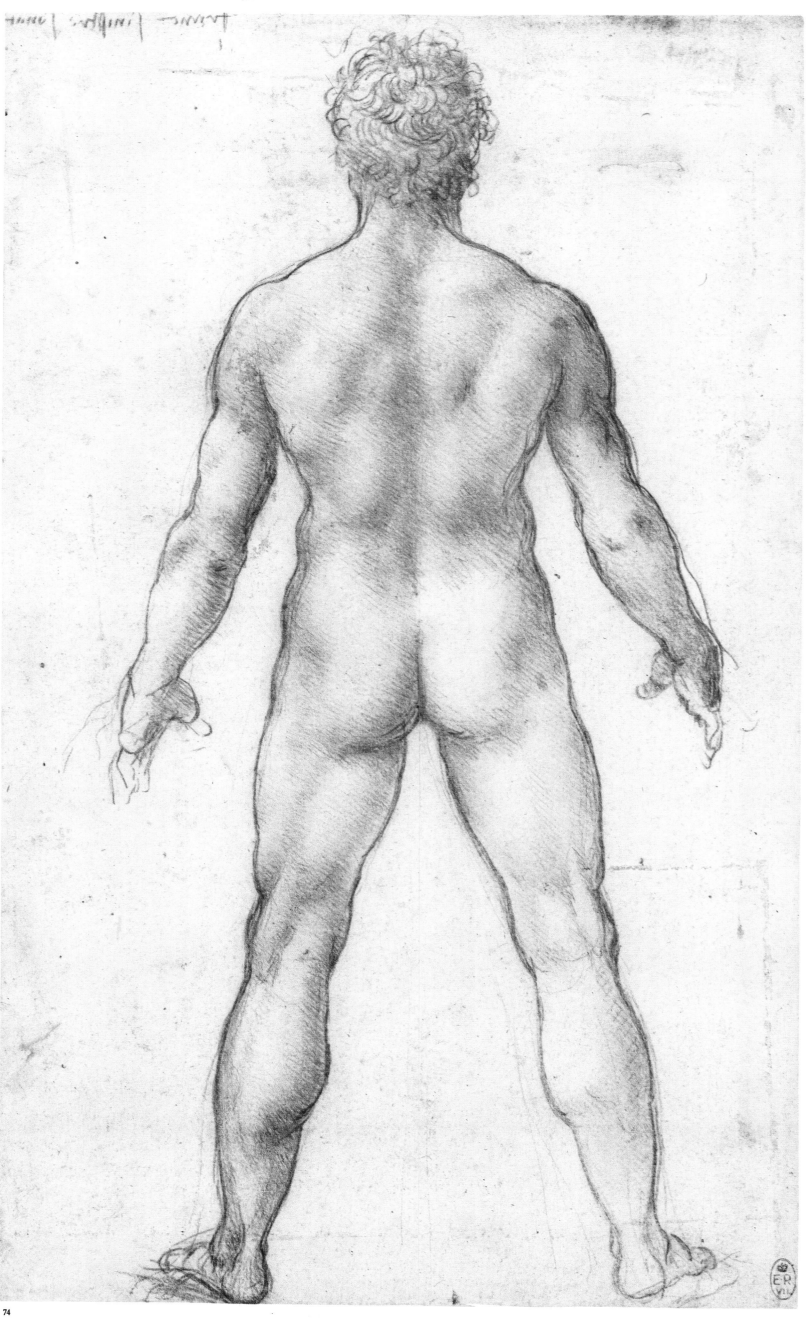

74

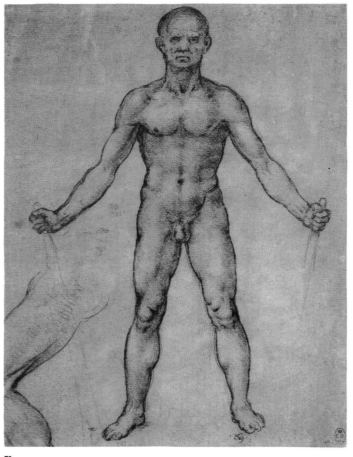

75

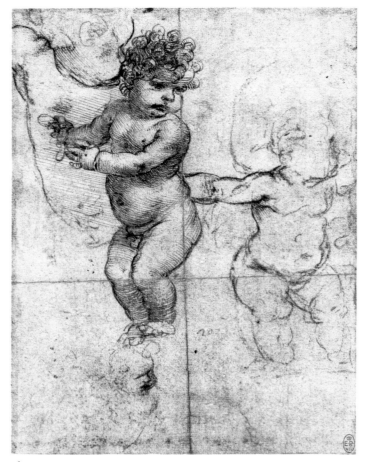

76

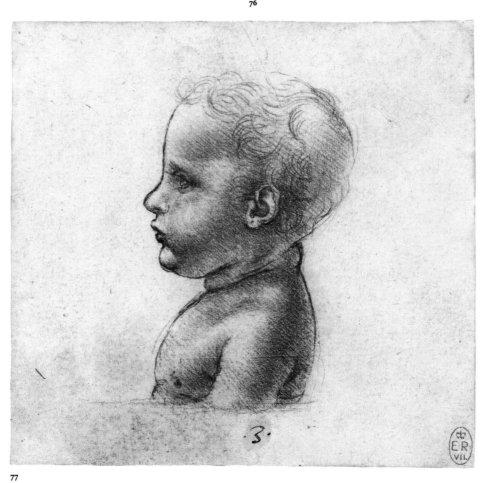

77

◄◄ **73 Study of a Male Nude Seen from the Front,** *c. 1503–1509*
*Red chalk, pen and ink,*
*236 x 146 mm*
*Windsor Castle, Royal Library*
*(RL 12594r)*

◄ **74 Study of a Male Nude Seen from Behind,** *c. 1503–1509*
*Red chalk, 270 x 160 mm*
*Windsor Castle, Royal Library*
*(RL 12596r)*

**75 Male Nude Seen from the Front,** *c. 1507*
*Red chalk on reddish prepared paper, 227 x 168 mm*
*Windsor Castle, Royal Library*
*(RL 12593r)*

**76 Study of a Naked Child,** *c. 1499 (?)*
*Pen and ink over black chalk, 205 x 152 mm*
*Windsor Castle, Royal Library*
*(RL 12562r)*

**77 Head and Shoulders of a Naked Child in Profile,** *c. 1495–1497*
*Red chalk, 100 x 100 mm*
*Windsor Castle, Royal Library*
*(RL 12519r)*

**78 Study of a Child's upper Chest and Shoulders, Seen from Front and Back,** *c. 1497–1499*
*Red chalk, 165 x 136 mm*
*Windsor Castle, Royal Library*
*(RL 12567r)*

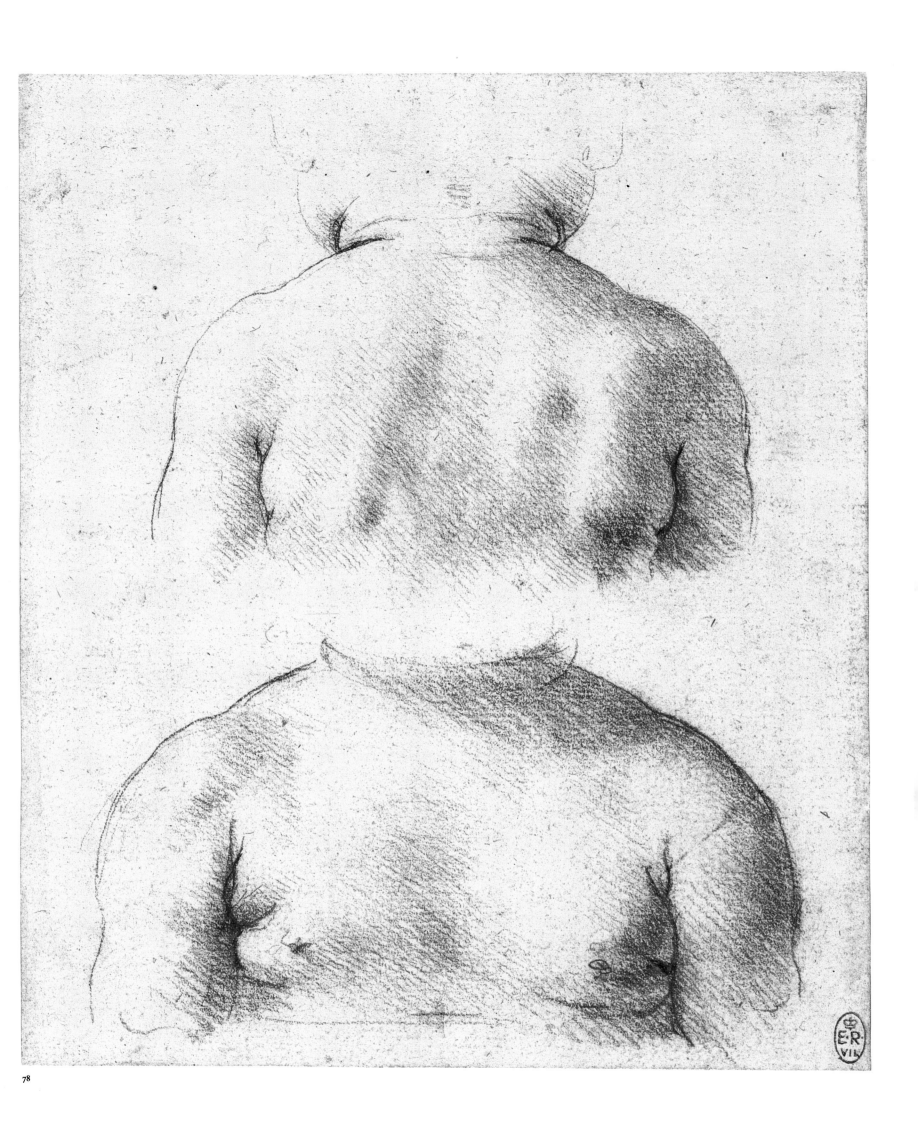

78

79

80

81

82

**79  Sheet of Studies of an Ox,
a Donkey and other Figures,
c. 1478–1480**
*Pen and ink over silverpoint,
164 x 177 mm
Windsor Castle, Royal Library
(RL 12362r)*

**80  Study of a Dog and Cat, c.
1480 (?)**
*Metalpoint, 140 x 105 mm
London, British Museum,
Inv. 1895-9-15-477*

**81  Drawing of the Head of
a Bear, c. 1480 (?)**
*Metalpoint on reddish prepared
paper, 70 x 70 mm
Private Collection*

**82  Study of a Bear, c. 1480 (?)**
*Metalpoint on reddish prepared
paper, 103 x 134 mm
New York, The Metropolitan
Museum of Art, Robert Lehman
Collection, 1975 (1975.1.369)*

83

84

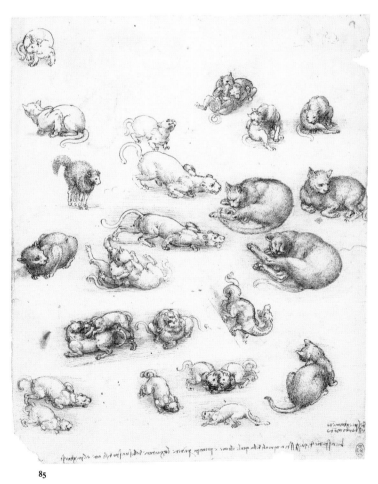

85

86

**83 Studies of the Paw of
a Dog or Wolf,** *c.* 1480 (?)
(recto of Cat. 84)
*Metalpoint on reddish prepared
paper, 135 x 105 mm
Edinburgh, The National Gallery
of Scotland, Inv. D 5189r*

**84 Studies of the Paw of
a Dog or Wolf,** *c.* 1480 (?)
(verso of Cat. 83)
*Metalpoint on reddish prepared
paper, 135 x 105 mm
Edinburgh, The National Gallery
of Scotland, Inv. D 5189v*

**85 Sheet of Studies of Cats, a
Dragon and other Animals,**
*c.* 1513–1515
*Pen and ink and wash over black
chalk, 270 x 210 mm
Windsor Castle, Royal Library
(RL 12363r)*

86 Copy after Leonardo
(Francesco Melzi)
**Drawing of a Monster with
Horns,** *c.* 1508
*Red, black and white chalk on
reddish prepared paper,
218 x 150 mm
Windsor Castle, Royal Library
(RL 12371r)*

# 4 Drapery studies

Despite a very great deal of research, the attribution of Renaissance works of art continues to pose great difficulties. The later practice of putting a signature to a work was still largely unknown in the 15th century; if an artist's name was recorded at all, it was in a more impersonal form, namely in an inscription (often in Latin) appearing within or beside the picture. In the case of drawings and sketches, on the other hand, which were valued far less highly than finished works of art, evidence of the artist's identity is found extremely rarely. The attribution of drawings thus relies upon a scholarly consideration of graphic style, comparisons with paintings and sculptures, materials used, documentary sources and – where known – the provenance of a sheet.

Thanks to a fortunate circumstance, however, Leonardo's graphic œuvre is relatively easy to identify: he was left-handed, something that reveals itself in his drawings by the fact that his hatching runs from top left to bottom right (right-handed hatching, by contrast, runs top right to bottom left). Since Leonardo made frequent use of hatching, it can in many cases provide unassailable proof of his authorship. A large number of drawings, and in particular those in the collection of the Royal Library at Windsor, can also be confidently attributed to Leonardo thanks to their clear and almost uninterrupted provenance.

In the case of the drapery studies, however, things look different. Only the drawing reproduced here as Cat. 93 includes hatching that proves it to be the work of a left-handed artist, and only the *Drapery Study for a Kneeling Figure* from Windsor (Cat. 94) has an unbroken provenance. In contrast, the other 16 studies (Cat. 88–92, 95) in many respects stand apart from Leonardo's œuvre, something we should look at before considering the difficult issue of attribution. These studies are all executed on linen, which meant they could not be worked using the usual materials of crayon or pen but only with a brush. The linen was first evenly coated with a brown or grey preparation, moreover, meaning that the draughtsman had to work from dark to light. After first laying down the outlines and areas of shadow in black, the study had to be built up in lighter shades, finishing off with white heightening. This method of working is thus the very opposite of the usual drawing by hand, for on paper the areas that are lightest are mostly those

that have been left blank, whereas the dark areas are those of particularly heavy sketching.

The method adopted in the present drapery studies is comparable, on the other hand, with the technique employed in contemporary 15th-century painting, in which areas destined to receive draperies were given a dark ground before the artist embarked on the actual painting. As the unfinished *Adoration of the Magi* shows, this was a technique that Leonardo clearly preferred, since he has in places applied the preparatory layer of paint so thickly that the corresponding areas appear almost black. In view of their technical similarity with painting, therefore, the present studies may represent exercises designed to introduce the artist to the technique of painting. This seems all the more likely considering that draperies even in painting are usually executed in just one colour; thus the practical procedure in both cases remains essentially the same.

Supporters of the attribution of these studies to Leonardo frequently refer to a passage from the *Life of Leonardo* (1568 edition) by the artist and biographer Giorgio Vasari (1511–1574). During his apprenticeship, Vasari writes, Leonardo sometimes "made clay models, draping the figures with rags dipped in plaster, and then drawing them painstakingly on fine Rheims cloth or prepared linen. These drawings were done in black and white with the point of the brush, and the results were marvellous, as one can see from the examples I have in my book of drawings." Vasari's information is valuable but can no longer entirely be checked, since the albums in his collection were broken up and the drawings scattered to the four winds. The few that survive, however, suggest that Vasari's attributions should be viewed with caution. Furthermore, the same author had already described a similar use of clay models in his *Vita* of Piero della Francesca (1416/17–1492), and it was also known to one of Piero's contemporaries, Antonio di Averlino Filarete (c. 1400–1469).

Historical sources are not alone in leaving the attribution of these drapery studies unresolved. Stylistic investigations are equally inconclusive, since the meticulous execution of the studies has left no room either for hatching or for the artist to develop his graphic style more freely. The situation is further complicated by the fact that the search for works of

art from the same period to which the studies might convincingly be linked has proved fruitless. While some have noted the similarities between Cat. 89 and the draperies of the Virgin in Leonardo's *Annunciation*, the drapery formation to which this study is devoted is typical of the day and is found in the works of other artists. More potent is the argument that another study (Cat. 87) comes closest to a work by one of Leonardo's contemporaries, Domenico Ghirlandaio (1449–1494). Despite intense debate, current scholarship thus seems to have reached a stalemate with regard to these drapery studies (and a few others not reproduced here). Ultimately, we simply do not have enough information to agree upon a definite attribution; all we can say is that, statistically, there is a good chance that several of the studies in this group were executed by Leonardo.

Although the mutual exchange of ideas between artists has attracted increasing interest amongst art historians in recent years, such processes have been taken into almost no consideration in the context of the present group of studies. The fact that several apprentices frequently trained under the same master, for example, meant that they were all given the same exemplars to copy from. Journeymen artists, meanwhile, took their most recent studies with them from place to place. New printing technology also contributed to the geographical spread of motifs and stylistic trends. Hence a similarity between Cat. 87 and the painting by Domenico Ghirlandaio does not necessarily mean that the two works are directly linked. Bearing in mind that a high proportion of Renaissance pictures – and particularly drawings – have since been lost, it seems more likely that the drapery study and the corresponding painting derive from a common prototype, and that many other drawings of this type were originally in circulation. The *Drapery Study for a Seated Figure* (Cat. 95), for example, also exists in another version, albeit executed on paper, by one of Leonardo's contemporaries (Paris, Institut Néerlandais, Inv. 2491).

*Johannes Nathan*

**Literature:** Degenhart,1934; Fahy, 1969; Ames-Lewis, 1981a; Cadogan, 1983; *Leonardo da Vinci. Die Gewandstudien*, 1989.

*One of the remarkable aspects of Leonardo's talent was the extremes he went to, in his anxiety to achieve solidity of modelling, in the use of inky shadows. Thus to get the darkest possible grounds Leonardo selected blacks that made deeper shadows and were indeed blacker than any other, endeavouring to make his lights all the brighter by contrast.*

GIORGIO VASARI, 1568

88

89

90

**87** Leonardo (or Domenico Ghirlandio ?)
**Drapery Study for a Seated Figure seen from the Front,** *c.* **1475–1478 (?)**
*Brush and greyish-brown tempera, with white heightening, on greyish-brown prepared canvas, 268 x 178 mm*
*Berlin, Staatliche Museen zu Berlin – Preussischer Kulturbesitz, Kupferstichkabinett, Inv. 5039*

**88 Drapery Study for a Kneeling Figure in Profile to the Right,** *c.* **1472–1475 (?)**
*Brush and grey tempera, with white heightening, on grey prepared canvas, 206 x 281 mm*
*Paris, Musée du Louvre, Cabinet des Dessins, R. F. 41904*

**89 Drapery Study for a Seated Figure Seen in Three-quarter Profile to the Left,** *c.* **1475/76 (?)**
*Brush and grey tempera, with white heightening, on grey prepared canvas, 220 x 139 mm*
*Paris, Musée du Louvre, Cabinet des Dessins, R. F. 41905*

**90 Study of Draperies falling over the Left Leg of a Seated Figure,** *c.* **1475/76 (?)**
*Brush and greyish-brown tempera, with white heightening, on grey prepared canvas, 240 x 193 mm*
*Paris, Institut Néerlandaise, Collection Frits Lugt, Inv. 6632*

91

92

93

94

**91** Leonardo (or Fra Bartolommeo?)
**Drapery Study for a Standing Figure Stepping forwards to the Right,**
*c.* **1475–1480 (?)**
*Brush and greyish-brown tempera, with white heightening, on grey prepared canvas, 286 x 212 mm*
*Rennes, Musée des Beaux-Arts, Inv. 794-1-2506*

**92** Leonardo (or Andrea del Verrocchio?)
**Drapery Study for a Standing Figure Seen from the Front, 1478–1480 (?)**
*Brush and greyish-brown tempera, with white heightening, on grey prepared canvas, 315 x 203 mm*
*Rennes, Musée des Beaux-Arts, Inv. 794-1-2507*

**93 Drapery Study for a Kneeling Figure turned to the Left,** *c.* **1475–1480 (?)**
*Metalpoint, charcoal and brown wash, with white heightening, on vermilion prepared paper, 257 x 190 mm*
*Rome, Gabinetto delle Stampe, Inv. F.C. 125770*

**94 Drapery Study for a Kneeling Figure,** *c.* **1475–1480 (?)**
*Lampblack with white heightening on bluish prepared paper, 213 x 159 mm*
*Windsor Castle, Royal Library (RL 12521r)*

95

**95** Leonardo (or Domenico
Ghirlandaio?)
**Drapery Study for a Seated
Figure,** *c.* 1475–1480 (?)
*Brush and greyish-brown tempera,*
*with white heightening, on grey*
*prepared canvas, 265 x 253 mm*
*Paris, Musée du Louvre,*
*Cabinet des Dessins, R. F. 2255*

# 5 Profile studies, character heads and grotesques

We have already encountered the second in this group of drawings (Cat. 97) in Chapter 3. Together with the recto of the same sheet (Cat. 65), it documents Leonardo's unusual interest in the human physiognomy. What is noteworthy about this sheet is not simply the sheer wealth of studies it contains, but also the fact that these can be divided without difficulty into two groups: on the one hand, the idealized youth, and on the other the often hideous old man, his face etched by experience. As so often with Leonardo, seemingly unorganized fields of interest reveal themselves, upon closer inspection, to be clearly defined.

It is not easy to determine the purpose of these studies. A glance at the *Adoration of the Magi* nevertheless shows that Leonardo evidently drew upon his reserves of such studies in his preliminary work on certain paintings. Amongst the drawings for the *Last Supper* and the *Battle of Anghiari*, we also find studies in a similar vein to the group seen here (cf. Cat. 12–15). The similarities are usually too generic, however, to permit us to conclude that direct links existed between them. Furthermore, the present types of study are evidently distributed very evenly throughout Leonardo's entire œuvre, making the suggestion that they belong to the preliminary phase of a specific work less plausible.

In view of this fact, art historians have proposed a series of hypotheses that seek to explain and categorize these sketches. Thus they have been seen by one as a symptom of a particular psychological disposition, and indeed deformation, on Leonardo's part, and by another as the remnants of a collection of standard types that Leonardo wanted to make available to his pupils. A further author has seen in them the beginnings of a systematic study of the human character. Since there is no overall evidence of any system to these studies, however, other than the fact that they concentrate upon two head types, the last two theories seem somewhat improbable. Can we then find no practical reasons for the execution of these drawings, and are they to be explained only by reference to some strange mentality on the part of the artist?

The study of Leonardo's drawings on the human physiognomy has shed light on his technique of combination. One of the chief instruments of this technique is Leonardo's supreme mastery of a limited range of motifs, a facility that also permits their rapid modulation. With regard to the human face, too,

Leonardo recommends the young artist to select and combine the best features that he has collected from studying the faces of the people around him (MK 530). Even if Leonardo may have borrowed this piece of advice from the ancient Greek painter Zeuxis (5th century BC; cf. Pliny, *Natural History* XXXV, 64), its relevance to his own practice cannot be ignored. In another passage, indeed, he even discusses in detail the three basic kinds of nose – straight, concave and convex – and the variations that are found within each of these categories (MK 535).

Leonardo's practice of combining features is demonstrated particularly clearly in the present drawings of grotesque heads (Cat. 107, 122–126). Thus we find a forehead – here flat, there bulging – married to a nose – now pug, now hooked – and finally a chin – here receding, there protruding. This method can be directly observed in the *Study of a Bearded Old Man in Profile* (Cat. 120): after trying out a number of variations, the artist has opted for a pronouncedly aquiline nose. Although, by its very nature, the idealized profile was unable to draw upon such an extreme range of options, comparisons reveal that even here, too, subtle variations were explored in different sketches. Leonardo's work on such drawings fitted seamlessly into his artistic practice. The question still remains, however, as to why Leonardo chose to combine strongly contrasting elements in these studies.

One answer may be provided by a remarkable sheet in the Uffizi (Cat. 106), which, in contrast to most of the other sketches in this series, has been executed with extreme care. Its appearance suggests that it was produced for a special occasion, perhaps as a gift or a presentation drawing. Whatever the case, the study was intended to impress – a consideration that would have influenced not just its formal composition but also its content. A bald-headed old man with a bent nose, down-turned mouth, protruding chin and wrinkled neck is gazing into the eyes of a youth with regular features and a mass of curly hair. Leonardo is here seeking to heighten the impact of his composition not just through meticulous draughtsmanship but also by contrasting two very different types. Not without reason does he recommend painters to combine the old and the ugly with the young and the beautiful: "I say that in narrative paintings you should closely intermingle direct opposites, because they offer a great contrast to each other, and the more so the more they are adjacent.

Thus, have the ugly one next to the beautiful, the large next to the small, the old next to the young, the strong next to the weak. In this way there is as much variety, as closely juxtaposed as possible" (MK 568).

If we accept, as the rationale behind Leonardo's emphasis upon contrast, a sober consideration of pictorial effect rather than a psychological state of tension, his general concentration upon two particularly distinctive, dissimilar types finds a logical artistic explanation. As in his studies of horses, in which he ultimately focused upon just a few particularly effective views, Leonardo's concentration clearly obeyed an economic logic: he had to rationalize his own labour. Although the large number of these studies might initially seem to refute this argument, the human figure ultimately occupied pride of place within the repertoire of Renaissance art, and expertise in the reproduction of faces and facial expressions was of supreme importance. Seen from this angle, Leonardo's volume of work in this area does not seem out of proportion – especially when we consider that he was by nature an indefatigable draughtsman. In other subject areas, too, such as his animal drawings (Cat. 85), he explored actions and poses in a manner fundamentally related to his studies of heads, (Cat. 97).

That this method of working was deeply ingrained can be clearly seen in the so-called *Self-portrait* in Turin (Cat. 121). Doubts as to whether this is truly a self-portrait are raised not least by a comparison with the captioned drawing of a less furrowed face with much more regular features in Windsor. Further comparisons, in particular with a series of large-format studies of a similar facial type (Cat. 116, 117, 119, 120), suggest that – should the Turin sheet really have been intended as a self-portrait – Leonardo's habit of improvising upon a profoundly familiar facial type has, in this late drawing, again got the upper hand over impartial observation. For here, too, we are looking at a motif that – as in the case of the early study of a *Warrior with Helmet and Breastplate in Profile* copied from a work by Andrea del Verrocchio (Cat. 103) – Leonardo had learnt long ago from his teacher.

*Johannes Nathan*

**Literature:** Gombrich, 1976a; Caroli, 1991; Kwakkelstein, 1994; Laurenza, 2001.

97

98

99

100

◄ **96 Head and Shoulders of a Youth in Profile,** *c.* 1486
*Pen and ink, 137 x 82 mm*
*Windsor Castle, Royal Library*
*(RL 12432r)*

**97 Studies of Heads in Profile,** *c.* 1478–1480
*(verso of Cat. 65)*
*Pen and ink, 405 x 290 mm*
*Windsor Castle, Royal Library*
*(RL 12276v)*

**98 Study of a Man with a Headpiece Seen in Profile,** *c.* 1485–1487
*Pen and ink, 73 x 49 mm*
*Windsor Castle, Royal Library*
*(RL 12442r)*

**99 Study of a Young Woman in Profile,** *c.* 1488–1492
*Metalpoint on reddish prepared paper, 320 x 200 mm*
*Windsor Castle, Royal Library*
*(RL 12505r)*

**100 Study of a Young Woman in Profile,** *c.* 1511/12
*Black and red chalk,*
*170 x 146 mm*
*Windsor Castle, Royal Library*
*(RL 12508r)*

101

102

103

**101  Profile Studies of Two
Warriors in Helmets,** *c.* **1472**
*Pen and ink, 60 x 102 mm*
*Windsor Castle, Royal Library*
*(RL 12590r)*

**102  Bearded Old Man in
Profile,** *c.* **1472 (?)**
*Pen and ink, 130 x 67 mm*
*Windsor Castle, Royal Library*
*(RL 12441r)*

**103  Warrior with Helmet
and Breastplate in Profile,**
*c.* **1472**
*Silverpoint on cream-coloured
prepared paper, 285 x 207 mm*
*London, British Museum,*
*Inv. 1895-9-15-474*

▶ **104  Drawing of Two Heads
in Profile and Studies of
Machines, December 1478**
*(recto of Cat. 336)*
*Pen and ink, 202 x 266 mm*
*Florence, Galleria degli Uffizi,*
*Gabinetto dei Disegni e delle*
*Stampe, Inv. 446 Ev*

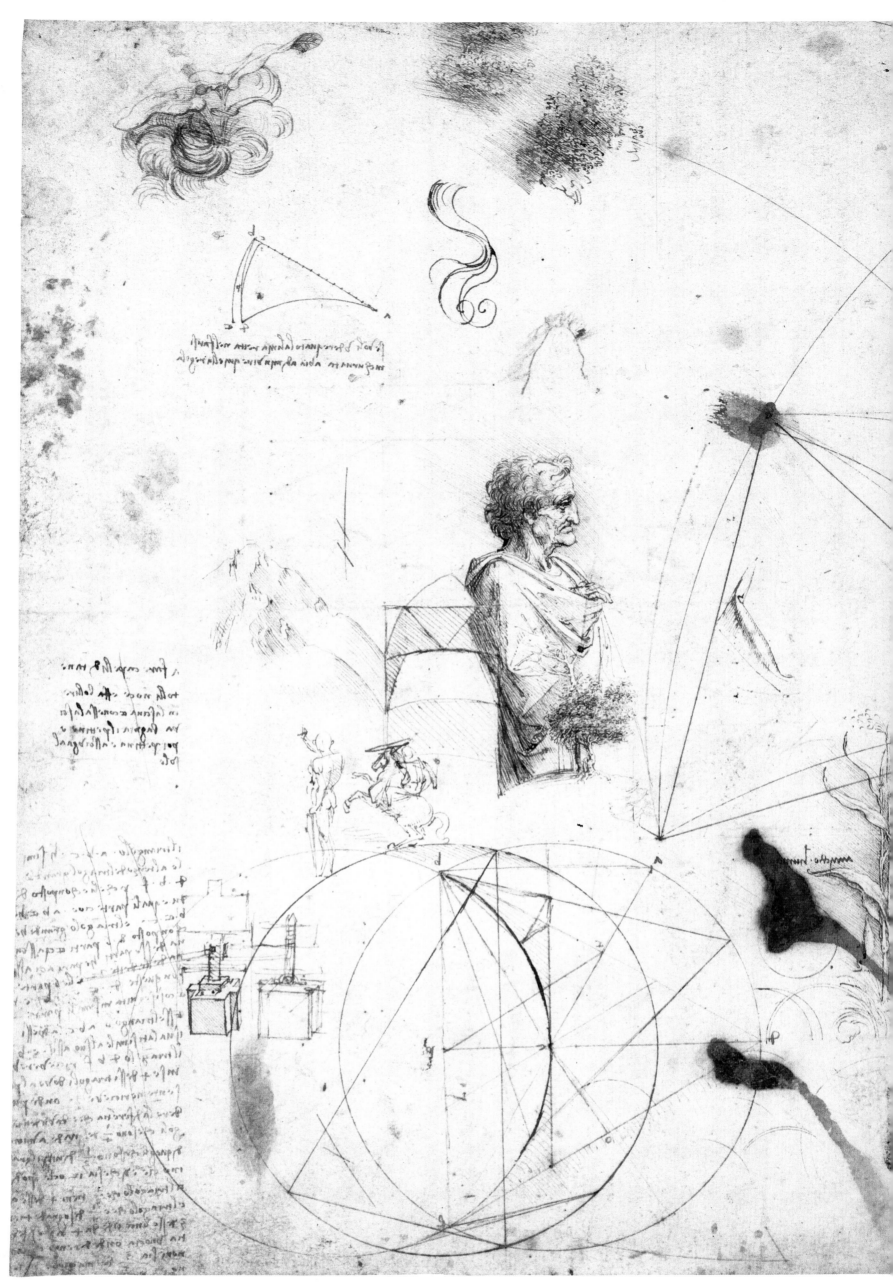

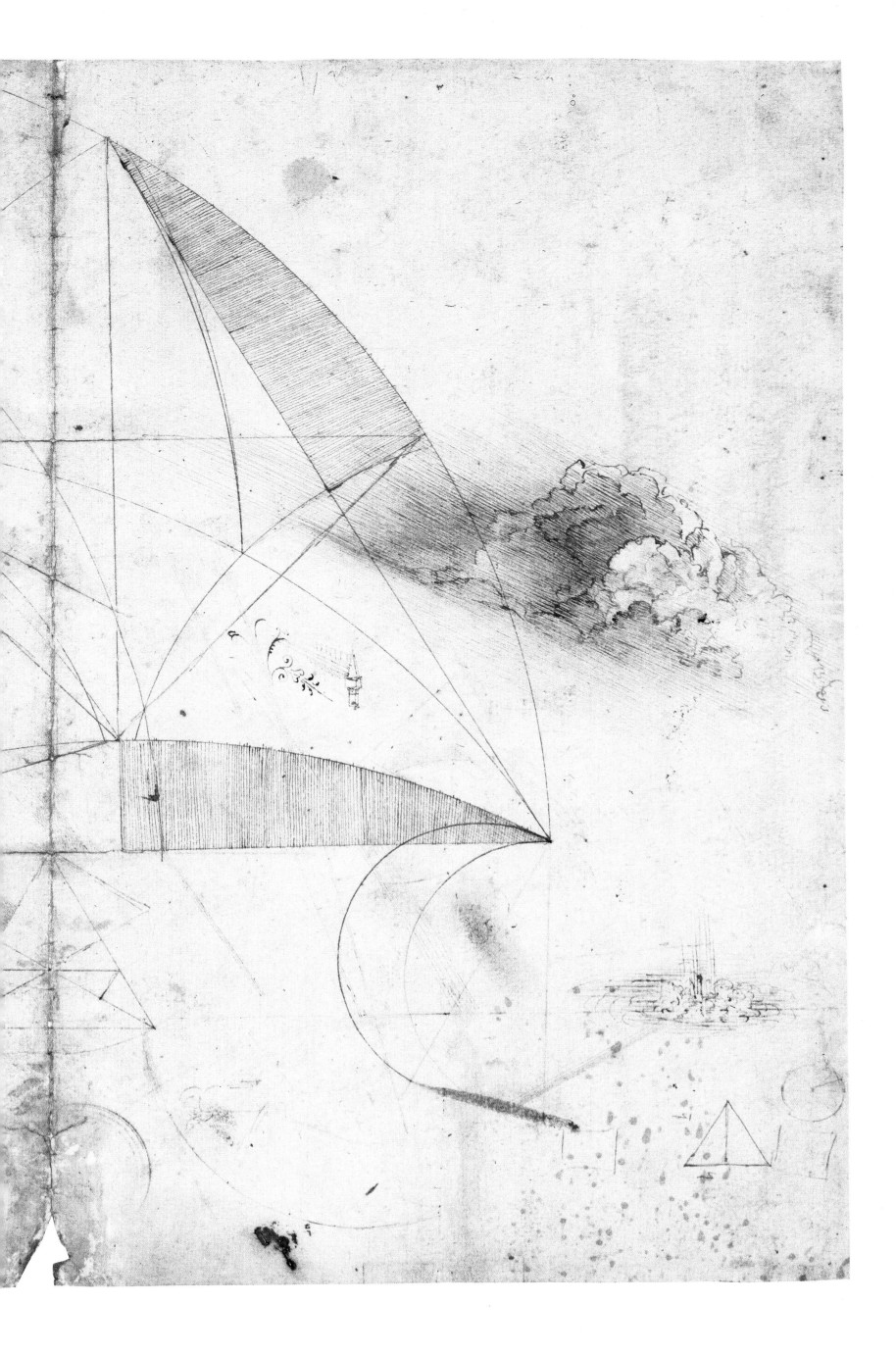

106

107

108

109

◄ 105  Sheet of Studies of
Geometric Figures and the
Bust of an Old Man in
Profile, *c. 1490*
*Pen and ink, 320 x 446 mm*
*Windsor Castle, Royal Library*
*(RL 12283r)*

106  Studies of an Old Man
and a Youth (Salai?) in
Profile, Facing each Other,
*c. 1500–1505*
*Red chalk, 210 x 150 mm*
*Florence, Galleria degli Uffizi,*
*Gabinetto dei Disegni e delle*
*Stampe*

107  Drawing of a Grotesque
Male Head and Sketch of a
Flying Machine, *c. 1485–1490*
*Pen and ink, 112 x 75 mm*
*Venice, Gallerie dell'Accademia,*
*Inv. 234*

108  Profile Study of an Old
Man with a Laurel Wreath,
*c. 1506–1508*
*Pen and ink and red chalk,*
*168 x 125 mm*
*Turin, Biblioteca Reale,*
*Inv. 15575*

109  Head of a Man in
Profile, *c. 1506–1508*
*Pen and ink and red and black*
*chalk, 147 x 104 mm*
*Venice, Gallerie dell'Accademia,*
*Inv. 264*

110

111

112

113

**110 Bust of an Older Man in Profile (Gian Giacomo Trivulzio?),** *c.* 1510
*Red and black chalk on reddish prepared paper, 222 x 159 mm*
*Windsor Castle, Royal Library*
*(RL 12556r)*

**111 Head and Shoulders of a Youth in Profile (Salaì?),** *c.* 1510
*Black chalk, 193 x 149 mm*
*Windsor Castle, Royal Library*
*(RL 12557r)*

**112 Profile Study of the Head and Upper Torso of a Man,** *c.* 1510/11
*Red chalk on reddish prepared paper, 198 x 146 mm*
*Windsor Castle, Royal Library*
*(RL 12598r)*

**113 Profile Study of a Youth (Salaì?),** *c.* 1510
*Red chalk on reddish prepared paper, 217 x 153 mm*
*Windsor Castle, Royal Library*
*(RL 12554r)*

114

115

116

117

**114 Head and Shoulders of
a Bearded Man in a Turban,**
*c.* **1510**
*Pen and ink, 154 x 205 mm*
*Windsor Castle, Royal Library*
*(RL 19106r)*

**115 Profile Study of a
Bearded Man,** *c.* **1513**
*Black chalk, 178 x 130 mm*
*Windsor Castle, Royal Library*
*(RL 12553r)*

**116 Head and Shoulders
of an Older Man,** *c.* **1510–1515**
*Red chalk on reddish prepared
paper, 178 x 136 mm*
*Windsor Castle, Royal Library*
*(RL 12503r)*

**117 Character Head of an
Older Man and Sketch of
a Lion's Head,** *c.* **1505–1510**
*Red chalk with white heightening
on pink prepared paper,
183 x 136 mm*
*Windsor Castle, Royal Library*
*(RL 12502r)*

118

119

120

121

**118 Portrait Drawing of
a Bearded Man (Cesare
Borgia),** *c.* 1502–1503
*Red chalk, 111 x 284 mm*
*Turin, Biblioteca Reale,*
*Inv. 15573*

**119 Profile Study of an
Old Man with a Beard and
Braided Hair,** *c.* 1511–1513
*Black chalk, 213 x 155 mm*
*Windsor Castle, Royal Library*
*(RL 12499r)*

**120 Study of a Bearded
Old Man in Profile,** *c.* 1513
*Black chalk, 253 x 182 mm*
*Windsor Castle, Royal Library*
*(RL 12500r)*

**121 Head of a Bearded
Man (so-called** *Self-portrait*),
*c.* 1510–1515 (?)
*Red chalk, 333 x 214 mm*
*Turin, Biblioteca Reale,*
*Inv. 15571*

122

123

124

125

**122  Five Grotesque Heads,**
**c. 1494**
*Pen and ink, 261 x 206 mm*
*Windsor Castle, Royal Library*
*(RL 12495r)*

**123  Profile Study of a**
**Grotesque Head, c. 1500–1505**
*Red chalk, 100 x 80 mm*
*Hamburg, Hamburger Kunsthalle,*
*Inv. 21482*

**124  Grotesque Portrait Study**
**of a Man, c. 1500–1505**
*Black chalk, reworked by foreign*
*hand (pricked), 390 x 280 mm*
*Oxford, Governing Body,*
*Christ Church, Inv. JBS 19*

**125** after Leonardo
(Francesco Melzi)
**Grotesque Portrait of an**
**Old Woman, c. 1490/91 (?)**
*Red chalk, 172 x 143 mm*
*Windsor Castle, Royal Library*
*(RL 12492r)*

**126** after Leonardo
(Francesco Melzi)
**Grotesque Portrait Studies**
**with a Caricature of Dante**
**(bottom right), c. 1492 (?)**
*Red chalk, 195 x 146 mm*
*Windsor Castle, Royal Library*
*(RL 12493r)*

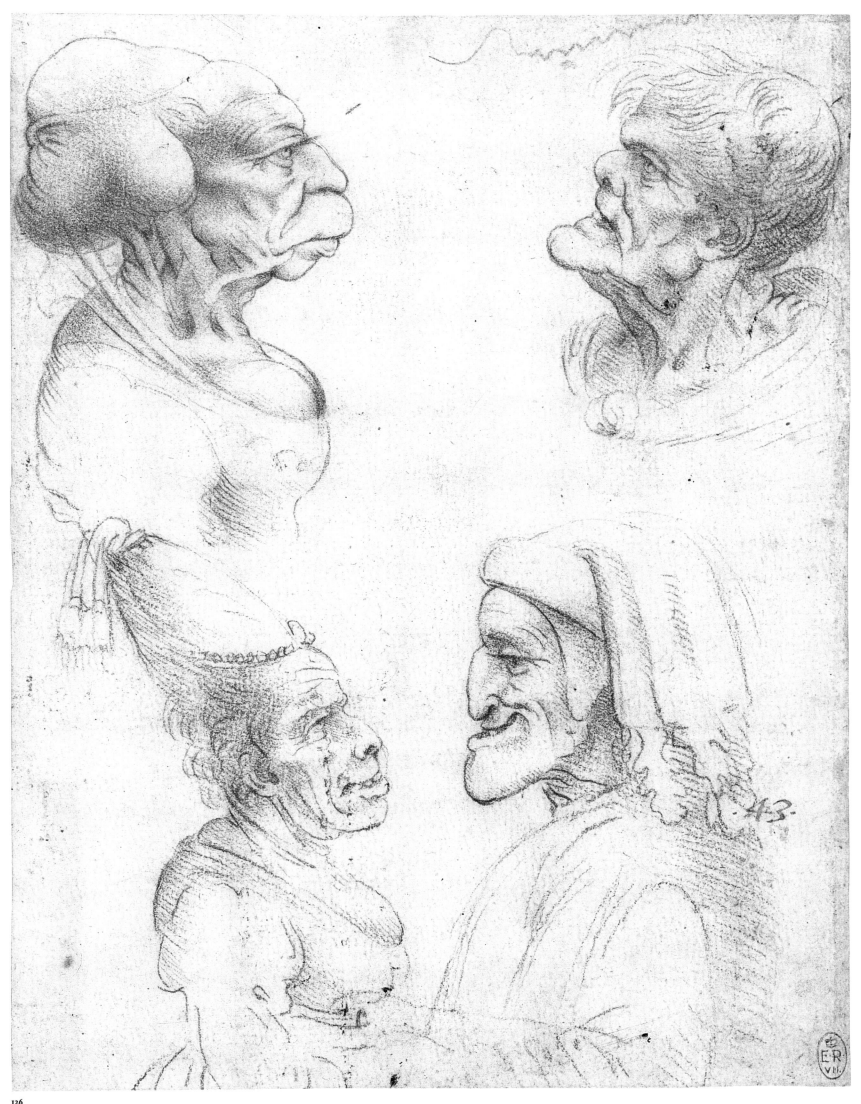

# 6 Proportion drawings

Leonardo's proportion drawings form a logical part of his studies of people and animals, and in particular horses, and appear within these subject areas in numbers that correspond closely to the size ratio of each subject area to Leonardo's total œuvre. Thus the majority are devoted to the proportions of the face and head and the human body in general (Cat. 127–137), while a considerable number relate to horses (Cat. 138–142). Other animals, by contrast, are virtually ignored. These studies represent a linear extension of Leonardo's artistic interests. Once again, they are far more numerous than comparable studies by Leonardo's contemporaries.

With his interest in proportion, Leonardo formed part of a long tradition. As long ago as classical antiquity, artists such as the famous sculptor Polyclitus had made detailed studies of the ideal proportions of the human body. In the Middle Ages, artists followed a less exact schema, the so-called Canon of Mount Athos, with its division of the height of a grown man into nine parts. Almost all artists of the 15th century oriented themselves towards this system. The first to adopt a truly new approach was the humanist Leon Battista Alberti (1404–1472), who in his treatise *De statua* (1434/35) corrected the earlier schemata, made his own measurements and also took into account the three-dimensional depth of the body.

It was probably without direct knowledge of Alberti's methods and results that, from about 1489, Leonardo began developing his own canon of proportion, one that aimed to express individual parts of the body as fractions either of the whole or of larger parts. His emphasis thus fell not on absolute measurements, but on the proportions of the individual parts of the body, one to the other. At the same time, Leonardo sought to impose a clear geometric schema above all on the human head. The first drawing reproduced here (Cat. 127) already points in this direction, but reveals differing points of departure in the verticals overlaying the face. The intersections of the horizontals and diagonals running across the brows, nose, upper lip and chin similarly float more or less in undefined space. The experimental nature of the sketch also reveals itself in the fact that Leonardo drew the head first, before trying to apply a regular grid to it. From an examination of other studies, it seems that in most cases this was the order in which Leonardo preferred to work. He drew the image he knew well first, and only then added the measurements, which he calculated by measuring either the sketch itself or a model. Even such an elaborate study as that of a magnificent horse by the name of "Ciciliano" from the stable of the Milanese commander Galeazzo da Sanseverino (Cat. 138) arose according to this principle, for if we remeasure the sheet we find that the proportions of the drawing do not agree with the measurements entered for the horse. When executing these sketches, Leonardo thus still did not accept a fixed schema of proportion of the kind that would find expression in the illustrations to the treatise on proportion by Albrecht Dürer (1471–1528) a few years later (1528). On the contrary, the majority of his studies testify to ongoing research and investigation. Only his famous drawing in Venice (Cat. 136), based on Vitruvius and consequently known as the "Vitruvian Man", ventures, in its perfect formal arrangement, a definitive statement of human proportions.

The unusually cleanly drawn "Vitruvian Man" marks the end of a long series of detailed measurements of the human body (Cat. 135). As a concept, however, it derives from Vitruvius (1st century BC), who in his treatise *De architectura libri decem* (3.1.) put forward measurements based on the Greek system of metrology. At the heart of this system is the assumption that the fathom (Gr. *orguia*) – a measure of length from the tip of one outstretched arm across the chest to the tip of the other outstretched arm – corresponds to the height of a grown man and can be subdivided into smaller units of length. Vitruvius likewise expressed his system of proportions in fractions of the height of a man and hence also of a fathom: one cubit equalled $\frac{1}{4}$ of the height of a man, one foot $\frac{1}{6}$, one hand's span $\frac{1}{8}$, one palm $\frac{1}{24}$ and one finger $\frac{1}{96}$. These divisions corresponded to the duodecimal system, which would remain in place right up till the introduction of the metre in the 19th century, and which as a rule operated with fractions with an even denominator: $\frac{1}{2}$, $\frac{1}{4}$, $\frac{1}{6}$, $\frac{1}{8}$, $\frac{1}{16}$ etc.

Leonardo's own anthropometric studies (Cat. 135) showed him that he could not agree with Vitruvius' canon in all its points. His own empiricism contradicted the simplifications implicit in Vitruvius' metrological system, whose measurements were rounded up into fractions with even denominators. In particular, he recognized that the measurement of one foot, taken to be $\frac{1}{6}$ of a man's height in metrology, was empirically incorrect. He therefore corrected it to $\frac{1}{7}$ and thus departed from the conventions of the duodecimal system embraced by Vitruvius. He otherwise sought to illustrate Vitruvius' text exactly; thus the calibrated scale beneath the drawing is given in *palmi* and *digiti* (palms and fingers), and the cubit ($\frac{1}{4}$) and the foot (here still $\frac{1}{6}$) are also indicated.

This polished drawing once again raises the question as to the purpose of Leonardo's studies of proportion. That they served more than simply a work-related function is beyond doubt, even if drawings such as Cat. 138 were executed as part of Leonardo's preparations for the equestrian monument to Francesco Sforza. Not even Leonardo can have thought that the job of artist demanded such detailed research into the measurements of man. The "Vitruvian Man" drawing is rather an indication of Leonardo's grander ambitions. The careful layout suggests that the sheet was intended for reproduction, and its reference to a classical authority – a convention of the day – would have made it suitable for the start of a series or treatise. Leonardo may even have planned to issue it as a single sheet, as had been done by the Florentine artist Antonio Pollaiuolo, who circulated prints of his famous *Battle of the Nudes* engraving amongst his contemporaries.

The degree of precision demonstrated in this drawing is matched by none of Leonardo's other studies on proportion. It is characteristic of Leonardo that he achieves this precision only in his illustration of someone else's ideas. When it came to his own research, on the other hand, it seems that Leonardo could never bring himself to formulate his conclusions in a definitive and comprehensive image – perhaps, too, because the deeper he probed into the subject, the more clearly he became aware of the insurmountable difficulties it posed.

*Johannes Nathan/Frank Zöllner*

**Literature:** Panofsky, 1921; Pedretti, 1965 (pp. 132–139); RLW, I (pp. 243–270); PRC, I (pp. 227–290); Zöllner, 1987; Berra, 1993; Alberti, 2000.

*Tolerance, it is true, demands that we respect differences of belief. But as already recognized by Leonardo da Vinci, to the degree that the truth becomes better known, so general consensus will come to replace individual opinions.*

THOMAS MANN, 1945

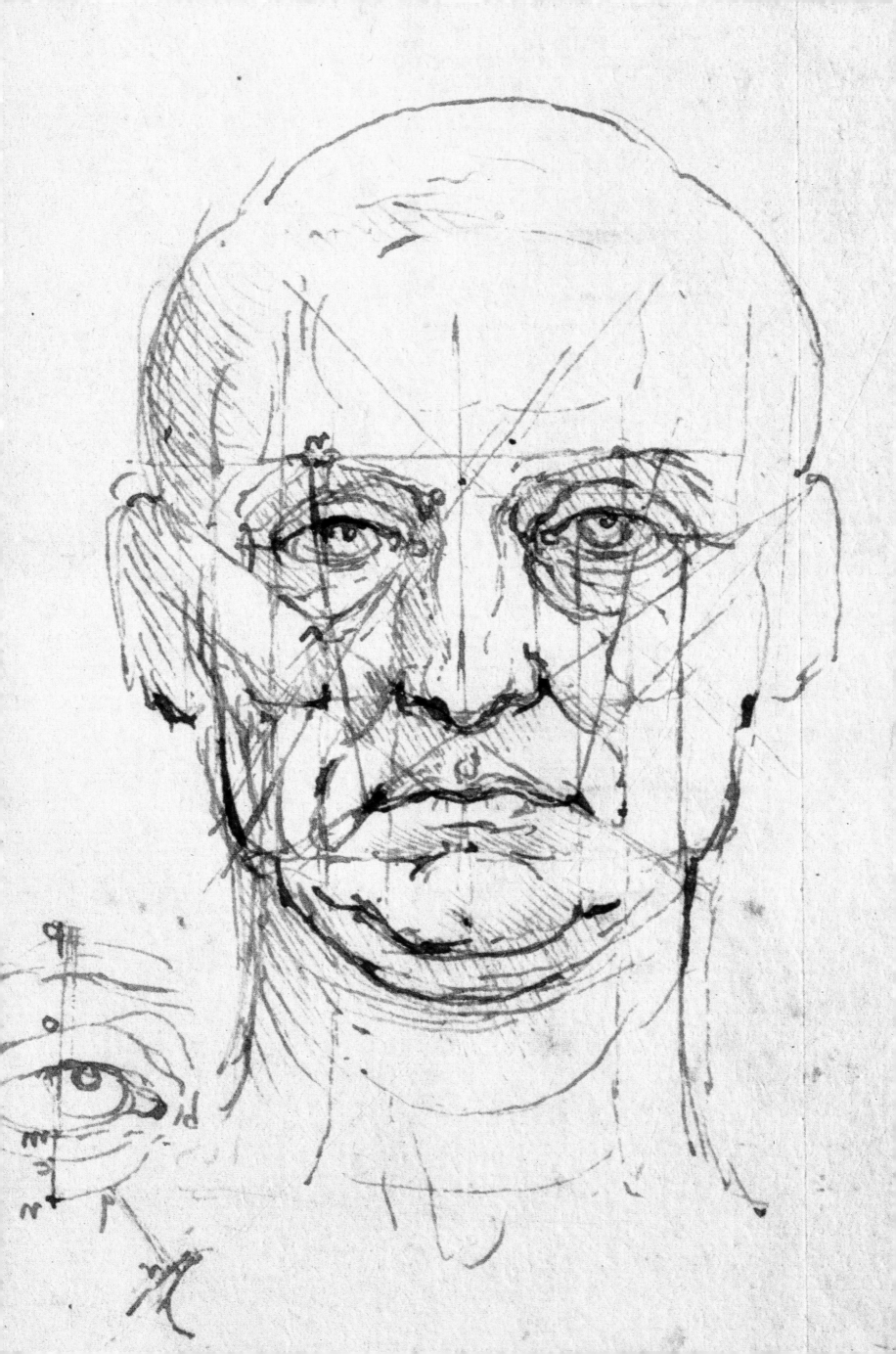

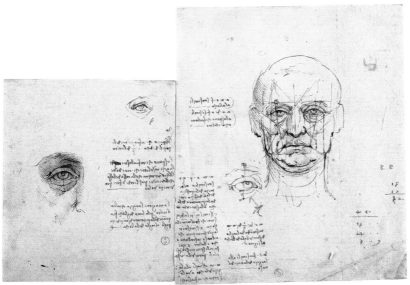

127

128

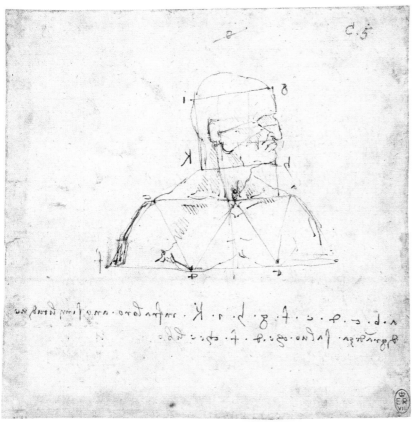

129

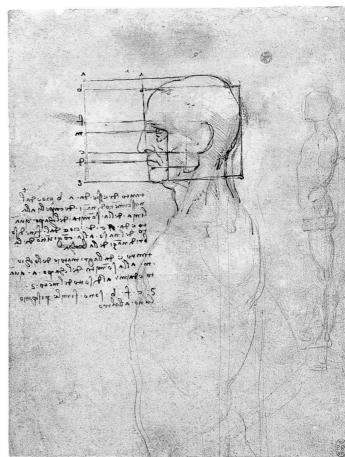

130

**127  Studies of the Proportions of the Face and Eye,**
*c. 1489/90*
*Pen and ink over metalpoint on yellowish prepared paper, 140 x 277 mm*
*Turin, Biblioteca Reale, Inv. 15574 D. C. recto*

**128  Study of the Proportions of the Head and Face,**
*c. 1489/90*
*Pen and dark brown ink over metalpoint on blue prepared paper, 213 x 153 mm*
*Windsor Castle, Royal Library (RL 12601r)*

**129  Study of the Proportions of the Head and Chest,**
*c. 1490*
*Pen and two shades of brown ink, 143 x 137 mm*
*Windsor Castle, Royal Library (RL 12607)*

**130  Bust of a Man in Profile, Squared for Proportion,**
*c. 1490*
*Pen and two shades of brown ink over metalpoint, 280 x 222 mm*
*Venice, Gallerie dell'Accademia, Inv. 236v*

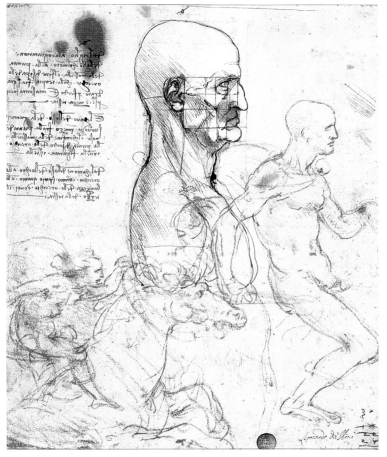

131

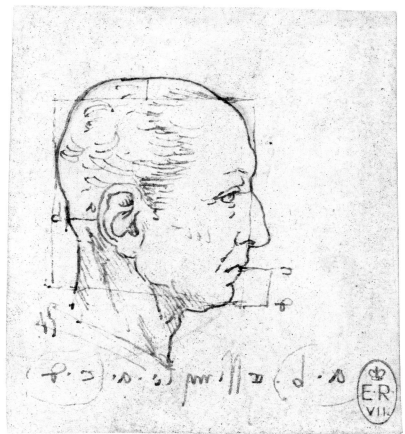

132

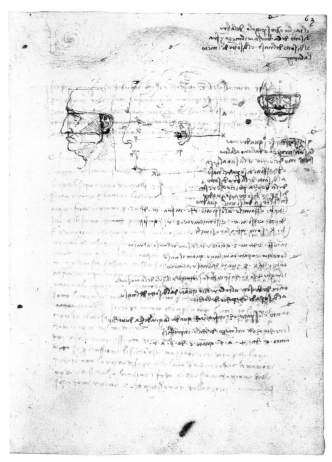

133

134

**131  Torso of a Man in Profile, the Head Squared for Proportion, and Sketches of Two Horsemen,** *c.* **1490 and** *c.* **1504**
*Pen and ink and red chalk over metalpoint, 280 x 222 mm*
*Venice, Gallerie dell'Accademia, Inv. 236r*

**132  Study of the Proportions of the Head,** *c.* **1490–1492**
*Pen and brown ink, 56 x 50 mm*
*Windsor Castle, Royal Library (RL 12606r)*

**133  Studies of the Proportions of the Head and Face,** *c.* **1490–1492**
*Pen and ink, 210 x 145 mm*
*Paris, Bibliothèque de l'Institut de France, MS 2172, fol. 63r*

**134  Studies of the Proportions of the Face, Head, Neck and Torso,** *c.* **1490**
*Pen and brown ink, 265 x 215 mm*
*Windsor Castle, Royal Library (RL 12304r)*

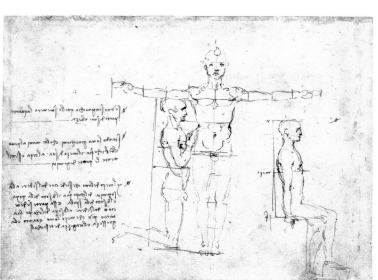

135

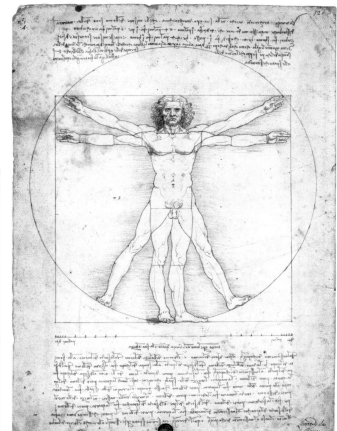

136

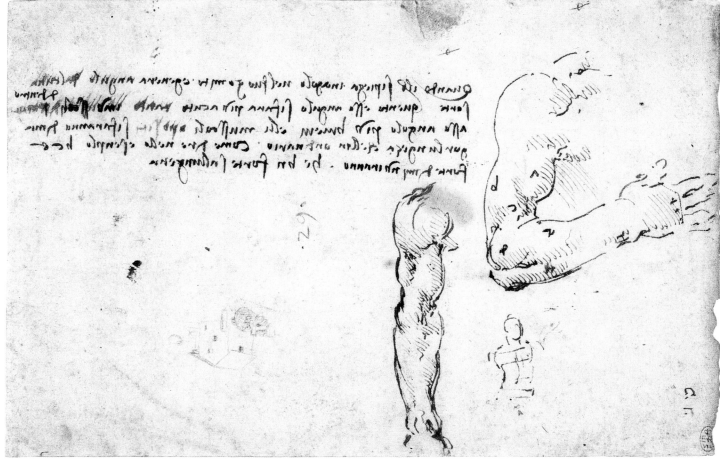

137

**135 Studies of the Propor-
tions of the Body when
Standing, Kneeling and
Sitting,** *c.* 1490
*Pen and two shades of brown ink,
160 x 218 mm
Windsor Castle, Royal Library
(RL 19132r)*

**136 The Proportions of
the Human Figure (after
Vitruvius),** *c.* 1490
*Pen and ink over metalpoint,
344 x 245 mm
Venice, Gallerie dell'Accademia,
Inv. 228*

**137 Study of the Proportions
of the Arm,** *c.* 1508
*Pen and brown ink and black
chalk, 155 x 230 mm
Windsor Castle, Royal Library
(RL 12614r)*

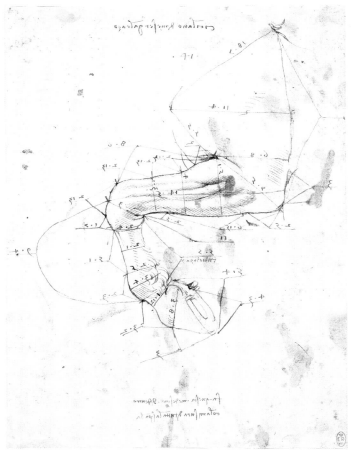

138

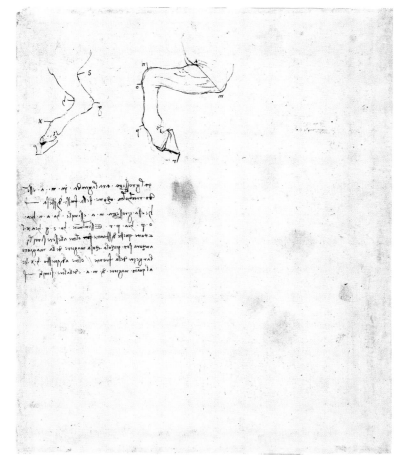

139

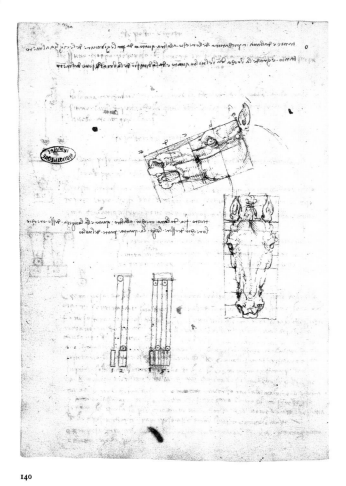

140

141

**138 Studies of the Proportions of a Horse's Leg,**
*c. 1485–1490*
*Pen, 250 x 187 mm*
*Windsor Castle, Royal Library*
*(RL 12294r)*

**139 Studies of the Proportions of a Horse's Leg,** *c. 1490*
*Pen and ink, 265 x 215 mm*
*Windsor Castle, Royal Library*
*(RL 12304v)*

**140 Studies of the Proportions of a Horse's Head,**
*c. 1490–1492*
*Pen and ink, 210 x 143 mm*
*Paris, Bibliothèque de l'Institut de France, MS A (2172), fol. 62v*

**141 Study of the Proportions of a Horse's Head,** *c. 1508–1511*
*Black chalk over red prepared paper, 275 x 197 mm*
*Windsor Castle, Royal Library*
*(RL 12286r)*

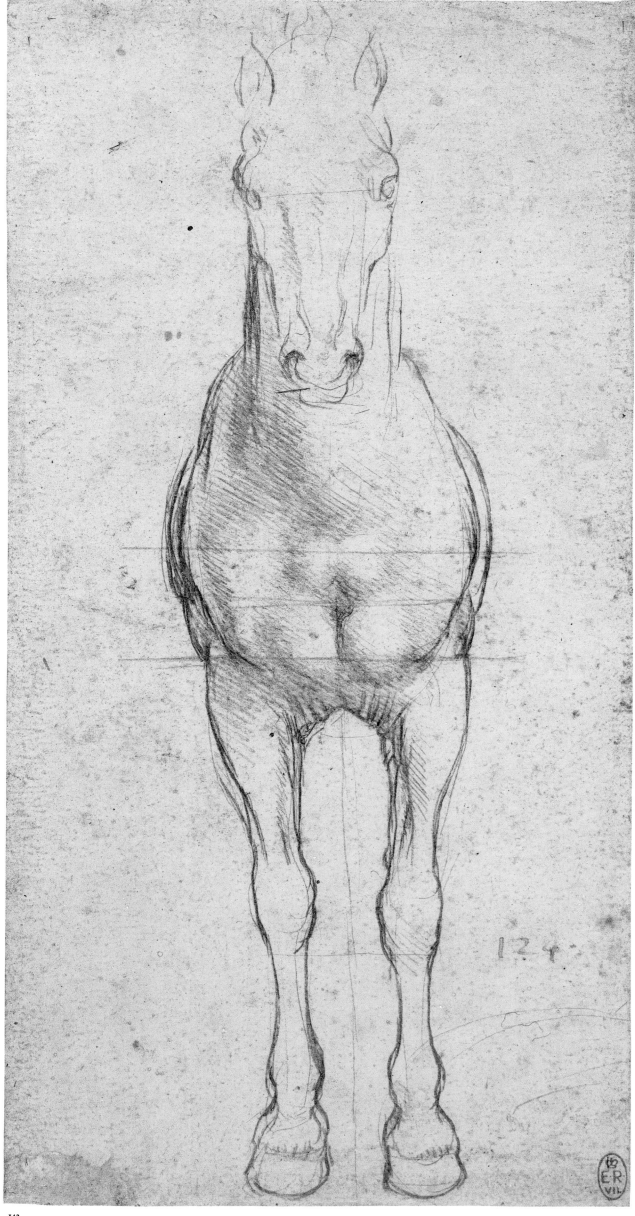

142

143

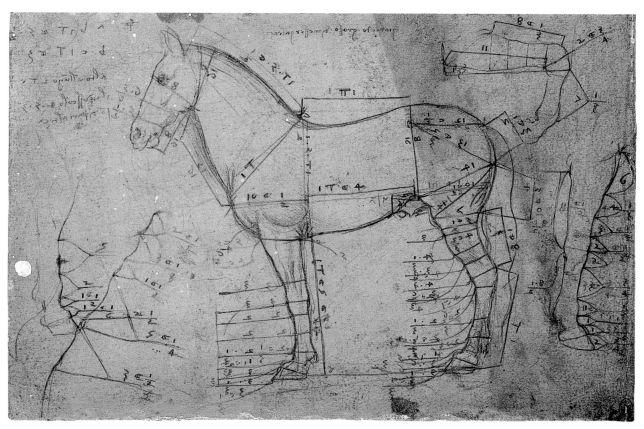

144

**142 Study of the Proportions
of a Horse,** *c.* **1481/82**
*Metalpoint on blue prepared paper,
221 x 110 mm*
*Windsor Castle, Royal Library*
*(RL 12290r)*

**143 Study of the Proportions
of a Horse,** *c.* **1489**
*Metalpoint on blue prepared paper,
150 x 189 mm*
*Windsor Castle, Royal Library*
*(RL 12320r)*

**144 Study of the Proportions
of a Horse,** *c.* **1489** (Detail)
*Metalpoint on blue prepared paper,
324 x 237 mm (total sheet)*
*Windsor Castle, Royal Library*
*(RL 12319r)*

# 7 Anatomical drawings

The main subject of the art of the late Middle Ages and the Renaissance was the human figure. It appeared in altarpieces, in Biblical, mythological and narrative paintings, and in portraits set in front of or inside buildings or, more rarely, within a landscape. Animals and plants served for the most part merely as accessories, and only in the sphere of drawing were landscape studies starting to emerge as an independent genre (cf. Cat. 229). Hence Leonardo's anatomical research sees art bordering on science – even if his study of the functioning of the body arose primarily out of an artistic desire to perfect his representation of the human figure. In this desire Leonardo was not alone amongst the artists of his day: Antonio Pollaiuolo, the Florentine master some 20 years older than Leonardo, was said to have dissected corpses, and even if this claim has failed to stand up to subsequent scrutiny, it is evident from Pollaiuolo's depictions of nudes that he must have made a thorough study of the human body. Michelangelo, Leonardo's younger contemporary, would also later think about compiling a work on anatomy, perhaps out of a sense of rivalry.

The field of superficial anatomy, covering the interplay of the muscles and bones visible just beneath the skin, is one naturally of interest to the artist. Unlike the study of deeper-lying parts of the body, surface anatomy was made a fixed part of artists' training soon after Leonardo's death, with apprentices required to make sketches of flayed human figures (later known as "écorchés"). Leonardo's own studies made him a forerunner in this field (cf. Cat. 151–154, etc.), and he emphasizes their vital importance for the artist in a note written on a schematic drawing of the cervical vertebra: "This illustration is as important for good draughtsmen as the derivation of Latin words for grammarians, since he who does not know which muscles cause what movements will draw the muscles of figures in motion and action in a poor fashion." Leonardo was nevertheless aware of the dangers of parading such anatomical knowledge in a painting, as he reveals in his warning to artists not to portray figures whose muscles are so bulging that they look like "a sack of walnuts".

Leonardo quickly turned his attention to the human body in its entirety. His advances into the subject went hand in hand with a notable shift in his approach as a draughtsman. Thus early sketches continue to reflect the ideas of the Greek anatomist Galen (AD 129–199), as repeated in Johannes de Ketham's *Fasciculus medicinae* (1495). Leonardo notes on this sheet that he wants to "cut through the middle of the heart, liver and lung and kidneys so that the tree of the vessels can be represented in its entirety". All the veins are here linked into a single system, in part via fictitious connections. Similarly simplified is Leonardo's portrayal of the sexual act (Cat.

204) and, to the lower left, the sketch of the human alimentary tract with two "stomachs", in which Leonardo simply applies his knowledge of animal anatomy to that of humans.

Later studies, on the other hand, are evidently the result of numerous dissections, of which Leonardo claimed, in a general introduction to anatomy written in his latter years, to have completed over 20 (RLW § 796). In the same passage, Leonardo sets out some of the deterrents to the study of anatomy, and in particular to the practice of dissection: "And if you should have a love for such things you might be prevented by loathing, and if that did not prevent you, you might be deterred by the fear of living in the night hours in the company of those corpses, quartered and flayed and horrible to see. And if this did not prevent you, perhaps you might not be able to draw so well […]."

There is no evidence in this passage to support the unfounded but often repeated claim that Leonardo's dissection of corpses caused him to be persecuted by the political or religious authorities; it nevertheless reveals how far he had distanced himself, with his anatomical studies, from the elegant world of the well-to-do painter as described in his treatise on painting (*The Works of the Eye and Ear Compared*, MK § 73). Considering the practical obstacles facing him in an age without disinfectants and preservatives, his aim to record the functioning of the human body in all its details appears all the more remarkable. His unusual efforts profoundly impressed his own contemporaries, as the earliest biography of Leonardo, written c. 1523–1527 by Paolo Giovio (1483–1552), makes clear: "In the doctors' schools of anatomy he dissected the corpses of criminals, undismayed by the brutal and repulsive nature of this study and only eager to learn how to portray in his painting the various limbs and muscles, their bending and stretching, in accordance with the laws of nature". While Leonardo's studies of limbs and muscles may indeed, as Giovio believed, have been intended to further his understanding as a painter, this seems unlikely to have been the reason for his investigations of the deeper-lying parts of the body (see below).

As an artist, Leonardo followed in his anatomical drawings a procedure that departed sharply from contemporary practice. Dissection at the universities continued to base itself upon traditional, mostly classical texts, which were read out and commented upon by the professor while an assistant sought to match the description to the appropriate limbs and organs. If authority thus lay within the academic world with textbooks largely written a long time ago, Leonardo started instead from the image. Thus he based his anatomical works on certain of the standard poses found in his artistic drawings. The contours of the head, torso and limbs employed in numerous

anatomical studies (Cat. 151, etc.) thereby reveal many correspondences with drawings in other areas of Leonardo's art (Cat. 74, 75, 108, etc.).

Leonardo's studies on anatomy can be roughly divided into an early (from c. 1487), a middle (1506–1510) and a late phase (after 1510). As already implied, the drawings from the early phase are based not on the dissection of corpses, but simply upon information that could be deduced from the surface of the human body, from the bodies of animals and from the human skeleton. Leading the way here are Leonardo's early skull studies (including one, Cat. 149, bearing the date 2 April 1489), which testify to his remarkable accomplishment as a draughtsman, both in his description of form and in his combination of view and section. Unprecedented for its day, for example, is the second sheet in this chapter (Cat. 146), in which Leonardo for the first time correctly represents the maxillary sinus in the cheekbone.

The task of illustrating how parts of the body moved was naturally more difficult than studying solid structures. In his sketches of muscles, Leonardo initially experimented with drawing them in cross-section (Cat. 150). That these cross-sections are little able to convey an understanding of the processes involved, however, is evidenced by a comparison with Leonardo's masterly studies of the hand from his mature years (Cat. 180). This latter drawing also reveals a tendency that would become even more pronounced in later studies: Leonardo increasingly refrains from portraying the muscles and sketches in their place the chords through which motive power is transmitted (Cat. 165, 167, 168).

Also dating from Leonardo's early years are a number of studies of the brain. An example here is found in Cat. 187, a sheet illustrating a number of Leonardo's early ideas on the functioning of the human body (including the vascular system, the alimentary tract and the skeleton). Next to the head in profile in the bottom left-hand corner is a section through a skull, which is intended to show the three successive "ventricles" in which the sense impressions received by the eye are processed, and which might be described as the switchboard and memory bank of the brain. The sense impressions received by the eye pass first to the *imprensiva* (which might be translated as "receiver"), where they are given a preliminary screening (cf. also RL 12 626). From the *imprensiva* they are sent on to the *sensus communis*, chief of all the senses, where they are processed by the faculty of judgement and the corresponding measures decided upon. Finally, certain data are stored in the *memoria*, the memory, to be kept for future use. Although the drawings, executed in metalpoint on blue prepared paper, have faded over time, it is still possible to see them, and to read the notes accompanying them, under ultraviolet light.

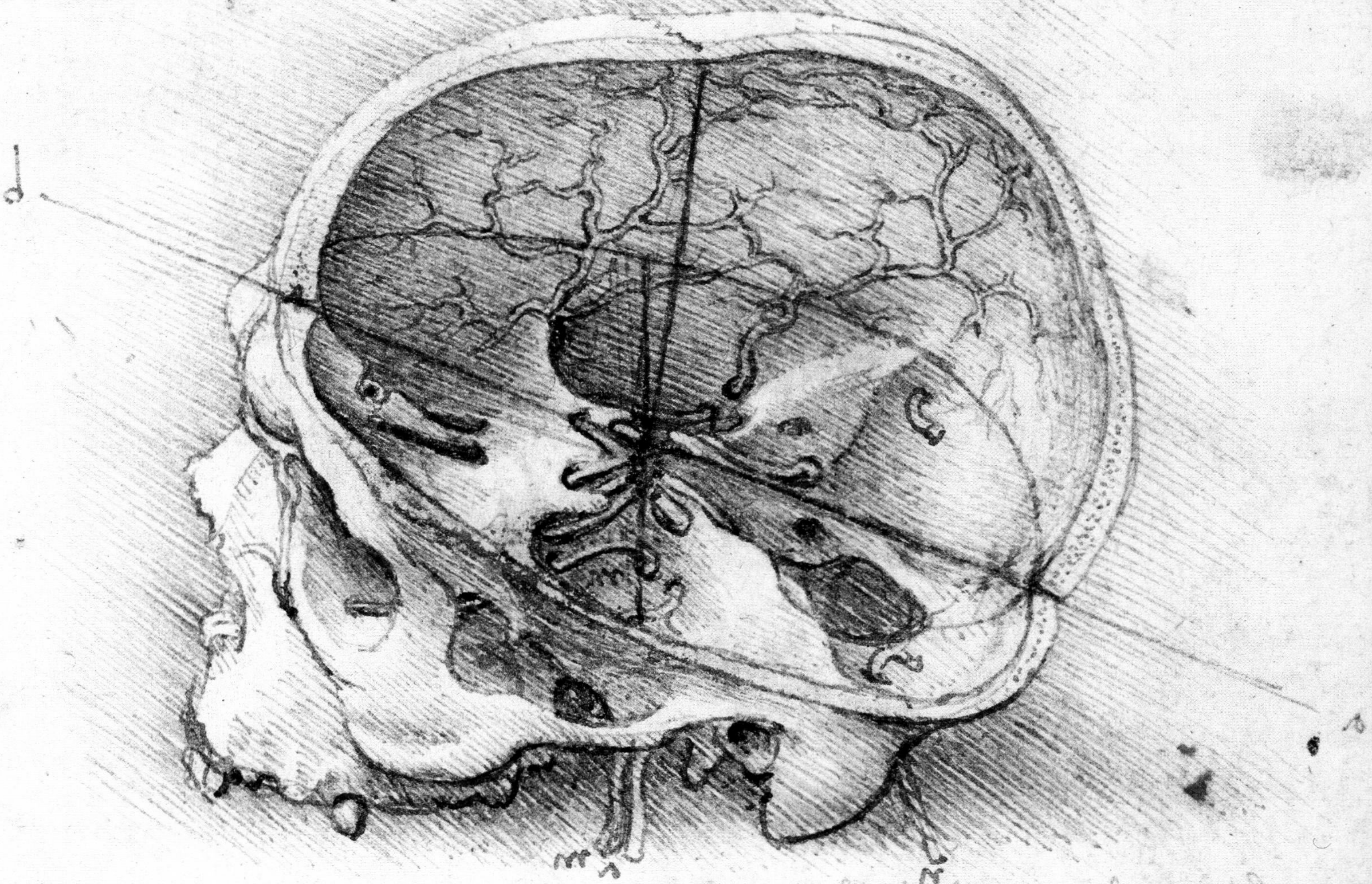
b
a

[illegible]

The diagrammatic illustration of the functioning of the brain seen in Cat. 187 essentially reflects traditional medieval interpretations of the writings of Aristotle. In his own version of this system, and in line with his conviction that the eye was the most important of all the senses, Leonardo concentrates first and foremost upon the route traced by visual impressions. This can also be seen in another anatomical study, in which the nerve leading to the eye is clearly drawn in. The connections to the ear, on the other hand, are only briefly indicated or are indeed omitted altogether. The directness of these early studies reflects the optimism with which Leonardo addressed himself to the most difficult and most fascinating areas of the human organism.

In contrast to these early studies, the anatomical drawings from Leonardo's mature years are founded on his first-hand observations of the dissected body. For a period Leonardo seems to have toyed with the idea of making an anatomical model of man, as a note on the sheet reproduced as Cat. 194 indicates. In an impressive, large-format drawing of the female body executed a good ten years later (Cat. 185), he attempted a synthesis in which the principal organs and their connections are shown in overall relation to one another. Although it is apparent from numerous details that, even here, Leonardo was still a long way from fully understanding the functioning and interaction of the organs, this fact pales in comparison with his ability to convey the complexity of the human body with such clarity, even while providing an enormous wealth of information.

At the end of 1509 or beginning of 1510, Leonardo noted on one of his studies that he hoped to complete his study of anatomy that same winter. The subject nevertheless continued to occupy him for several more years, as the remarkable anatomical drawings from his latter years demonstrate. His famous study of a developing foetus (Cat. 211), which Leonardo estimated to be about four months old, conveys not just an extremely three-dimensional impression of the typical foetal position, but also seeks to clarify the composition of the placenta in a series of accompanying sketches. The masterly nature of the drawing can easily cause us to overlook the fact that, even in this late phase, Leonardo was still obliged to draw upon his knowledge of animal anatomy to supplement his human studies. Thus the lobules (cotyledons) extending out from the placenta, illustrated in the top right-hand part of the sheet, are found not in the female body but in the cow, whose uterus (with embryonic calf) forms the subject of a similar study (Cat. 214).

Leonardo devoted particular attention in his late anatomical studies to the composition of the heart, as for example in the drawings in Cat. 198. Although these again illustrate the anatomy of the ox, Leonardo was clearly of the view that certain anatomical features applied equally to man and beast – here, for example, he describes the "refining" of the blood by means of a complicated process of osmosis between the chambers of the heart. Revealingly, his anatomical work also includes studies that attempt to establish a direct comparison between man and animal: amongst his drawings of the muscles of the legs seen in Cat. 152, for example, the skeletal structure of the human leg in the bottom right-hand corner appears beside a corresponding sketch of the leg of a horse.

The positioning of the captions and explanatory notes within Leonardo's anatomical studies in general reveals that the drawings were executed first, and the notes added afterwards. The text thereby serves for the most part to supplement the information provided by the illustration. Leonardo's science is thus a science of visual understanding, and the instrument of his research is the recording of information in pictorial form. His ambition for what he termed the science of painting was thereby less to place the representation of the human figure in painting on a scientific basis – although this aim may have played a role in the context of the rivalry between painting and the other arts. Rather, Leonardo must have been aware that his profound revelations far exceeded not just the knowledge of other artists, but also that of the medical experts. For not until the publication of the groundbreaking work by Vesalius (1514/15–1564), *De humani corporis fabrica*, in 1543 would the anatomical textbooks of the Renaissance begin to approach the standard of the studies from Leonardo's mature and late years. It is a significant fact that illustrations make up a substantial proportion of Vesalius' work, thereby confirming the importance of pictorial representation as a tool of anatomical teaching and research – the very method pioneered decades earlier by Leonardo. His vast corpus of anatomical studies thus stands as a testament to his ambition to establish drawing as the supreme vehicle of scientific knowledge. In his biography of the artist mentioned earlier, Paolo Giovio indeed writes that Leonardo harboured concrete plans to publish his studies in the shape of a series of copperplate engravings. The fact that the importance of the image in the medical sciences has risen continuously ever since, and indeed continues to rise, bears witness to Leonardo's extraordinary foresight as to the importance of the anatomical illustration.

*Johannes Nathan*

**Literature:** O'Malley/ Saunders, 1952; Braunfels-Esche, 1961; Clark/ Pedretti, 1968–1969 [RL]; *Anatomische Zeichnungen,* 1979; Keele/ Pedretti, 1979–1980; Kemp, 1981; Kemp/ Roberts, 1989; Laurenza, 2001.

◀ **145  Side View of Human Skull in Sagittal Section, with Cranial Nerves, 1489**
*Pen and brown ink, 190 x 137 mm*
*Windsor Castle, Royal Library*
*(RL 19058r)*

**146  Anatomical Study of the Human Skull in Sagittal Section, Seen from the Front, 1489**
*Pen and brown ink over traces of black chalk, 183 x 130 mm*
*Windsor Castle, Royal Library*
*(RL 19058v)*

**147  Anatomical Study of the Human Skull in Side View, showing the Eye Sockets and Maxillary Sinus, 1489**
*Pen and brown ink over black pencil, 188 x 134 mm*
*Windsor Castle, Royal Library*
*(RL 19057v)*

**148  Anatomical Study of the Human Skull in Sagittal Section, Seen from the Side, 1489**
*Pen and two shades of brown ink over black chalk, 188 x 134 mm*
*Windsor Castle, Royal Library*
*(RL 19057r)*

**149  Anatomical Study of the Human Skull with Blood Vessels (Cranial and Maxillary Veins), 2 April 1489**
*Pen and brown ink, 188 x 139 mm*
*Windsor Castle, Royal Library*
*(RL 19059r)*

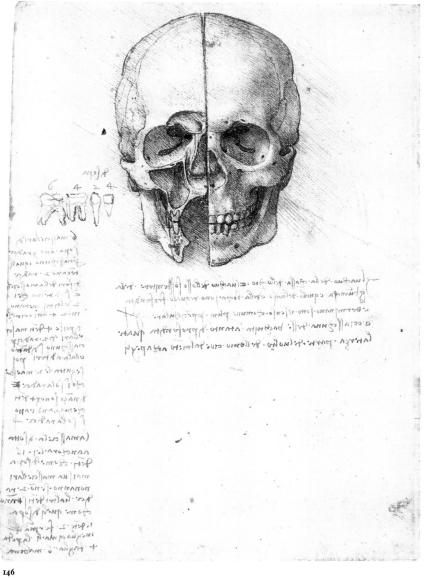

146

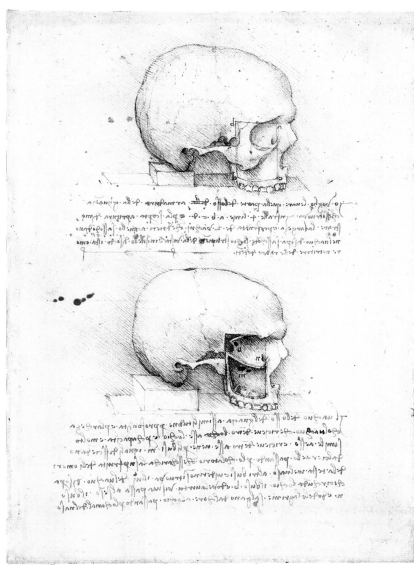

147

148

149

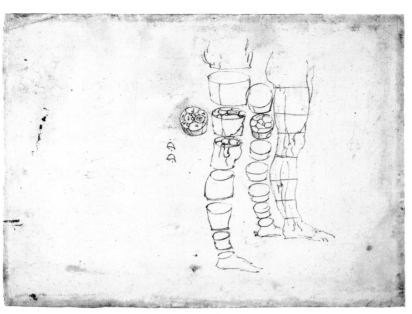

**150**

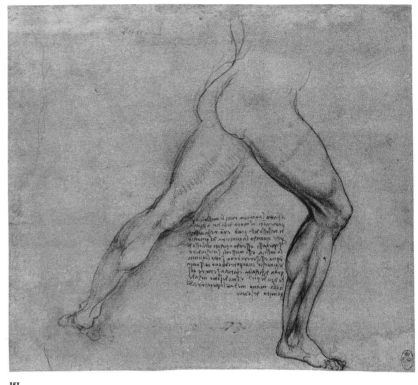

**151**

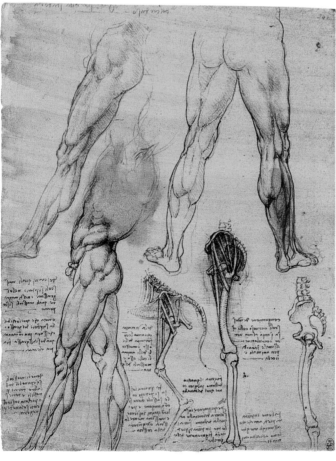

**152**

**153**

**150  Cross-sections of the Human Leg**, *c.* **1485**
*Pen and brown ink, 222 x 290 mm*
*Windsor Castle, Royal Library*
*(RL.12627v)*

**151  Study of the Muscles of the Legs in Action**, *c.* **1507**
*Pen and brown ink and red chalk*
*on red prepared paper,*
*157 x 166 mm*
*Windsor Castle, Royal Library*
*(RL 12623r)*

**152  Anatomical Studies of the Muscles of the Legs and a Comparison of these Muscles in Man and Horse,** *c.* **1507**
*Pen, two shades of brown ink and*
*red chalk on red prepared paper,*
*282 x 204 mm*
*Windsor Castle, Royal Library*
*(RL 12625r)*

**153  Anatomical Study of the Muscles of the Legs**, *c.* **1507**
*Pen and brown ink and black*
*chalk, 305 x 190 mm*
*Windsor Castle, Royal Library*
*(RL 12631r)*

**154  Anatomical Study of the Muscles of the Leg**, *c.* **1490**
*Pen and brown ink over traces*
*of black chalk, 196 x 313 mm*
*(dimensions of restored sheet)*
*Windsor Castle, Royal Library*
*(RL 12632r)*

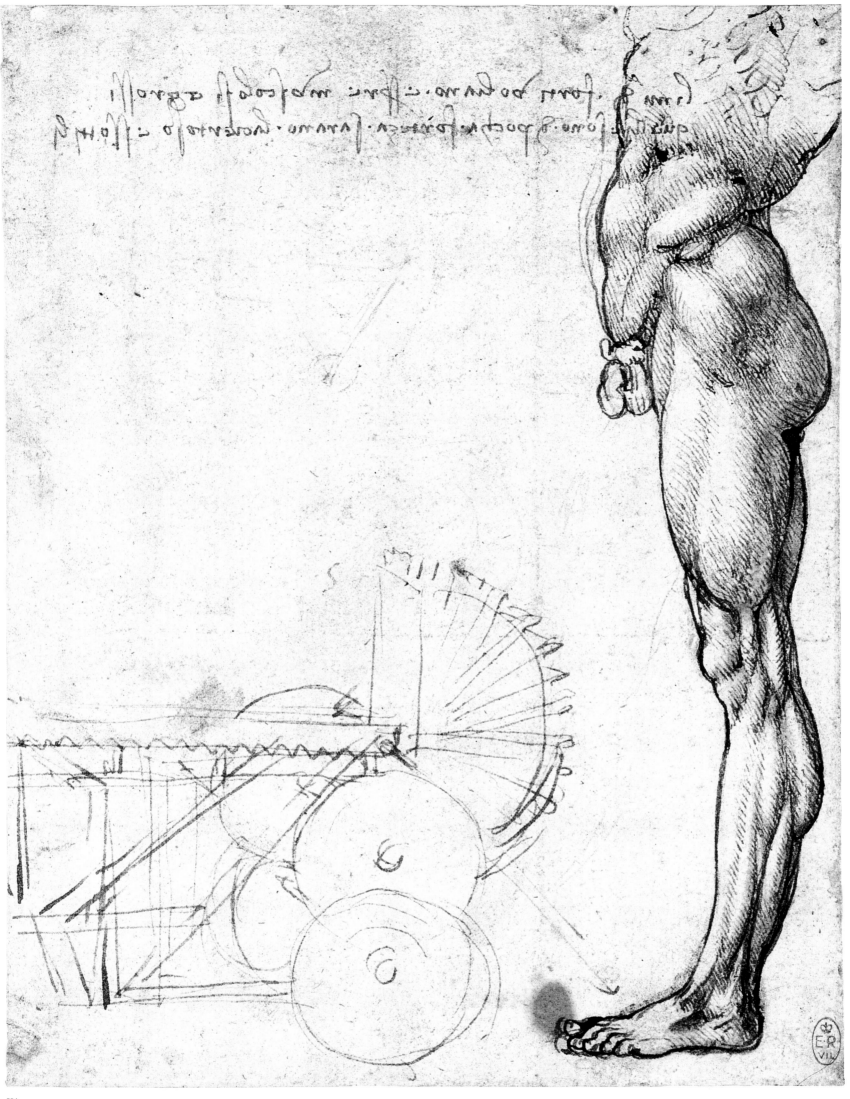

154

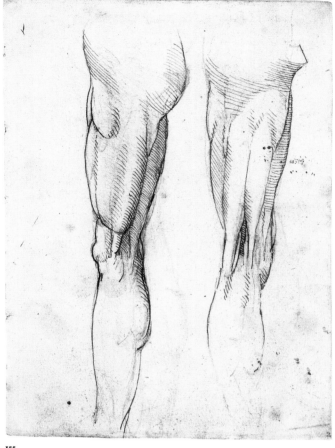

155

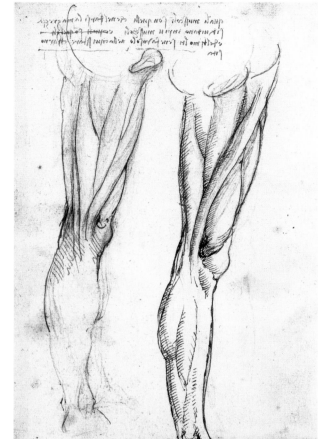

156

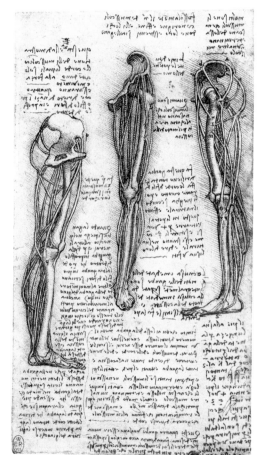

157

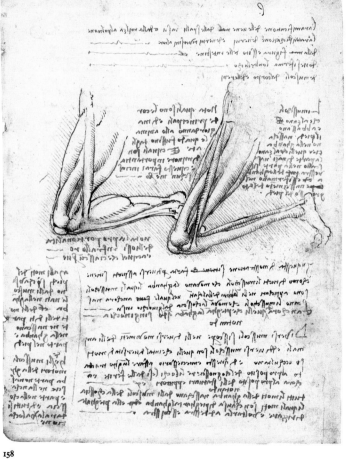

158

**155** Anatomical Studies
of the Muscles of the Leg,
*c.* 1507
*Pen and brown ink over traces*
*of black chalk, 191 x 136 mm*
*Windsor Castle, Royal Library*
*(RL 19036r)*

**156** Anatomical Studies
of the Muscles of the Leg,
*c.* 1507
*Pen and brown ink over black*
*chalk, 191 x 136 mm*
*Windsor Castle, Royal Library*
*(RL 19036v)*

**157** Anatomical Studies
of the Muscles of the Leg,
*c.* 1509/10
*Pen and brown ink over traces*
*of black chalk, 215 x 110 mm*
*Windsor Castle, Royal Library*
*(RL 12619r)*

**158** Studies of the Muscles
of the Leg with Knee Bent,
1489 and *c.* 1508
*Pen and two shades of brown ink,*
*190 x 138 mm*
*Windsor Castle, Royal Library*
*(RL 19037v)*

**159** Anatomical Studies
of the Muscles of the Leg,
*c.* 1507–1510
*Pen and two shades of brown ink*
*over traces of black chalk,*
*192 x 140 mm*
*Windsor Castle, Royal Library*
*(RL 19035v)*

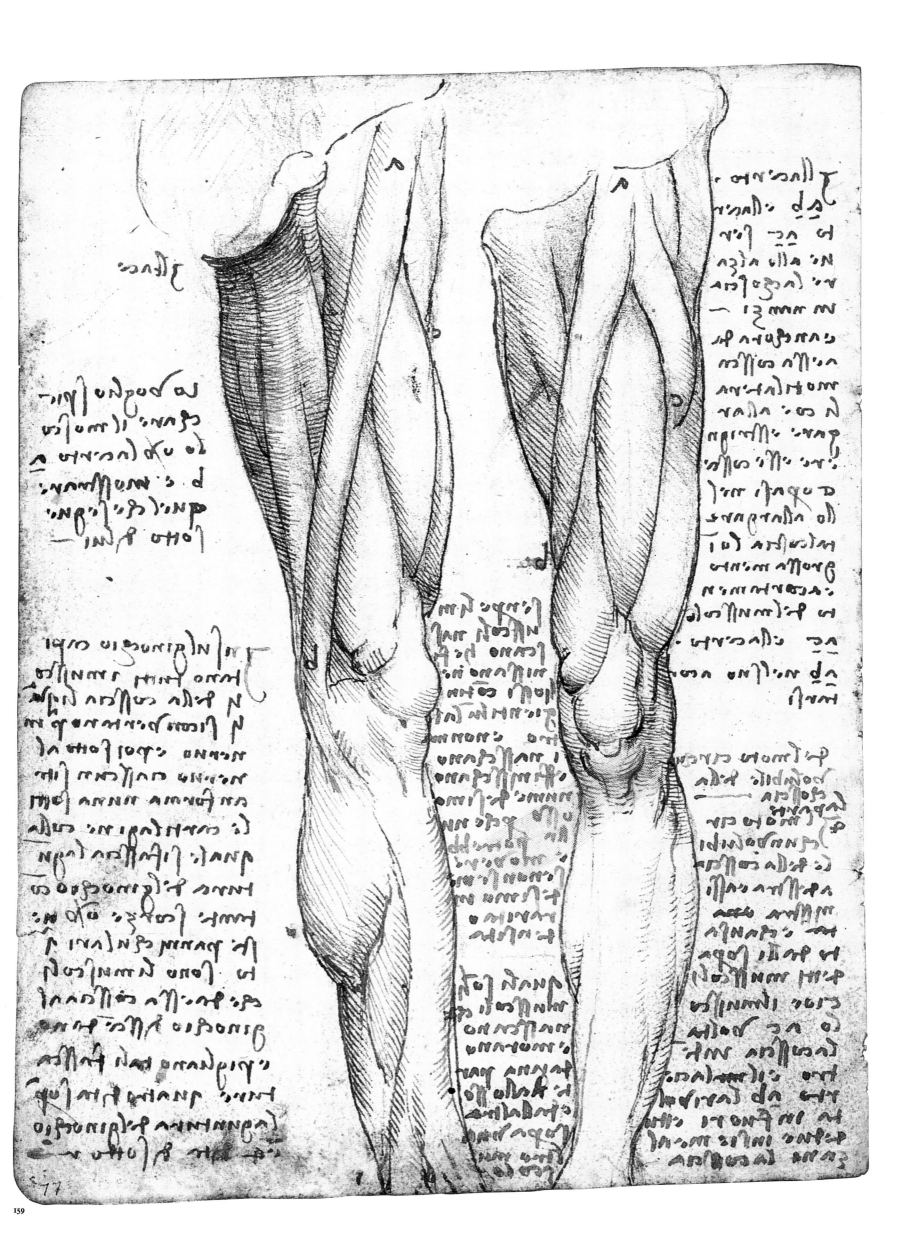

160

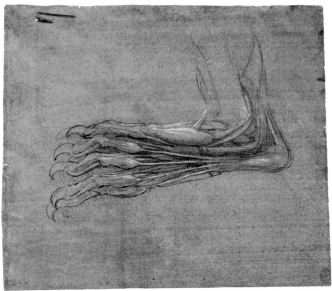

161

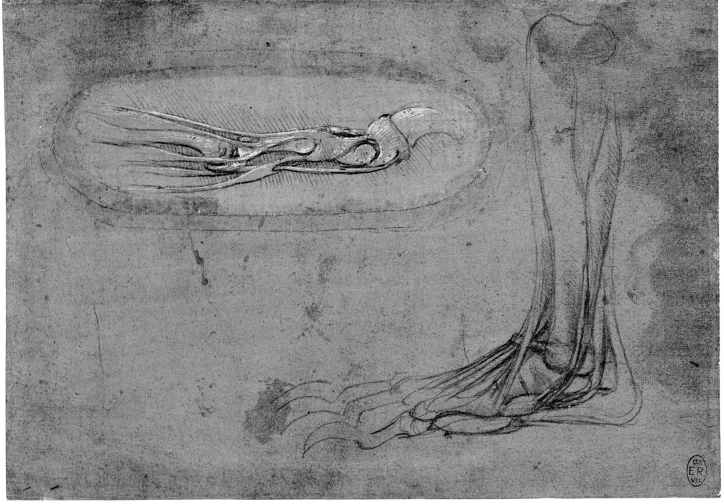

162

**160 Anatomical Study of a Bear's Foot**, *c.* **1490**
*Pen and brown ink over metalpoint, heightened with white, on blue prepared paper, 141 x 181 mm*
*Windsor Castle, Royal Library (RL 12374r)*

**161 Anatomical Study of a Bear's Foot**, *c.* **1490**
*Pen and brown ink over metalpoint, heightened with white, on blue prepared paper, 155 x 173 mm*
*Windsor Castle, Royal Library (RL 12375r)*

**162 Anatomical Studies of a Bear's Foot**, *c.* **1490**
*Pen and brown ink, heightened with white, over metalpoint on blue prepared paper, 48 x 121 mm and 136 x 186 mm*
*Windsor Castle, Royal Library (RL 12373 ar, RL 12373r)*

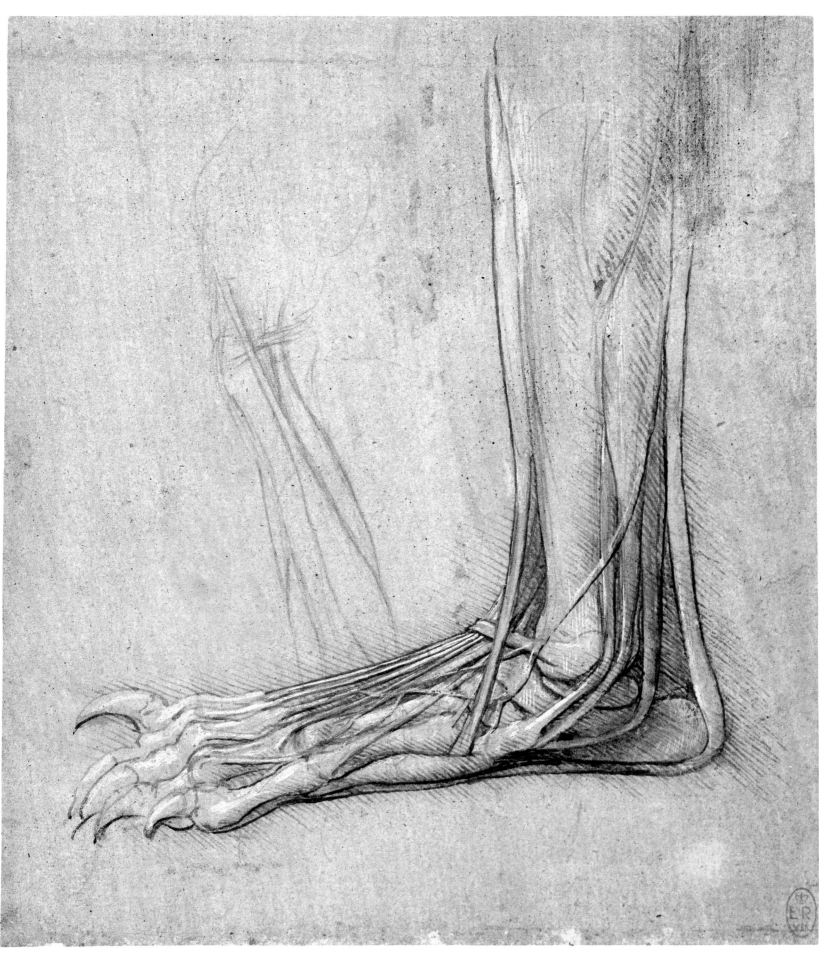

**163**

**163 Anatomical Study of
a Bear's Foot,** *c.* **1490**
*Metalpoint with pen and brown
ink, heightened with white, on
blue prepared paper, 161 x 137 mm
Windsor Castle, Royal Library
(RL 12372r)*

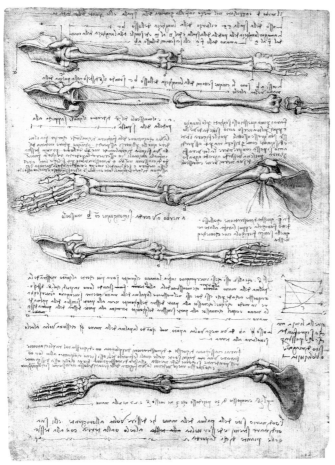

164

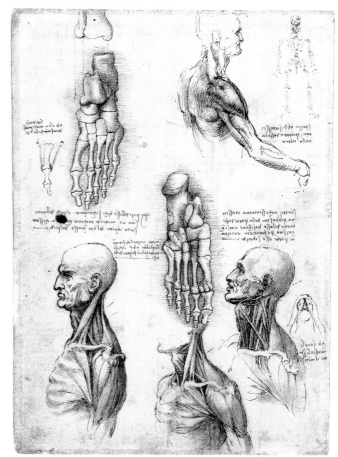

165

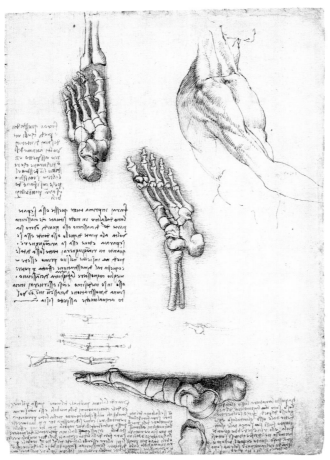

166

167

**164 Anatomical Studies on the Rotation of the Arm (Pronation and Supination),** *c.* 1509/10
*Pen, two shades of brown ink and wash over traces of black chalk, 293 x 201 mm*
*Windsor Castle, Royal Library (RL 19000v)*

**165 Anatomical Studies of the Muscles of the Shoulder and Neck and of the Skeletal Structure of the Foot,** *c.* 1509/10
*Pen, two shades of brown ink and wash over black chalk, 290 x 196 mm*
*Windsor Castle, Royal Library (RL 19002v)*

**166 Anatomical Studies of the Bones of the Foot and Study of the Shoulder,** *c.* 1509/10
*Pen, two shades of brown ink and wash over traces of black chalk, 293 x 201 mm*
*Windsor Castle, Royal Library (RL 19000r)*

**167 Studies of the Muscles of the Shoulder and of the Movement of the Foot and Shoulder Joints,** *c.* 1509/10
*Pen, two shades of brown ink and wash over traces of black chalk, 289 x 198 mm*
*Windsor Castle, Royal Library (RL 19001r)*

**168 The "Instruments" of Breathing, Swallowing and Speaking (Uvula, Pharynx, Tongue with Trachea, Larynx and Oesophagus),** *c.* 1509/10
*Pen, three shades of brown ink and wash over black chalk; red chalk (sketches top right), 290 x 196 mm*
*Windsor Castle, Royal Library (RL 19002r)*

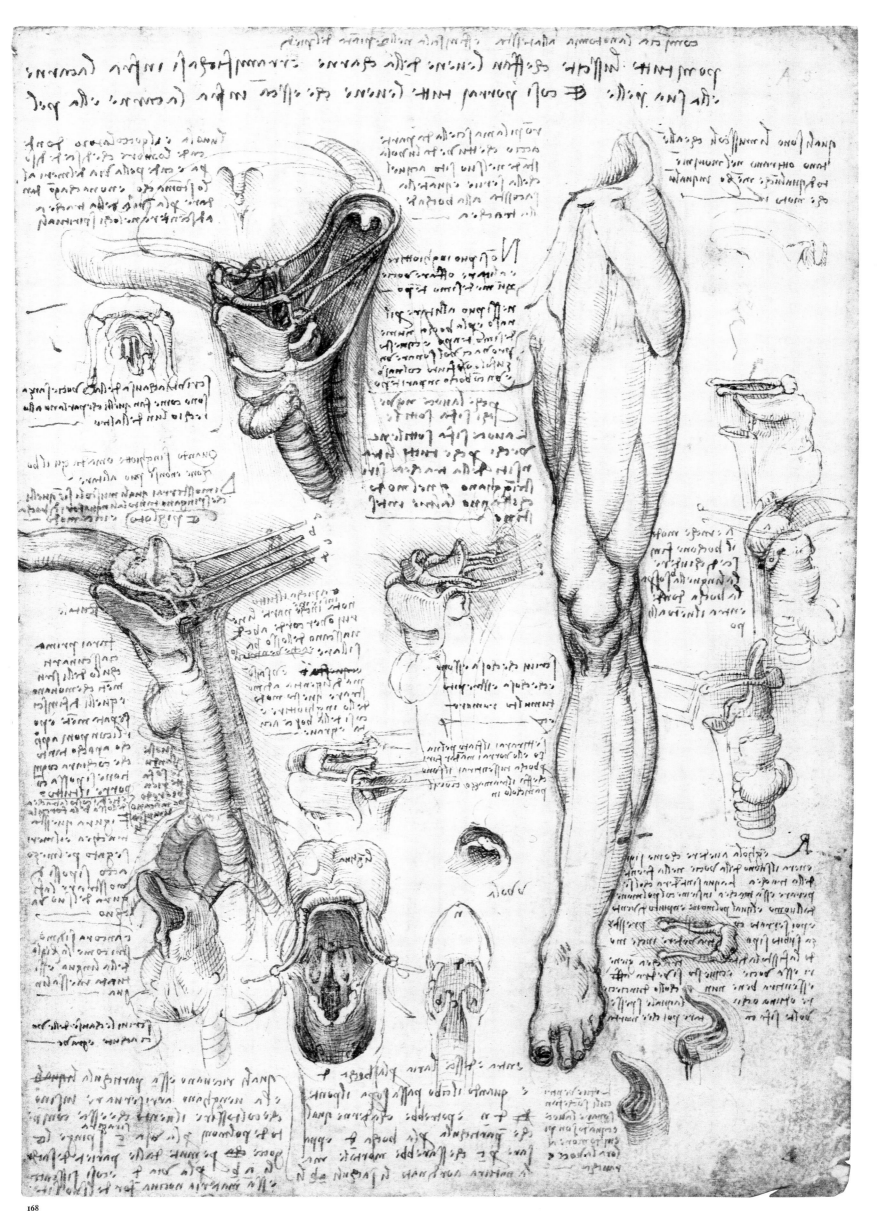

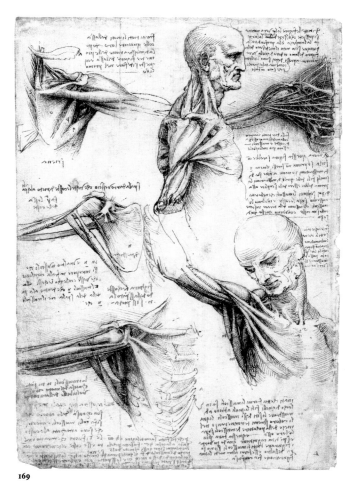

169

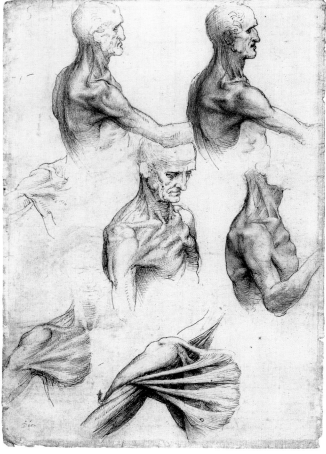

170

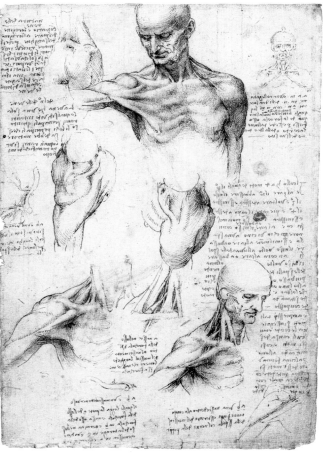

171

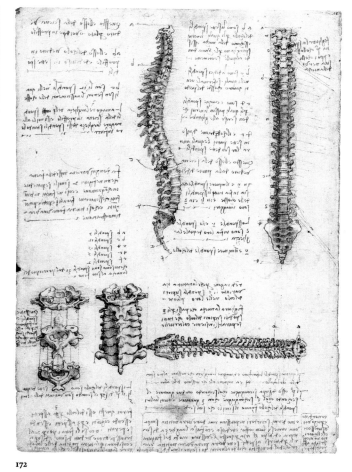

172

**169 Anatomical Analysis of the Movements of the Shoulder and Neck,** *c.* **1509/10**
*Pen, three shades of brown ink and wash over black chalk, 292 x 198 mm*
*Windsor Castle, Royal Library (RL 19003v)*

**170 Anatomical Studies of the Muscles of the Shoulder, Neck and Chest,** *c.* **1509/10**
*Pen, two shades of brown ink and wash over black chalk, 289 x 198 mm*
*Windsor Castle, Royal Library (RL 19001v)*

**171 Anatomical Studies of the Muscles of the Shoulder and of the Mechanics of Stabilizing the Clavicle Joint,** *c.* **1509/10**
*Pen, two shades of brown ink and wash over traces of black chalk, 292 x 198 mm*
*Windsor Castle, Royal Library (RL 19003r)*

**172 Anatomical Studies of the Spine,** *c.* **1509/10**
*Pen, two shades of brown ink and wash over traces of black chalk, 286 x 200 mm*
*Windsor Castle, Royal Library (RL 19007v)*

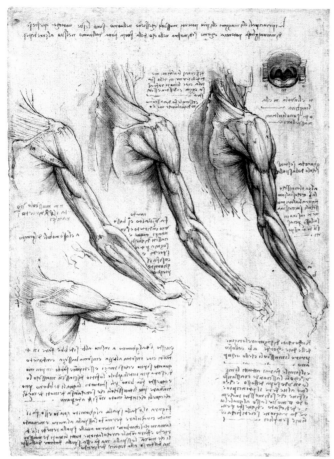

173

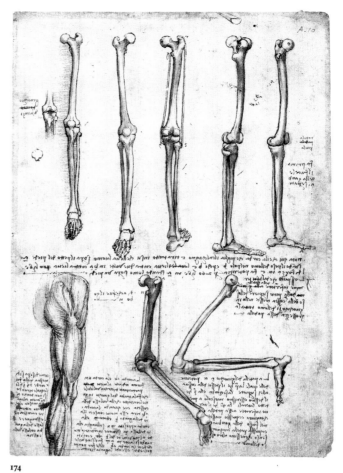

174

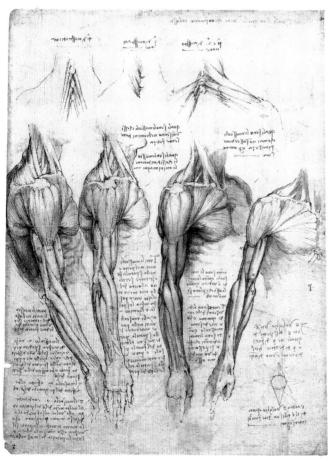

175

176

**173 Anatomical Studies of the Muscles of the Shoulder and Arm**, *c.* 1509/10
*Pen, two shades of brown ink and wash over black chalk,*
*289 x 199 mm*
*Windsor Castle, Royal Library*
*(RL 19005v)*

**174 The Skeletal Structure of the Lower Limbs and the Movement of the Foot and Knee Joints,** *c.* 1509/10
*Pen, brown ink and wash over traces of black chalk,*
*288 x 202 mm*
*Windsor Castle, Royal Library*
*(RL 19008r)*

**175 Anatomical Studies of the Muscles of the Neck, Shoulder, Chest and Arm,** *c.* 1509/10
*Pen, brown ink and wash over traces of black chalk with small red chalk strokes between the main figures, 288 x 202 mm*
*Windsor Castle, Royal Library*
*(RL 19008v)*

**176 Anatomical Drawings of the Muscles and Veins of the Arm and Chest, and the Head of an Old Man,** *c.* 1509/10
*Pen, brown ink and wash over traces of black chalk,*
*289 x 199 mm*
*Windsor Castle, Royal Library*
*(RL 19005r)*

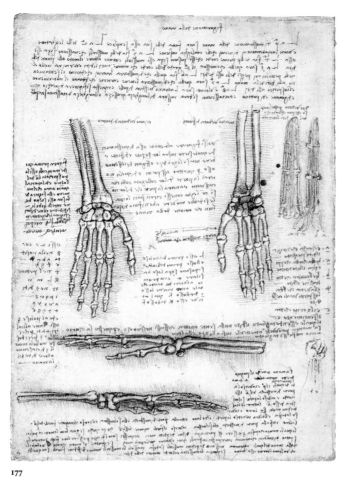

177

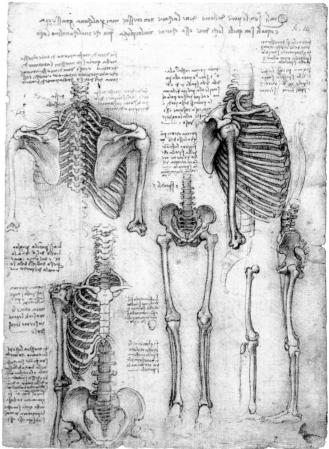

178

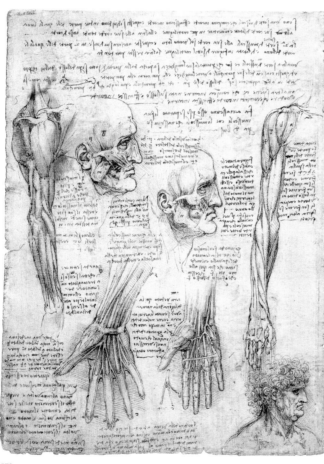

179

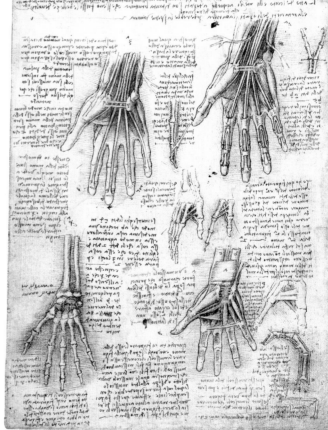

180

**177 Anatomical Studies of the Hand**, *c.* 1509/10
*Pen, two shades of brown ink and wash over traces of black chalk,*
*288 x 202 mm*
*Windsor Castle, Royal Library*
*(RL 19009v)*

**178 Anatomical Studies of the Human Skeleton,**
*c.* 1509/10
*Pen, three shades of brown ink and wash over traces of black chalk,*
*288 x 200 mm*
*Windsor Castle, Royal Library*
*(RL 19012r)*

**179 Studies of the Muscles of the Arm, Hand and Face,**
*c.* 1509/10
*Pen, three shades of brown ink and wash over traces of black chalk,*
*288 x 200 mm*
*Windsor Castle, Royal Library*
*(RL 19012v)*

**180 Anatomical Studies of the Hand,** *c.* 1509/10
*Pen, three shades of brown ink and wash over traces of black chalk,*
*288 x 202 mm*
*Windsor Castle, Royal Library*
*(RL 19009r)*

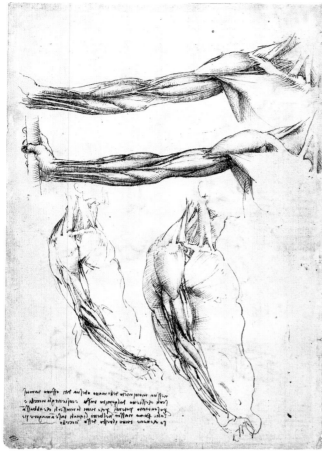

181

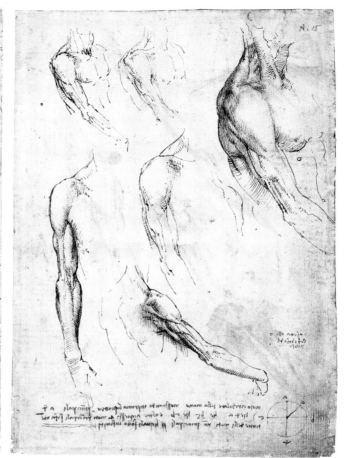

182

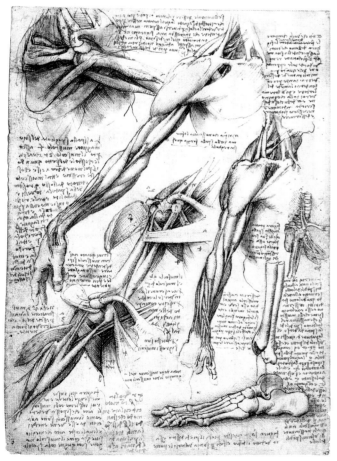

183

184

**181 Studies of the Muscles of the Neck, Shoulder and Arm,** *c.* **1509/10**
*Pen and brown ink, 287 x 198 mm*
*Windsor Castle, Royal Library*
*(RL 19011v)*

**182 Studies of the Muscles of the Neck, Shoulder and Arm,** *c.* **1509/10**
*Pen and brown ink, 289 x 201 mm*
*Windsor Castle, Royal Library*
*(RL 19013r)*

**183 Anatomical Studies of the Muscles of the Shoulder and Arm,** *c.* **1509/10**
*Pen, three shades of brown ink and wash over traces of black chalk, 289 x 201 mm*
*Windsor Castle, Royal Library*
*(RL 19013v)*

**184 Studies of the Anatomy of the Shoulder and the Foot,** *c.* **1509/10**
*Pen, two shades of brown ink and wash over black chalk, 287 x 198 mm*
*Windsor Castle, Royal Library*
*(RL 19011r)*

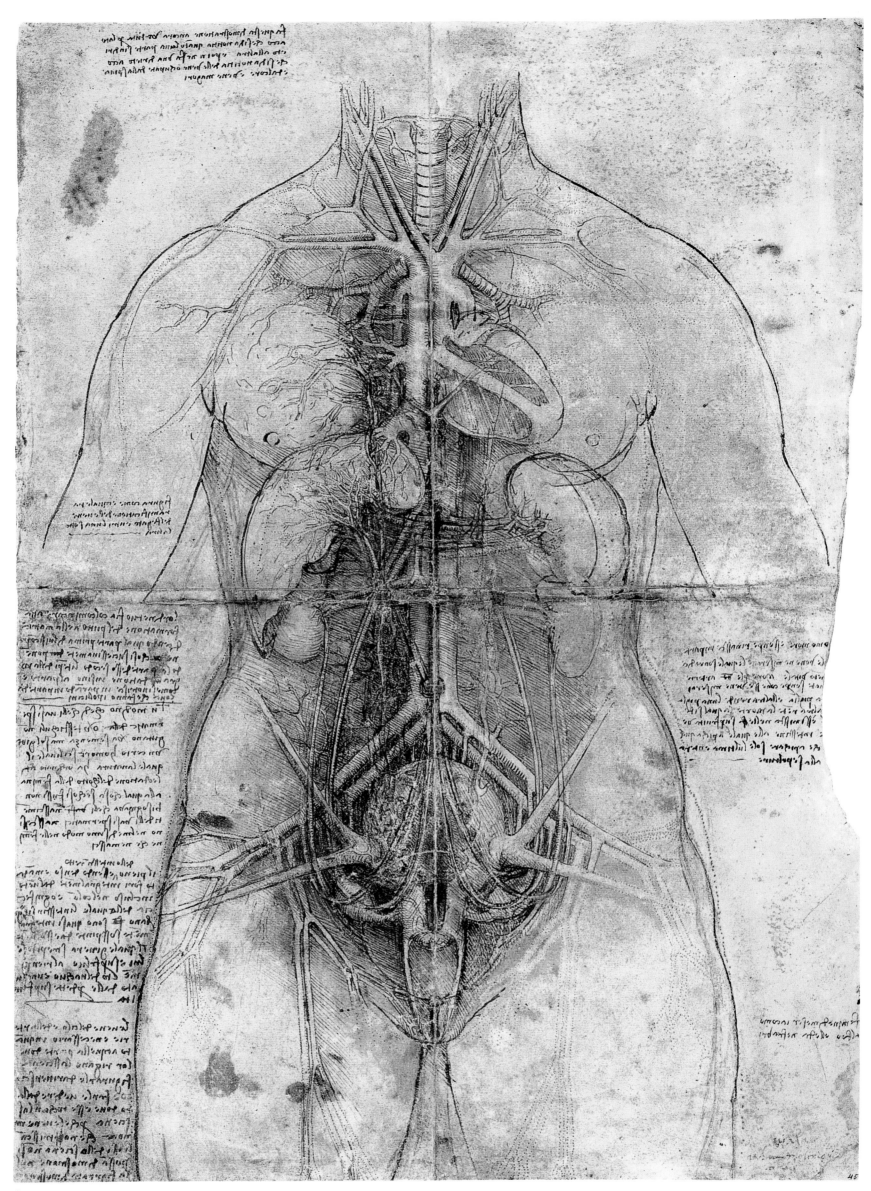

185

186

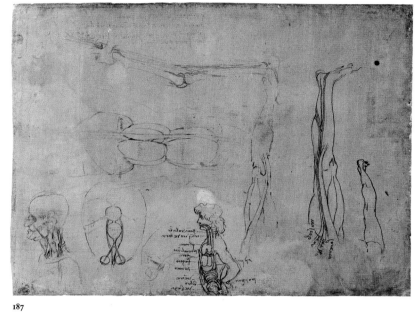

187

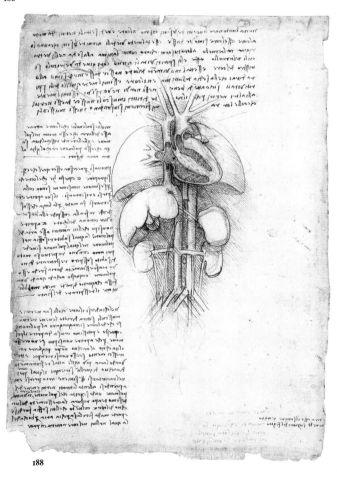

188

189

**185 View of the Organs of the Chest and Abdomen and of the Vascular System of a Woman,** *c.* **1508**
(recto of Cat. 186)
*Pen, brown ink and wash, with traces of black and red chalk and yellow wash, on ochre-washed paper, pricked for transfer, 476 x 332 mm*
*Windsor Castle, Royal Library*
*(RL 12281r)*

**186 View of the Organs of the Chest and Abdomen and of the Vascular System of a Woman,** *c.* **1508**
(verso of Cat. 185)
*Pricked, 476 x 332 mm*
*Windsor Castle, Royal Library*
*(RL 12281v)*

**187 Various Anatomical Studies with the Drawing of a Human Figure, on which all the Vital Organs are indicated,** *c.* **1485–1489**
*Pen and two shades of brown ink over metalpoint on blue prepared paper, 222 x 290 mm*
*Windsor Castle, Royal Library*
*(RL 12627r)*

**188 Anatomical Study of the Heart and Lungs,** *c.* **1508/09**
*Pen, two shades of brown ink and black chalk, 275 x 190 mm*
*Windsor Castle, Royal Library*
*(RL 19112r)*

**189 Studies of the Organs of the Abdomen and Chest,** *c.* **1508/09**
*Pen, two shades of brown ink and black chalk, 283 x 219 mm*
*Windsor Castle, Royal Library*
*(RL 19104v)*

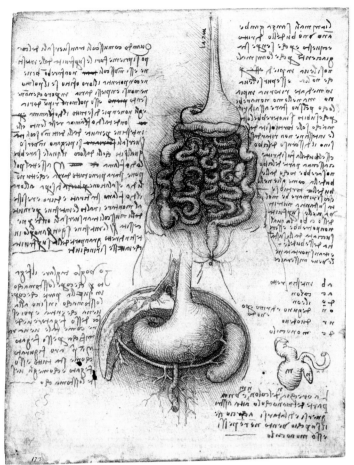

190

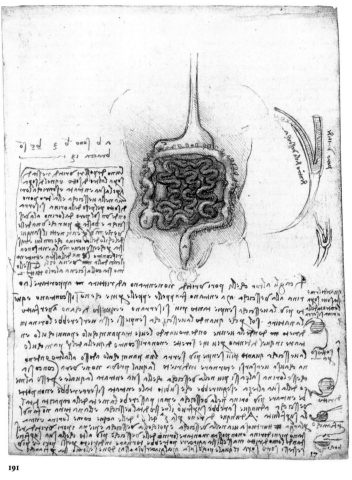

191

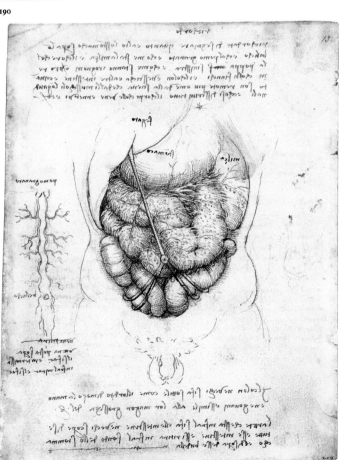

192

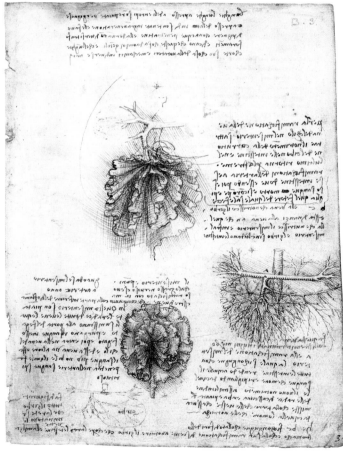

193

**190  Anatomical Drawing of the Stomach and Intestines,** *c.* 1506
*Pen and brown ink over traces of black chalk, 192 x 138 mm*
*Windsor Castle, Royal Library*
*(RL 19031v)*

**191  Anatomical Study of the Stomach, Intestines and Physiology of the Kidneys and Bladder,** *c.* 1506
*Pen and two shades of brown ink over black chalk, 192 x 138 mm*
*Windsor Castle, Royal Library*
*(RL 19031r)*

**192  Anatomical drawing of the Liver, Stomach, Spleen and Large Intestine,** *c.* 1506
*Pen and two shades of brown ink over traces of black chalk,*
*192 x 141 mm*
*Windsor Castle, Royal Library*
*(RL 19039v)*

**193  The Mesentery of the Bowel and its Blood Supply,** *c.* 1506
*Pen and two shades of brown ink over traces of black chalk,*
*193 x 143 mm*
*Windsor Castle, Royal Library*
*(RL 19020r)*

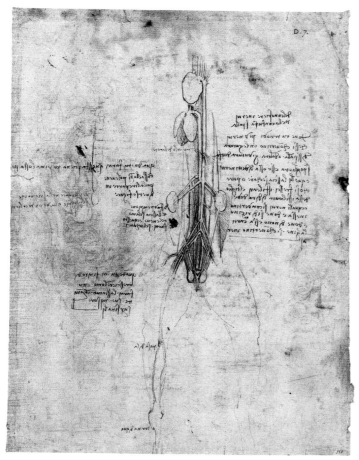

194

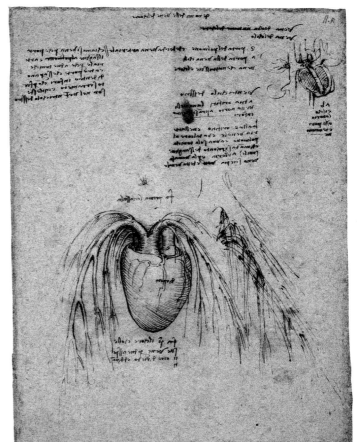

195

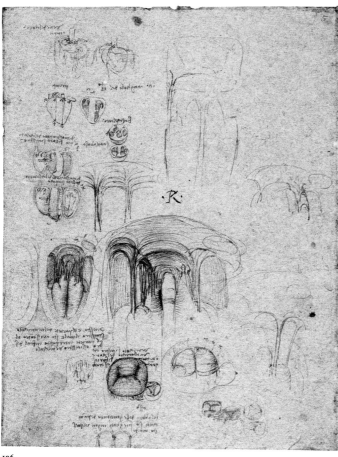

196

197

**194 Anatomical Study of the Heart, Liver and Blood Vessels of the Abdomen and Testicles of an Animal, probably a Horse, c. 1493**
*Pen and two shades of brown ink, 276 x 204 mm*
*Windsor Castle, Royal Library (RL 19097)*

**195 Anatomical Drawing of the Heart and its Blood Vessels, c. 1513**
*Pen and brown ink, 285 x 208 mm*
*Windsor Castle, Royal Library (RL 19072v)*

**196 Section of the Heart with the Left Ventricle and Mitral Valve, c. 1513**
*Pen and brown ink on blue paper, 284 x 209 mm*
*Windsor Castle, Royal Library (RL 19080r)*

**197 Study of the Valves and Muscles of the Heart, c. 1513**
*Pen and brown ink on blue paper, 260 x 200 mm*
*Windsor Castle, Royal Library (RL 19093r)*

**▶ 198 Anatomical Drawings of the Heart and its Blood Vessels, c. 1513**
*Pen and brown ink, 288 x 413 mm*
*Windsor Castle, Royal Library (RL 19073r–RL 19074v)*

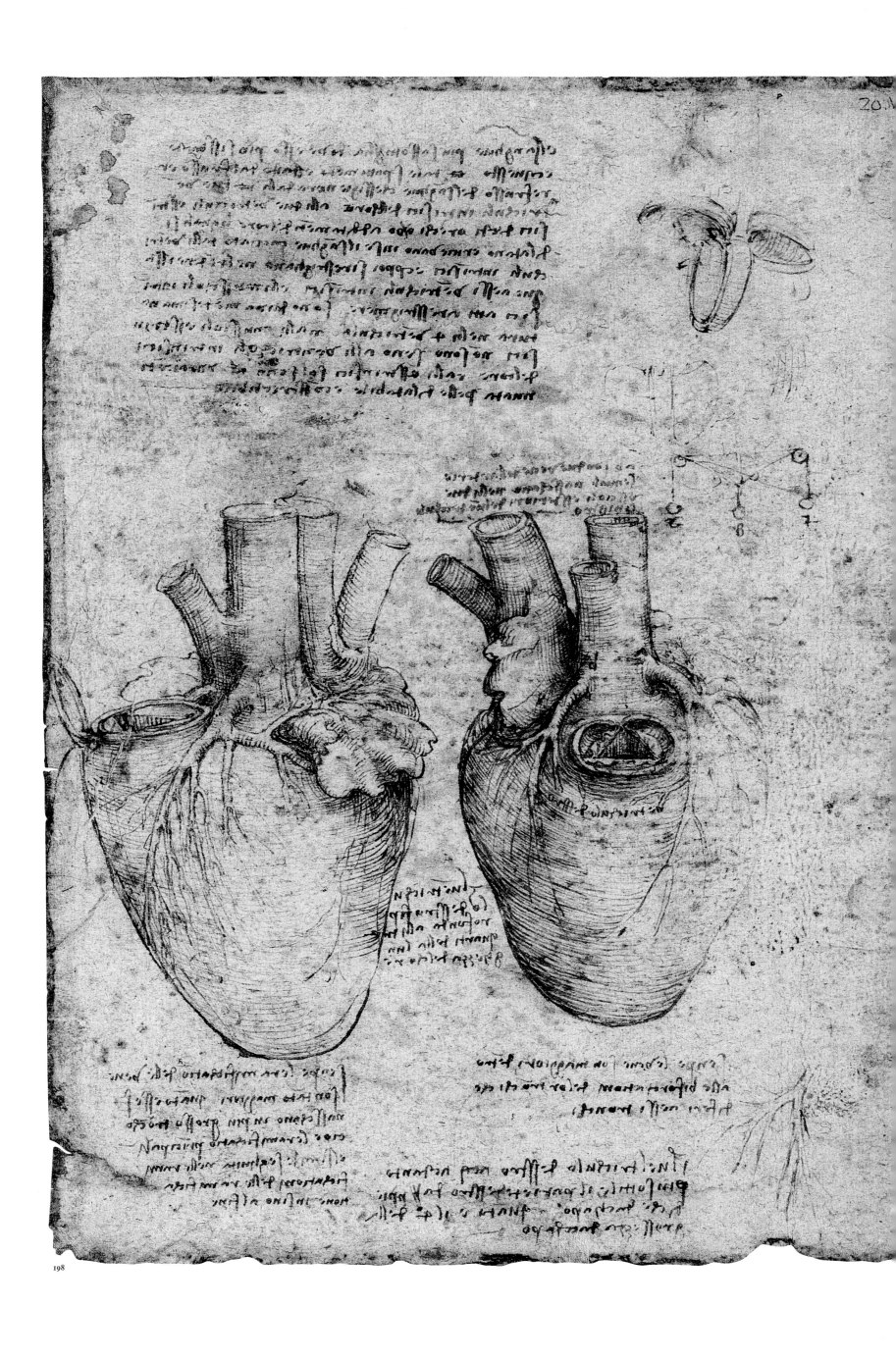

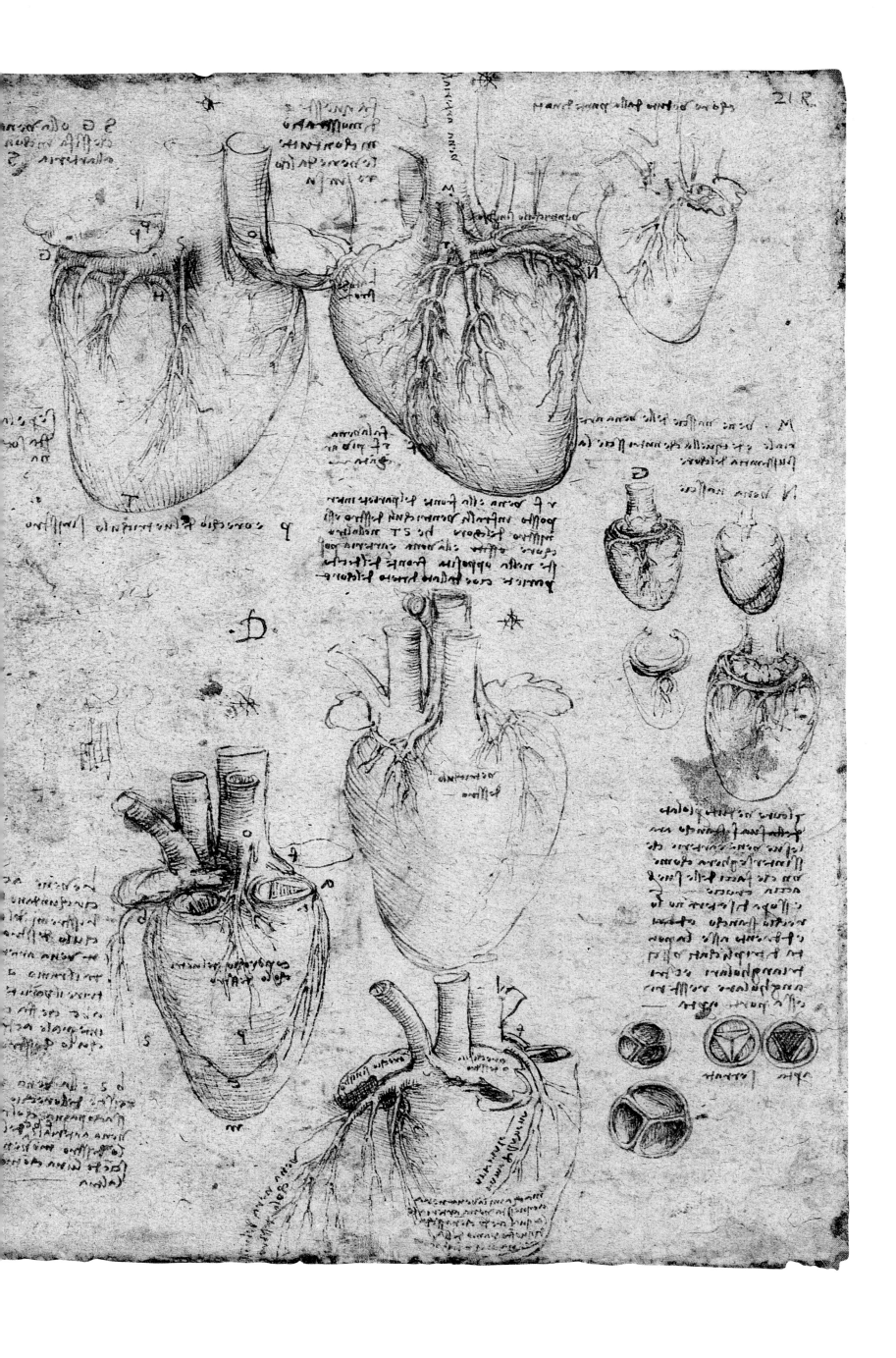

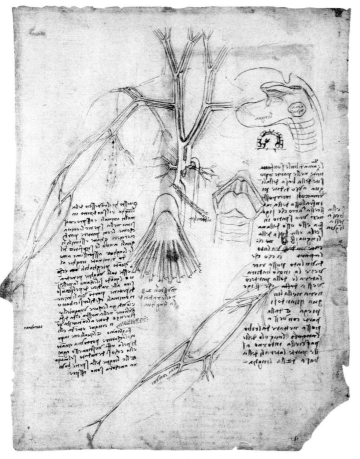

199

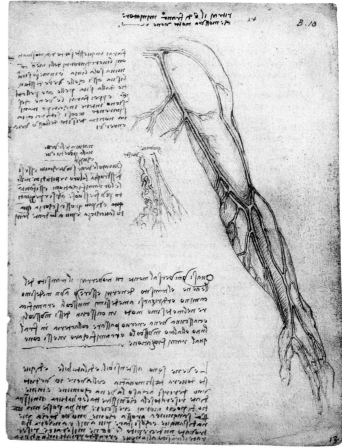

200

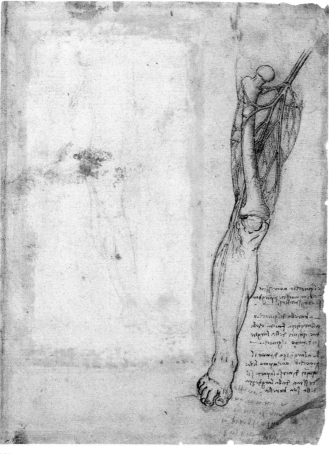

201

202

**199 Anatomical Studies of the Veins, Tongue and Throat,** *c. 1504*
*Pen, three shades of brown ink and black chalk, 282 x 207 mm*
*Windsor Castle, Royal Library*
*(RL 19114v)*

**200 Study of the Veins of the Left Arm,** *c. 1506*
*Pen and two shades of brown ink over traces of black chalk,*
*192 x 141 mm*
*Windsor Castle, Royal Library*
*(RL 19027r)*

**201 The Blood Supply to the Upper Leg,** *c. 1508*
*Pen, brown ink and black chalk,*
*275 x 195 mm*
*Windsor Castle, Royal Library*
*(RL 12624v)*

**202 Studies of the Trachea Oesophagus, Larynx and Stomach,** *c. 1506*
*Pen and two shades of brown ink over traces of black chalk,*
*193 x 133 mm*
*Windsor Castle, Royal Library*
*(RL 19050v)*

**▶ 203 Umbilical Artery in the Foetus of a Calf (upper right), a Child (lower right) and an Old Man (centre),** *c. 1506*
*Pen and two shades of brown ink over traces of black chalk,*
*193 x 138 mm*
*Windsor Castle, Royal Library*
*(RL 19021r)*

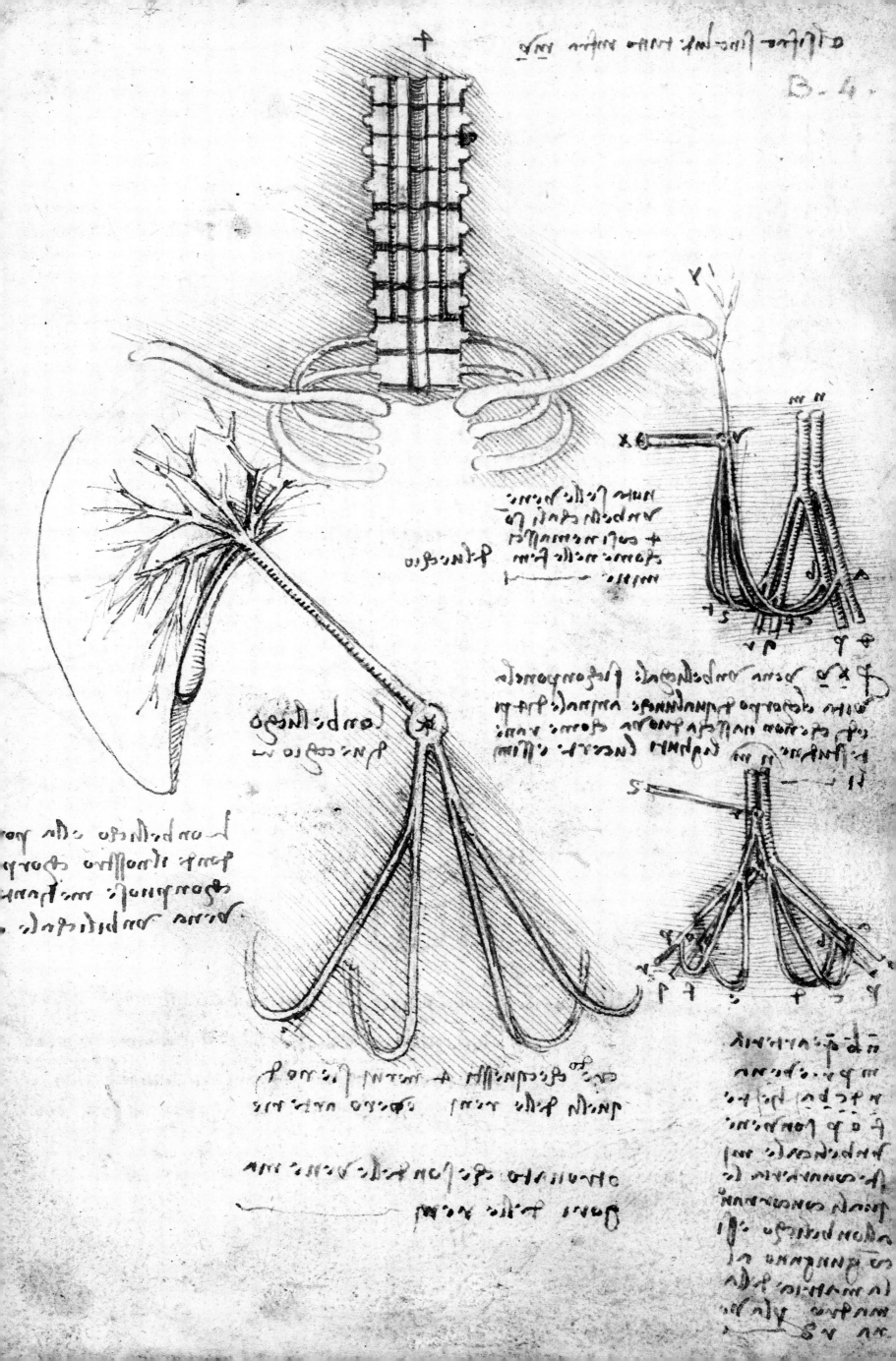

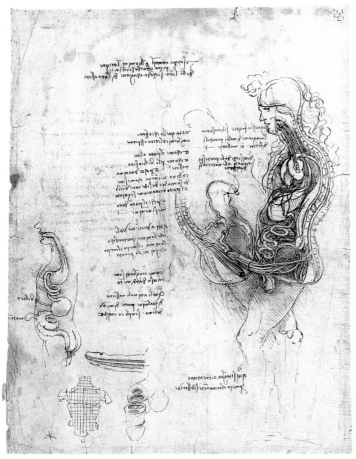

204

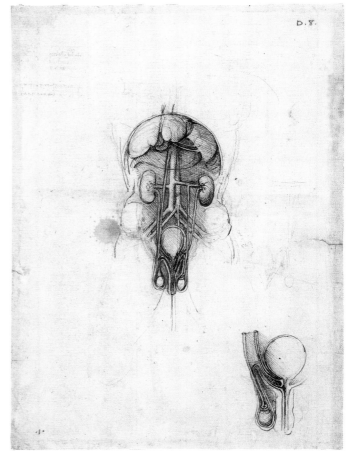

205

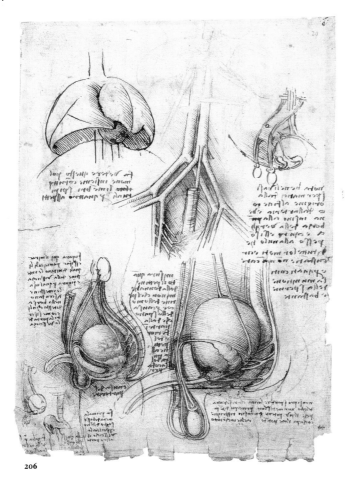

206

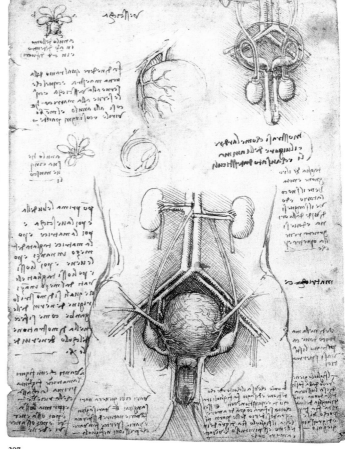

207

**204  The Sexual Act in
Vertical Section,** *c.* **1490**
*Pen and brown ink, 276 x 204 mm*
*Windsor Castle, Royal Library*
*(RL 19097v)*

**205  Anatomical Drawings
of the Male Genitalia with
Spermatic Ducts,** *c.* **1508/09**
*Pen, brown ink and black chalk,*
*263 x 189 mm*
*Windsor Castle, Royal Library*
*(RL 19099r)*

**206  Anatomical Drawings
of the Male Genitalia with
Blood Vessels and Spermatic
Ducts,** *c.* **1508/09**
*Pen, three shades of brown ink*
*and black chalk, 272 x 192 mm*
*Windsor Castle, Royal Library*
*(RL 19098v)*

**207  The Male Genital
Organs,** *c.* **1508**
*Pen and brown ink, 192 x 135 mm*
*Weimar, Kunstsammlungen*
*zu Weimar, Schlossmuseum,*
*Inv. KK 6287r*

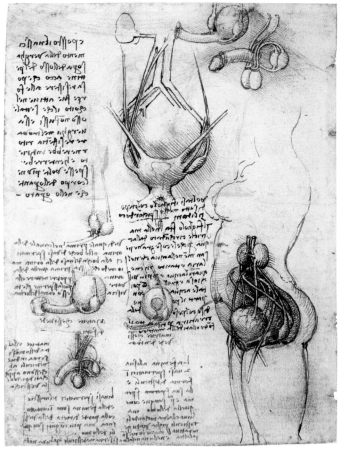

208

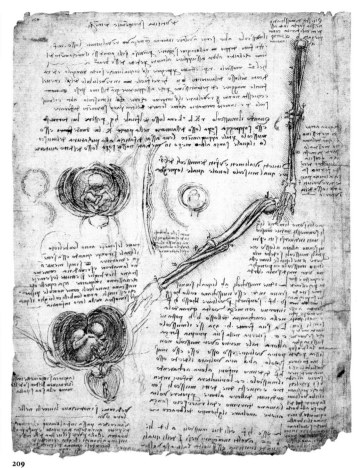

209

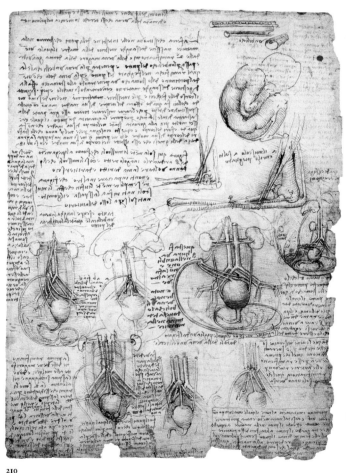

210

211

**208 Comparative Drawing of the Male and Female Genitalia,** *c.* 1508/09
*Pen and two shades of brown ink over traces of black chalk,*
*191 x 138 mm*
*Windsor Castle, Royal Library*
*(RL 19095v)*

**209 Drawings of the Foetus** *in utero* **and the three surrounding Membranes, and of the Movements of the Elbow Joint,** *c.* 1510–1512
*Pen and two shades of brown ink over black chalk, 287 x 211 mm*
*Windsor Castle, Royal Library*
*(RL 19103v)*

**210 Anatomical Studies of the Developing Foetus,** *c.* 1510
*Pen and two shades of brown ink,*
*304 x 213 mm*
*Windsor Castle, Royal Library*
*(RL 19101v)*

**211 Foetus in the Womb,** *c.* 1510
*Pen, two shades of brown ink and wash, with red chalk,*
*304 x 220 mm*
*Windsor Castle, Royal Library*
*(RL 19102r)*

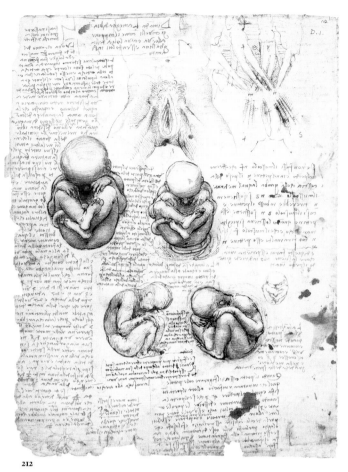

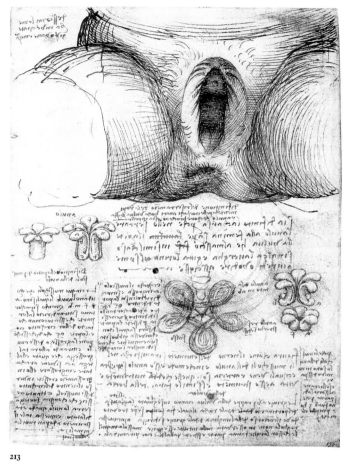

**212 Studies of the Foetus in the Womb and of the Structure and Size of the Female Genitalia,** *c.* **1510**
*Pen and two shades of brown ink with black and red chalk,*
*304 x 213 mm*
*Windsor Castle, Royal Library*
*(RL 19101r)*

**213 Studies of the Mechanics of the Muscles of Body Orifices such as the Vulva, Anus and Penis,** *c.* **1508/09**
*Pen and two shades of brown ink over black chalk, 191 x 138 mm*
*Windsor Castle, Royal Library*
*(RL 19095r)*

**214 Studies of the Blood Supply of a Foetal Calf** *in utero, c.* **1506**
*Pen and brown ink over traces of black chalk, 192 x 142 mm*
*Windsor Castle, Royal Library*
*(RL 19055r)*

**215 Study of the Male Bladder with Ureter and Kidneys,** *c.* **1506**
*Pen and two shades of brown ink over black chalk, 194 x 142 mm*
*Windsor Castle, Royal Library*
*(RL 19054r)*

# 8 Plant studies

Leonardo's plant studies formed part of his graphic repertoire from an early stage (RLW § 680) and fall within the tradition of contemporary herbals, with which the artist was undoubtedly familiar (RLW § 1386) and of which he owned at least one, the *erbario grande* (CM II, fol. 2v). They must of course also be seen against the backdrop of the natural studies undertaken by artists of the generation before Leonardo and known to us in a small number of surviving drawings, such as those by Pisanello (Montauban, Musée Ingres) dating from *c.* 1438–1442 and by Jacopo Bellini (Paris, Louvre, fol. 56) from around the same time. These studies subsequently provided the botanical details in larger paintings, of which prominent Florentine examples include Gentile da Fabriano's *Adoration of the Magi* of 1423, with its copious, detailed representations of plants in the ornamental fields of the frame, and Sandro Botticelli's *Primavera* of *c.* 1482 (both Florence, Uffizi). A similar wealth of flora can be found not least, of course, in Leonardo's own paintings, in particular the *Annunciation*, the two versions of the *Virgin of the Rocks* and the decorative scheme for the Sala delle Asse.

The first sheet in this section (Cat. 216) can be dated to Leonardo's early career. It shows the study of a lily, executed with extreme care. The outlines of the flower were first sketched in black chalk and then redrawn with a pen. A wash in several shades of brown was then applied with a brush, and lastly the lightest areas "heightened" with white. This conscientious process of execution has so greatly obscured all stylistic clues as to the hand of the draughtsman that, did it not form part of the Leoni volume in Windsor, which contains almost exclusively original drawings, its attribution to Leonardo would today be difficult to argue. The technical qualities of the study illustrate how solidly Leonardo's origins were anchored in the workshop tradition of the 15th century. Thus it can be concluded both from its subject and its detailed execution that the study is based on a specimen drawing: on the one hand it portrays a flower that, as a symbol of purity, regularly appeared in painting – as, for example, in Leonardo's own *Annunciation*; on the other hand, the size and fidelity to nature of the study, and in particular the fact that it reveals signs of transfer, indicate that it either served as a specimen or was copied from another original. The lily has namely been pricked with a needle along its outlines and thus bears the traces of one of the earliest forms of mechanical reproduction.

This technique of transferring a drawing to another surface consisted of using a needle to prick a hole at regular intervals along the outlines of a design. According to one method, a second sheet was thereby laid beneath the first and was perforated by the needle at the same time; the holes left behind were subsequently joined up into lines. Alternatively, the surface of the pricked drawing was dusted with a dark pounce which passed through the perforations onto the surface beneath, be it another sheet of paper or the support for a painting. When the top drawing was removed, it left behind a string of chalk dots from which the draughtsman or painter could then take his lead.

It is a striking fact in the present drawing that not all the outlines of the flower have been pricked: the top of the stem carrying the closed buds has been omitted from this procedure. This and the fact that the actual outlines do not always coincide precisely with the pricked holes suggest that the sheet did not itself serve as an original, but that its outlines were transferred by the pricking method from another design *before* Leonardo commenced drawing. The purpose of the study was thus to elaborate and refine the original subject, a process that led to several clearly visible changes. This does not exclude the possibility that the sheet later served as the basis for a reworking of the motif by Leonardo himself or as an original for his pupils to copy. The study in question thus offers a useful illustration of the process whereby pictorial motifs were passed on and developed in workshops in the 15th century. This process of development was not impulsive and disjointed, but slow and gradual, comparable with the measured, careful approach that Leonardo would later adopt in his studies for equestrian monuments (cf. Ch. 2).

While this process is by no means found in every sphere of Leonardo's art – his working rhythms are elsewhere far more impulsive – it appears to have remained characteristic of his plant studies. As can be seen from the drawings in the present section, he adopts a deliberate approach, patiently piecing together the – in most cases – finely detailed elements of his subject. Whereas the sheets of sketches of individual blooms reproduced here as Cat. 217, 218 reflect a relatively early phase in this process, the drawings of Cat. 219–224 have reached an advanced stage of development. These latter reveal Leonardo's outstanding sensitivity as an artist: despite their meticulous, additive process of execution, they manage to convey an astonishing sense of realism, achieved in the majority of cases by means of a skilful use of lighting, through which Leonardo lends depth and plasticity to his forms.

It may have been his interest in achieving such plasticity that motivated Leonardo's work on the particularly captivating study of a Star of Bethlehem (Cat. 224). The leaves at the base of the plant are swirling, as if caught by a wind gusting in from the left. The lines of motion traced by the elongated leaves thereby recall Leonardo's studies of water, which are discussed in the next chapter. Here, as there, Leonardo reveals his remarkable ability to adapt his method of working, and indeed even his style of draughtsmanship, to his subject – something that is also illustrated by the final two sheets in this section (Cat. 226 and 227). In these studies of trees viewed at a distance, he develops a graphic technique that captures the flickering of the light reflecting off a thousand leaves with greater fidelity to life than any more detailed rendering could do. Leonardo thereby anticipates later artistic developments by several centuries.

*Johannes Nathan*

**Literature:** de Toni, 1922; Popham, 1946 (1994; pp. 74–76); Morley, 1979; *Leonardo da Vinci: Natur und Landschaft*, 1983; Beyer/ Prinz, 1987; Emboden, 1987; Kemp/Roberts, 1989.

*But since we know that painting embraces and contains within itself all things produced by nature or whatever results from man's passing actions – and ultimately everything that can be taken in by the eyes – he seems to me to be a pitiful master who can only do one thing well.*

LEONARDO DA VINCI, MK 522

217

◄ **216 Study of a Lily (*Lilium candidum*), *c.* 1480–1485**
*Pen and ink over black chalk with white heightening, 314 x 177 mm*
*Windsor Castle, Royal Library*
*(RL 12418r)*

**217 Studies of the Flowers of Grass-like Plants (*Briza maxima*), *c.* 1481–1483**
*Pen and ink over metalpoint on brownish prepared paper,*
*183 x 210 mm*
*Venice, Gallerie dell'Accademia,*
*Inv. 237*

▶ **218 Studies of Violas (*Viola odorata* and *Viola canina*), *c.* 1487–1490**
*Pen and ink, 233 x 168 mm*
*Paris, Bibliothèque de l'Institut de France, MS B 2173, fol. 14r*

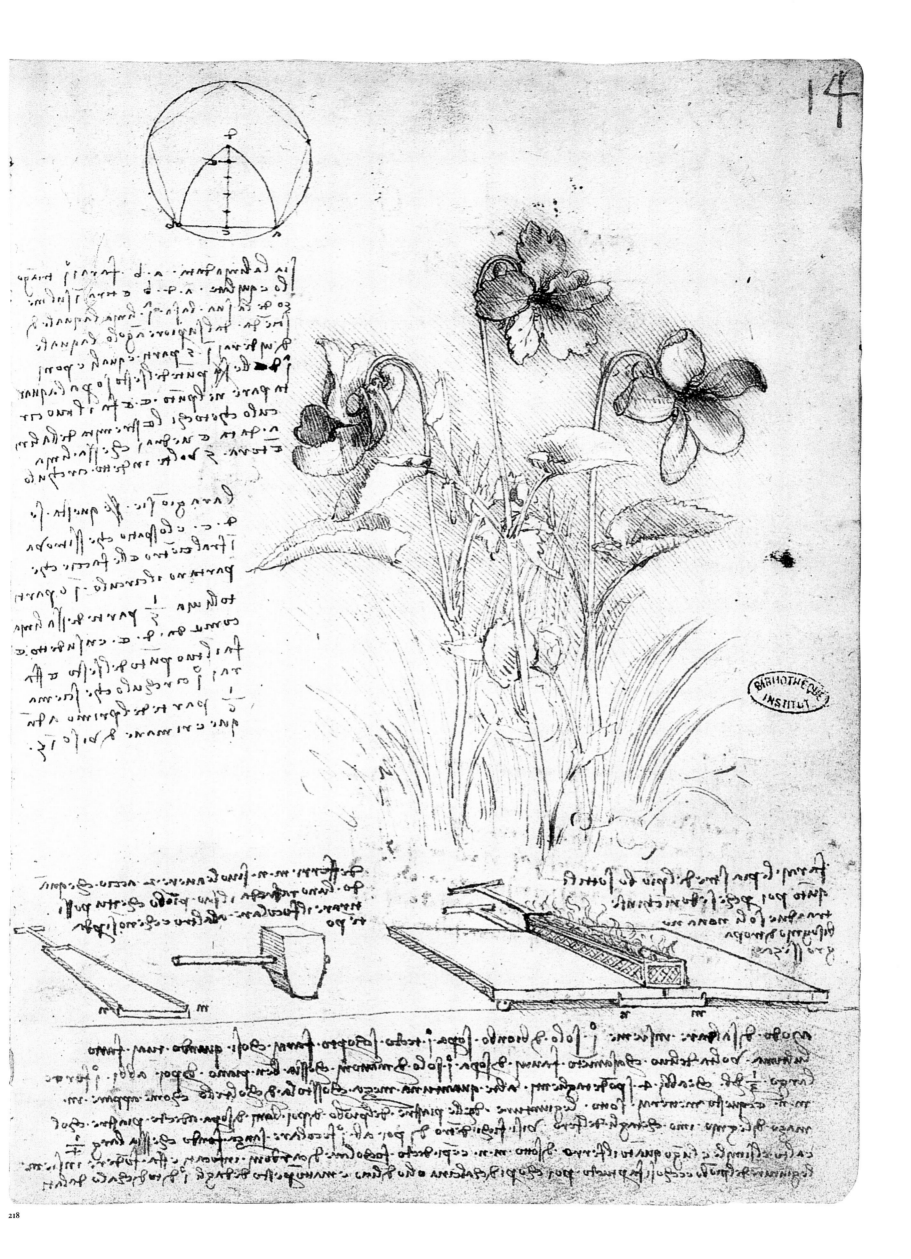

219

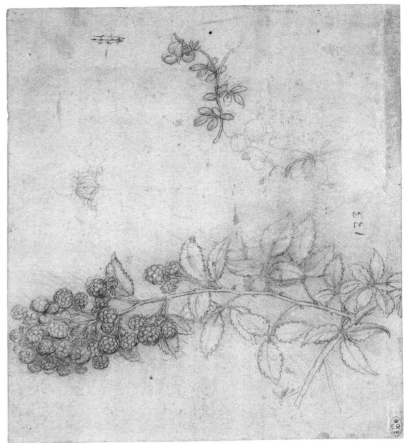

220

221

222

**219  Study of a Spray of
Blackberry (*Rubus fruticosus*),
*c.* 1505**
*Red chalk with white heightening
on red prepared paper,
155 x 162 mm
Windsor Castle, Royal Library
(RL 12419r)*

**220  Study of a Spray of
Blackberry (*Rubus fruticosus*),
*c.* 1505–1508**
*Red chalk on red prepared paper,
188 x 165 mm
Windsor Castle, Royal Library
(RL 12420r)*

**221  Spray of a Plant with
a Cluster of Berries (from
the *Acer* Family? *Acer
platanoides?*), *c.* 1506–1508**
*Red chalk with white heightening
on red prepared paper,
144 x 143 mm
Windsor Castle, Royal Library
(RL 12421r)*

**222  A Small Oak Branch
with a Spray of Dyer's
Greenweed (*Genista
tinctoria*), *c.* 1506–1508**
*Red chalk with traces of white
heightening on red prepared paper,
188 x 154 mm
Windsor Castle, Royal Library
(RL 12422r)*

**223  Study of a Spray of
Blackberry (*Rubus fruticosus*),
*c.* 1505**
*Pen and red chalk, 90 x 60 mm
Windsor Castle, Royal Library
(RL 12425r)*

131

. 130.

224

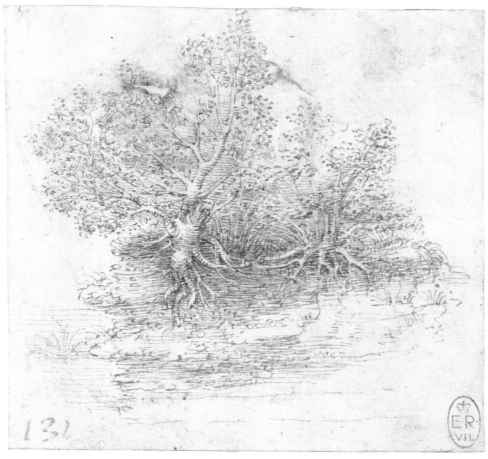

225

226

227

**224 Star of Bethlehem**
**(*Ornithogalum umbellatum*)**
**and Anemones (*Anemone***
***bulbosa, Anemone***
***ranunculoides*), *c.* 1506–1508**
*Pen and ink over red chalk,*
*198 x 160 mm*
*Windsor Castle, Royal Library*
*(RL 12424r)*

**225 Study of Two Trees**
**Growing beside a**
**Stream, *c.* 1505–1510 (?)**
*Pen and light-coloured ink,*
*70 x 74 mm*
*Windsor Castle, Royal Library*
*(RL 12402r)*

**226 A Copse of Trees, *c.* 1508**
*Red chalk, 191 x 153 mm*
*Windsor Castle, Royal Library*
*(RL 12431r)*

**227 Study of a Tree, *c.* 1508 (?)**
*Red chalk, 191 x 153 mm*
*Windsor Castle, Royal Library*
*(RL 12431v)*

# 9 Studies of landscapes, water and "natural catastrophes"

The subjects of the studies brought together in this chapter are only seemingly heterogeneous. With just a few exceptions, the drawings are all linked by Leonardo's particular interest in the portrayal of currents and their effects. This interest, which we have already encountered in a plant study (Cat. 224), reflects Leonardo's ambition to illustrate, in a static picture, sequences of movement. It is in this sense that we should also understand his insistence that a good painter should portray not just the physical appearance of man, but also the intentions of his mind (cf. Ch. 1).

Long before the invention of "moving pictures" in film, Leonardo was seeking to suggest the potential of immanent motion in his art – for example, by including in his *Portrait of Cecilia Gallerani* an ermine, which is apparently in the process of shifting its pose and which in so doing implies that Cecilia Gallerani herself is also moving.

Leonardo strove to illustrate the effects of sequences of action, both past and in some cases imminent, not just in his representations of people, animals and plants, but also in his studies of the seemingly static landscape. That he saw the landscape as the mirror of dynamic processes emerges from his description of the formation of mountains: "The shapes of mountains [...] are produced by the courses of the rivers that are born of rain, snow, hail and ice, melted by the solar rays in the summer. This melting produces the waters which join together in many small rivulets, running from various directions into larger streams, growing in magnitude as they acquire motion, until they converge on the great oceanic sea, always eroding one of the river banks and building up the other, as long as they go on seeking out the breadth of their valleys. And they do not rest content with this, and consume the bases of the flanking mountains. The mountains, collapsing into the rivers, close the valleys, and, as if wishing to be avenged, prohibit the course of such a river and convert it into a lake in which the slow-moving water appears to be subdued [...]" (MK 460). Within this geographical theatre, rivers and mountains become the protagonists who are each pursuing their own ends and whose intentions it is the task of the painter, as far as possible, to render visible.

Leonardo's first surviving landscape drawing (Cat. 229) may already reflect some of these ideas, since the opening in the foreground, leading down to the lower-lying valley floor, and the overhanging cliff-top in the middle ground can evidently be traced back to the erosive forces of the waterfall to the right. From this point of view this early drawing appears to herald the astonishing developments of Leonardo's later landscapes. It is unusual in another respect, too, however, for in contrast to the majority of Leonardo's sketches, this *Arno Landscape*, as it is known, can be precisely dated to his 22nd year: the top left-hand corner shows the date 5 August 1473. As the study is also the first pure landscape drawing to be handed down to us from the Renaissance, the fact that the sheet is dated has attracted great attention, for it seems to suggest that Leonardo – like the artists of the 19th century – went off to the Arno valley one summer's day, sketched a view of the scenery and then gave it a date.

The arguments for and against this attractive hypothesis are too many to discuss here; suffice to say that the view in the drawing has failed to be matched to a real location in the vicinity of Florence, but on the other hand can be aligned with the imaginary landscapes in the paintings of Leonardo and his predecessors. Even if Leonardo did indeed execute this drawing in the open air, it remains indebted both to existing landscape conventions and to Leonardo's own personal landscape preferences, such as for bizarre rock formations.

The tension between personal preference and the impartial observation of nature is even more evident in the majority of Leonardo's later landscape drawings. If the sheer-sided mountains and plunging ravines that Leonardo drew again and again throughout his life (Cat. 228, 230–233) are indeed real locations (as is sometimes claimed), Leonardo would have had to travel a very long way to find them. No such geological formations are to be found in the region of Florence, Milan or Rome, where the artist spent the large part of his life. Leonardo's landscapes thus probably owe their appearance less to direct observation of nature than to his goal to render visible the shaping influence of the elements on the topography. This is illustrated in particularly impressive fashion by the study of an outcrop of stratified rock (Cat. 236), whose horizontal layers, eroded from beneath, seem in imminent danger of collapse. The rocks themselves thereby trace a rolling movement similar to waves and water.

Comparable interests determine even those drawings that exude the character of a real topography, such as the *View of a River Valley* (Cat. 234), which shows a river meandering through a cultivated landscape, or Cat. 246, which portrays a storm in a mountain valley – perhaps in the southern foothills of the Alps. Only a small handful of these studies have been successfully matched with real locations. They include a sheet showing a view of the alpine peaks visible from Milan and the study of a river with a ferry (Cat. 242). On the basis of its details – in particular the small stone bridge carried on three arches, leading from the right shore across to a rocky outcrop – this latter study has been identified with a stretch of

▶ **228 A Stream Running through a Rocky Ravine,** *c.* **1483**
*Pen and ink, 220 x 158 mm*
*Windsor Castle, Royal Library*
*(RL 12395r)*

200

the Adda river between Canonica and Vaprio d'Adda. It corresponds to the view from the Villa Melzi, the family home of Leonardo's favourite pupil and later heir, Francesco Melzi, where the master evidently stayed on several occasions during his second Milanese period. In this drawing, too, Leonardo's interest in the erosion of land by water seems to manifest itself.

Over the course of his career, this same interest would lead Leonardo to devote himself increasingly to the study of water. He evidently hoped to extrapolate from his studies the principles underlying the processes of motion, as emerges from a note accompanying the drawing reproduced here as Cat. 245: "Observe the motion of the surface of water, which resembles the behaviour of hair, which has two motions, of which one depends on the weight of the strands, the other on the line of its revolving; thus water makes revolving eddies, one part of which depends upon the impetus of the principle current, and the other depends on the incident and reflected motions."

In view of his analogy between the motion of water and hair (cf. also Cat. 31–34), it seems likely that Leonardo suspected similar patterns of motion in other materials, too. In his above-mentioned study of a stratified rocky outcrop (Cat. 236), parts of the rock convey an impression of undulating and swirling movement. In another drawing (Cat. 240), similar vortices can be found in the smoke rising from two fires, lit – as the accompanying note informs us – by the Swiss during their siege of Milan in December 1511. Here, too, Leonardo's pen serves an ordering function, insofar as it captures a motion that is essentially largely chaotic as a pattern of spirals.

What we have said thus far may help us to cut through the thicket of interpretations surrounding Leonardo's "Deluge Drawings" (Cat. 247–255). Why this remarkable series of drawings should have held such a fascination for the 20th-century viewer in particular is easy to see: as representations of catastrophes of gigantic proportions, they speak to the modern sense of pessimism about the future, as shaped by the historical events of the last hundred years. Indeed, in several of these studies Leonardo shows the annihilation of great trees and forests and even people and towns. The destructive forces of nature are clearly in evidence in the drawing reproduced here as Cat. 255. The word "deluge" is here at its most appropriate, for the swirling, tempestuous mass of water is seen alone, in the absence of rocks or mountains.

By contrast, the other drawings in the series (Cat. 247–254) sketch events that might equally well relate to Leonardo's observations on the erosion of mountains, as cited above. Interpreted in this light, the occasional appearance of trees and houses should not necessarily be read as the expression of a pessimistic view of the future of civilization, but primarily as indicators of scale. The function of the series would in this case be to demonstrate how Leonardo's understanding of the movement of water could be applied even to natural events on the grandest scale.

It would be dangerous, in classifying Leonardo's "Deluge Drawings", to see them as exclusively one thing or another. The notable persistence with which Leonardo pursued this series suggests that his fascination for this unusual subject was fuelled not just by purely scientific interests, but also by aesthetic concerns. The notes – most of them coolly observational in style – which he wrote to accompany these drawings, however, suggest that he was aiming at an objective realism to a greater extent than is generally assumed. Noteworthy is an astonishingly impartial note written above the particularly violent sketch reproduced here as Cat. 248: "On rain: show the degrees of rain falling at various distances and of varied darkness; and the darker part will be closer to the middle of its thickness."

Perhaps it was precisely the contrast between cool scientific analysis and emotional emphasis that spurred Leonardo on to execute these drawings.

*Johannes Nathan*

**Literature:** Gantner, 1958; Perrig, 1981; Castelfranco, 1966 (pp. 125–152); Gombrich, 1976 (pp. 33–35); Kemp, 1989; Kemp/Roberts, 1989; Nathan, 1995; Fehrenbach, 1997.

*Just as the case of Arcimboldi remains inexplicable in the context of his time, so we may perhaps think of Leonardo, who is said to have read figurations into cloud formations and old walls. The fantastical images of our master [Arcimboldi] are related to these on account of their same "as if" quality, insofar as they lack all relationship to the reality of creation.*

OSKAR KOKOSCHKA, 1951

229

230

**229 Arno Landscape,**
**5 August 1473**
*Pen and ink, 190 x 285 mm*
*Florence, Galleria degli Uffizi,*
*Gabinetto dei Disegni e delle*
*Stampe, Inv. 436E*

**230 Mountains and Foothills,**
*c. 1506*
*Black chalk, 96 x 137 mm*
*Windsor Castle, Royal Library*
*(RL 12408r)*

231

232

**231 Rolling Hills and Rocky**
**Pinnacles,** *c.* **1506**
*Red chalk, 93 x 152 mm*
*Windsor Castle, Royal Library*
*(RL 12405r)*

**232 Mountain Peaks and**
**Foothills with a River in**
**the Foreground,** *c.* **1506**
*Red chalk, 87 x 151 mm*
*Windsor Castle, Royal Library*
*(RL 12406r)*

**233**

**234**

233 **Town on a Valley Floor**
**in front of Mountains,** *c.* 1506
*Black chalk, 88 x 145 mm*
*Windsor Castle, Royal Library*
*(RL 12407r)*

234 **View of a River Valley**
**with a Canal,** *c.* 1505–1510
*Pen and ink over black chalk,*
*85 x 160 mm*
*Windsor Castle, Royal Library*
*(RL 12398r)*

235

236

**235 Houses above a Canal Running alongside a Winding River,** *c.* 1505–1510
*Pen and ink, 100 x 147 mm*
*Windsor Castle, Royal Library*
*(RL 12399r)*

**236 Horizontal Strata of Rock,** *c.* 1510–1513
*Pen and ink over black chalk, 185 x 268 mm*
*Windsor Castle, Royal Library*
*(RL 12394r)*

237

238

**237 Drawing of Two
Mountain Ranges and
Notes,** *c.* 1511
*Red chalk on red prepared paper,*
*159 x 240 mm*
*Windsor Castle, Royal Library*
*(RL 12414r)*

**238 A Marshy Plain, Seen
from Above, and Notes,**
*c.* 1511
*Red chalk on red prepared paper,*
*150 x 235 mm*
*Windsor Castle, Royal Library*
*(RL 12412r)*

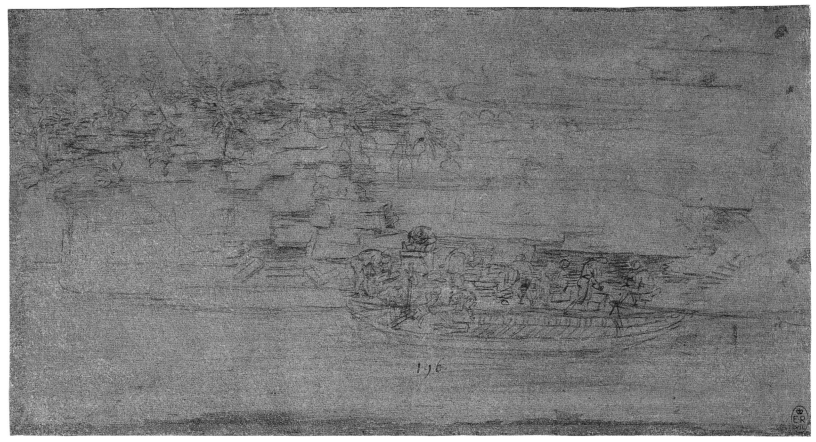

239

240

**239 Study of a Quarry beside**
**a River,** *c.* **1511**
*Red chalk on red prepared paper,*
*133 x 240 mm*
*Windsor Castle, Royal Library*
*(RL 12415r)*

**240 Drawing showing Two**
**Fires in the Landscape,**
**16 December 1511 (?)**
*Red chalk on red prepared paper,*
*146 x 233 mm*
*Windsor Castle, Royal Library*
*(RL 12416r)*

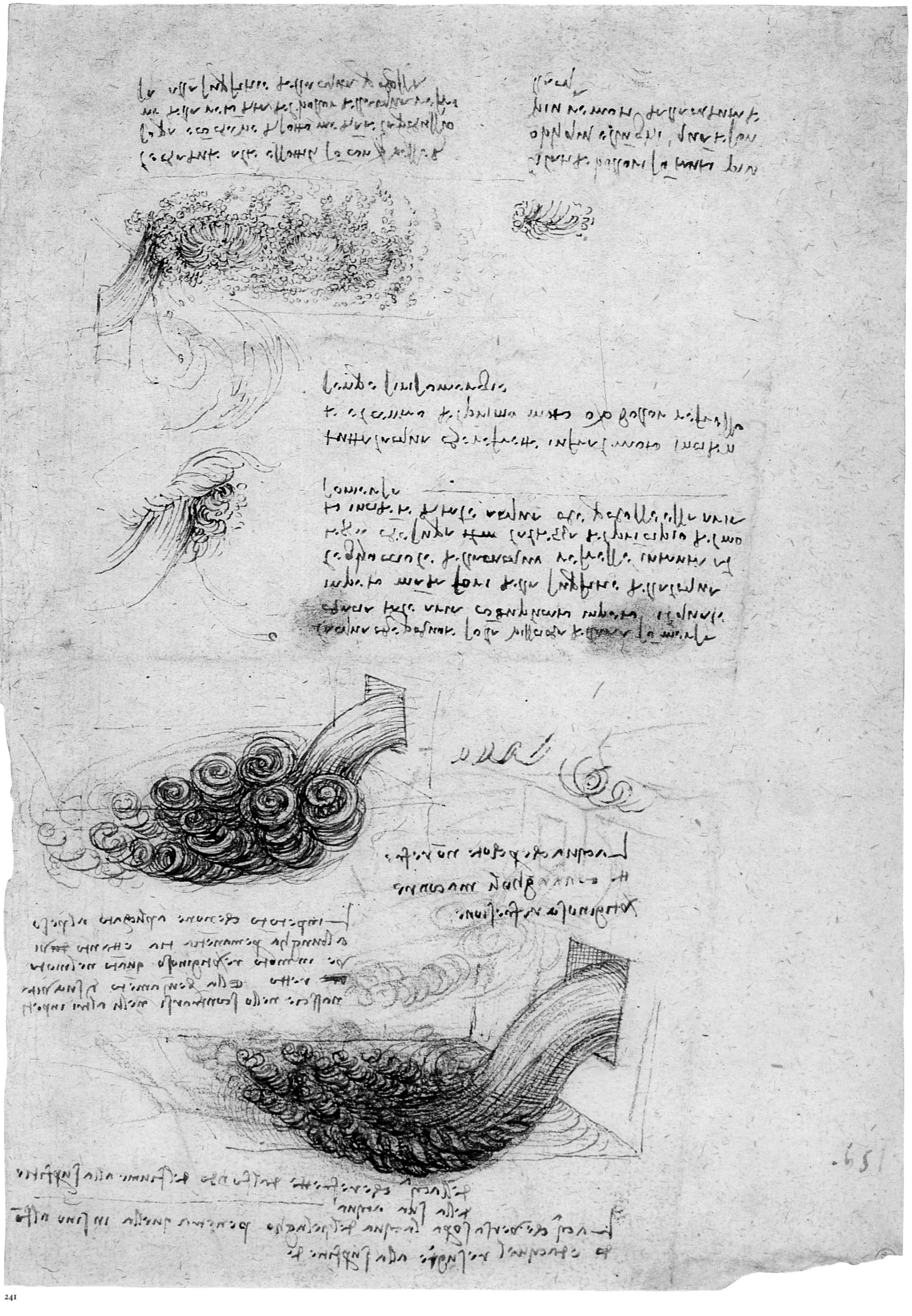

241

241

242

243

245

244

241 **Sheet of Studies of Water**, *c.* 1508–1510
*Pen and ink over red chalk,*
*268 x 182 mm*
*Windsor Castle, Royal Library*
*(RL 12662r)*

242 **View of the River Adda with the Ferry between Vaprio and Canonica, 1513**
*Pen and ink, 100 x 128 mm*
*Windsor Castle, Royal Library*
*(RL 12400r)*

243 **Sheet of Studies of Water**, *c.* 1508–1510
*Pen and ink over red chalk,*
*205 x 203 mm*
*Windsor Castle, Royal Library*
*(RL 12661r)*

244 **Sheet of Studies of Water Flowing past Obstacles**, *c.* 1508–1510
*Pen and ink over red chalk,*
*290 x 202 mm*
*Windsor Castle, Royal Library*
*(RL 12660r)*

245 **Old Man Seated on a Rocky Outcrop, Seen in Profile to the Right, with Water Studies**, *c.* 1510–1513
*Pen and ink, 152 x 213 mm*
*Windsor Castle, Royal Library*
*(RL 12579r)*

·137·

247

248

**246  Storm over a Valley
in the Foothills of the Alps,**
*c.* **1506**
*Red chalk, 200 x 150 mm*
*Windsor Castle, Royal Library*
*(RL 12409r)*

**247  Explosion of Rock
caused by the Bursting of
a Water Vein,** *c.* **1508–1511**
*Black chalk, 178 x 278 mm*
*Windsor Castle, Royal Library*
*(RL 12387r)*

**248  Explosion of Rock
caused by the Bursting of a
Water Vein and Creation of
Waves in a Lake by Falling
Boulders,** *c.* **1515 (?)**
*Pen and two inks (brown and
yellow) over black chalk,*
*162 x 203 mm*
*Windsor Castle, Royal Library*
*(RL 12380r)*

249

250

249 Deluge over the Sea,
c. 1515 (?)
*Black chalk, 158 x 210 mm*
*Windsor Castle, Royal Library*
*(RL 12383r)*

250 Storm Clouds, Vortices
and Torrents of Water over a
Rocky Landscape, c. 1508–1511
or c. 1515 (?)
*Black chalk, 158 x 203 mm*
*Windsor Castle, Royal Library*
*(RL 12377r)*

251

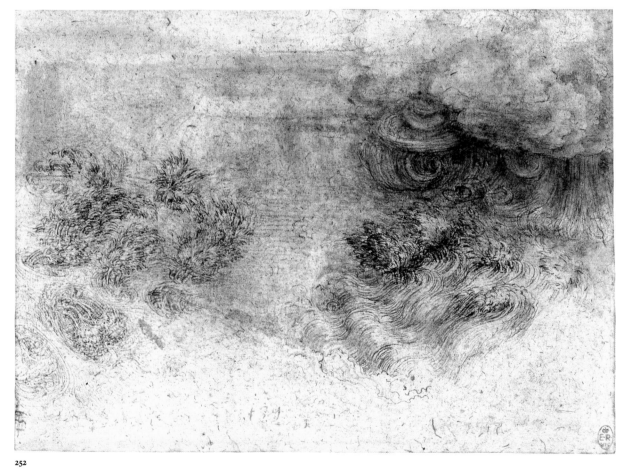

252

**251  A Town at the Centre of the Cloudburst,** *c.* 1508–1511 or *c.* 1515 (?)
*Black chalk, 163 x 210 mm*
*Windsor Castle, Royal Library*
*(RL 12378r)*

**252  Storm Clouds over a River or Lake and Trees,** *c.* 1514 (?)
*Pen and ink and brown washes over black chalk, 157 x 203 mm*
*Windsor Castle, Royal Library*
*(RL 12379r)*

253

254

255

**253 Sheet of Various Studies of Destruction and Rocks,** c. 1511/12 (?)
*Pen and ink over traces of black chalk, 300 x 203 mm*
*Windsor Castle, Royal Library (RL 12388r)*

**254 Storm and Flood in a Bay with Castle and Viaduct,** c. 1515 (?)
*Pen and ink over black chalk, 163 x 206 mm*
*Windsor Castle, Royal Library (RL 12401r)*

**255 Tempest over Horsemen and Trees with Enormous Waves,** c. 1514 (?)
*Pen and ink over black chalk with touches of wash and white heightening, on grey prepared paper, 270 x 408 mm*
*Windsor Castle, Royal Library (RL 12376r)*

# 10 Drawings of maps and plans

Leonardo's drawings of maps and plans number amongst the most magnificent of the period around 1500. They were executed in some cases for military purposes and in others to satisfy the need for reliable topographical maps for peacetime projects, such as the draining of marshes and the canalization of rivers. Leonardo's studies also reflect the interest in recording the exact topography of Upper and Central Italy, which had been increasing since the 14th century. Specific centres of this interest in cartography included Florence, which since the middle of the 15th century had been producing the best maps for manuscripts and printed editions of Ptolemy's *Geographia*. Leonardo would also have learned the great practical value of cartography in Lombardy; during his many years in Milan, he worked on the expansion and improvement of the existing network of shipping and irrigation canals, a task that clearly highlighted the need for accurate maps. It was in Milan, too, that he executed a small, rapidly sketched view of the city below a crude, schematic plan drawing.

Alongside simple pen drawings of the Italian topography, Leonardo's surviving œuvre includes several maps executed in colour and dating probably from after 1500. These include bird's-eye views of the Chiana valley and the surrounding Tuscan hills (Cat. 256–258), which the artist produced in 1502 either in conjunction with the military campaigns being mounted by his then employer, Cesare Borgia, or soon afterwards for other reasons. Leonardo thereby based his maps of Tuscany on the maps and landscape views in Ptolemy's *Geographia*, mentioned above. These already contained all the most important topographical features, such as the chains of hills, the major rivers and the marshes and lakes dotting the Chiana valley. Somewhat elongated in Leonardo's drawings, the Chiana valley runs to the southeast of Florence from Arezzo to Lake Trasimeno – a route today followed by the *autostrada del sole* between the Arezzo and Chiusi exits. In the most strongly coloured of these drawings (Cat. 258), Leonardo modified the actual area covered by the map to include the course of the Tiber at the top of the picture, a stretch of the Upper Arno on the left and, on the far right, the Lago di Bolsena and a glimpse of the Tyrrhenian coast. Numerous towns appear in the shape of small *vedute*: Arezzo, to the east Anghiari and Borgo Sansepolcro, further south Cortona and Perugia, and in the lower half of the map Volterra and Siena.

The artist's prime focus, however, falls upon the numerous rivers and their identification; clearly recognizable are the watersheds from where the smaller rivers flow either into the Tiber (top), the Chiana valley (centre) or the Mediterranean (bottom right). In view of its hydrographical emphasis, the map can probably be linked with plans to transform the marshy Chiana valley into an enormous lake with the aid of several dams (Cat. 256 and 258). The artificial lake would have incorporated the present-day lakes of Montepulciano and Chiusi to the south and would have extended northwards almost as far as the Arno, whose level it was intended to regulate through the controlled release of water. The project to create an artificial reservoir at the same time recalls the vast ocean of prehistory that Leonardo would describe a few years later in the Codex Leicester (fol. 9r).

Of the two large-format views of the Chiana valley and its surrounding region, the less eye-catching map comes closest to the principles of modern cartography (Cat. 256). Here the elevations are no longer seen in the conventional "relief" view, but are portrayed with orographic accuracy in different shades of brown, with high ground indicated by darker shading. A number of the maps that Leonardo produced in 1503–1504 in conjunction with the regulation and diversion of the Arno (Cat. 259–263) similarly turn away from the traditional technique of showing elevations in oblique view.

Leonardo's studies and proposals for the regulation of the Arno were originally linked with the idea of providing Florence with a waterway to the sea. Other plans included literally cutting off Pisa – at that time at war with Florence – both from its water supply and the sea. Proposals to regulate the Arno for peaceful purposes had already been discussed in the 15th century and extended both to the straightening of the watercourse and to the building of a canal, enabling shipping to bypass the river's innumerable shallows and meanders (Cat. 259, 261, 262). In further drawings, Leonardo takes a detailed look at the river's bifurcations and flow conditions and at the effect of breakwaters on siltation and water currents (Cat. 262).

The course of the proposed canal is sketched somewhat approximately in several drawings and leads from Florence, via Prato and Pistoia, to Serravalla. From here it traverses the marshy region above Fucécchio, identifiable by its two shallow lakes (Lago di Biéntina and Lago di Fucécchio), and finally continues further westwards to rejoin the Arno (Cat. 259–261). Had it been built, the canal would have brought the added advantage of draining the above-mentioned marshes. In the end, however, the project went beyond the bounds of what was then technically possible – a fact that even the enormous earthworking machines designed by Leonardo and other engineers to excavate the soil were unable to change (Cat. 322).

*If I remember correctly, da Vinci advised his pupils
to stimulate their imagination by looking at cloud
formations and random shapes in nature.*

ROBERT MUSIL, 1924

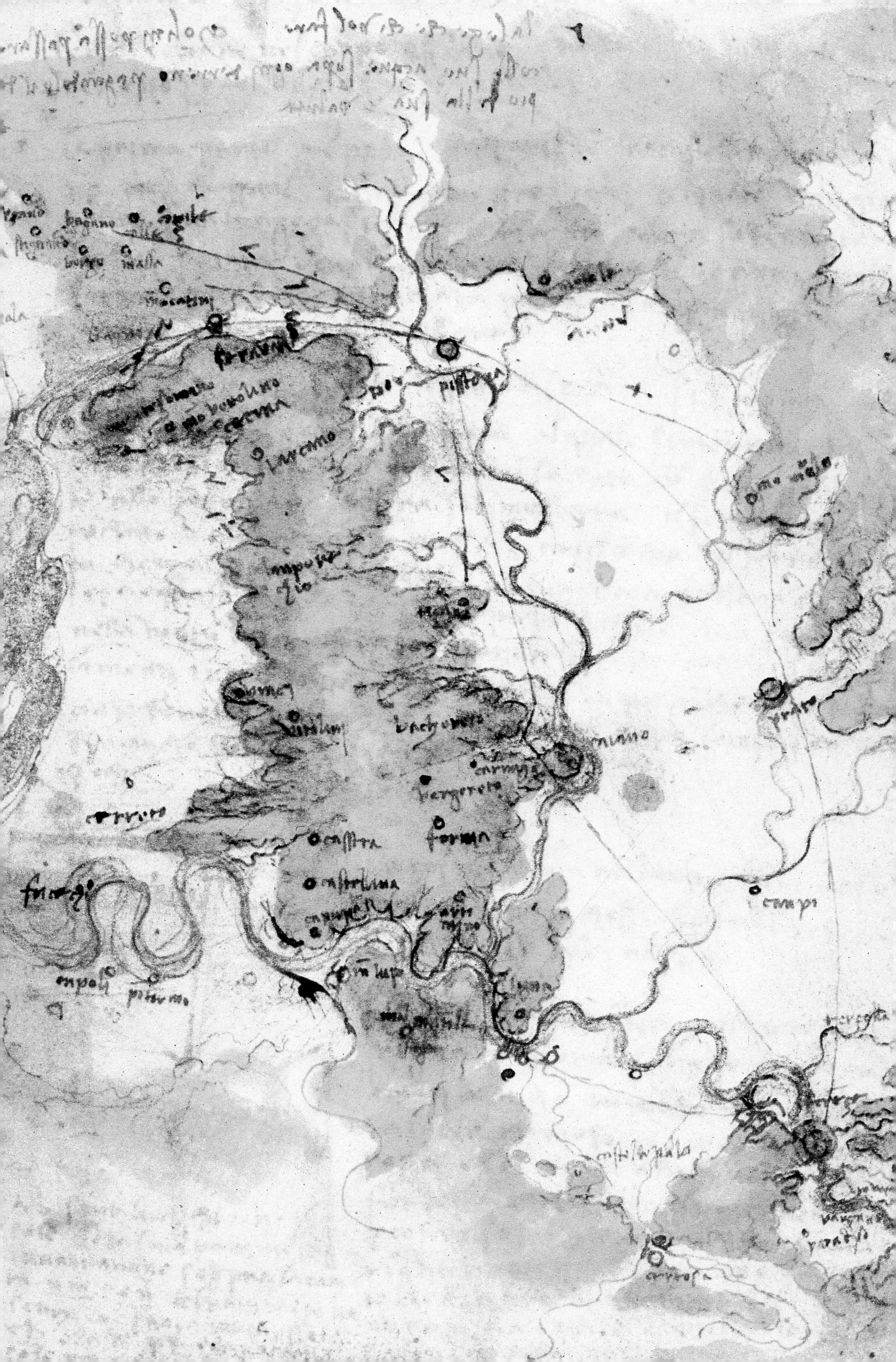

Another grandiose vision that remained unrealized was the plan by Leonardo's patron, Giuliano de'Medici, to drain the Pontine marshes south of Rome. The map reproduced here as Cat. 264 documents the start of Leonardo's work on the project, which was headed by Fra Giovanni Scotti from Como. Leonardo's map covers the marshy region extending from the west of the Volscian hills (Monti Lepini) to the Tyrrhenian coast. Drainage of the Pontine marshes had been attempted on a number of occasions since Roman times, but would finally succeed as late as the 20th century.

The main hydrological problem facing such a project is described by Goethe in an entry in his *Italian Journey* of 23.2.1787: owing to the shallow incline of the plain and the height of the coastline, the water coming down from the hills was unable to run off fast enough. The water moving along the rivers with their countless meanders was also travelling too slowly. Leonardo takes account of these problems in his drawing: the old drainage channel running parallel to the Via Appia – the "Nympha fl[umen]" – has been widened to allow it to absorb the waters coming down from the mountains around Sermonetta, Sezze and Priverno and to carry them to the sea west of Terracina. The Rio Martino running at right angles to the Via Appia has also been widened and corrected. The clearly legible inscriptions on the map were added by Francesco Melzi. The possibility cannot be excluded that here, too, Leonardo drew on earlier cartography.

The largest and at the same time most important of Leonardo's maps and plans is his bird's-eye view of Imola (Cat. 265), a town lying to the southeast of Bologna. Measuring over 60 cm wide and executed in great detail and in splendid colour, it is a true forerunner of modern town plans. The drawing arose at the end of 1502, when Leonardo spent several months in Imola with his then employer Cesare Borgia and thus had ample time for his topographical studies.

Although he drew upon an earlier map in producing his bird's-eye plan of the town, preparatory sketches demonstrate that the artist made detailed studies in Imola itself in order to augment his existing material and perhaps also to emphasize the fortifications around the citadel. In the inscription, Leonardo gives the distances to the nearest large towns as well as the names of the four points of the compass and the four winds. The circle drawn around Imola is divided up evenly into eight main segments and 32 subsidiary segments, all of whose lines intersect at the centre of the circle. Leonardo hereby follows a surveying system that he would have known from humanist Leon Battista Alberti's *Ludi matematici* (1450). In measuring the individual buildings and streets from this exact central point, Leonardo ultimately anticipates the principles of modern cartography.

The majority of Leonardo's maps and plans served no practical purpose in his lifetime. The significance of these monumental drawings seems to lie in their projection of ambitious ideas that would be realized in only one case (Cat. 264) and at a much later date.

That the artist was guided by his visionary powers far more than by his sense of the achievable is illustrated by another look at his map of the Chiana valley (Cat. 258). The outlines of the artificial lake in blue seem to resemble the silhouette of a bird cir-cling over the land, just as if Leonardo were trying in his aerial views to simulate or subsume within a symbol the dream of flying, which in reality was doomed to fail.

*Frank Zöllner*

**Literature:** Baratta, 1911, 1941; Clark/Pedretti, 1968–1969; RLW, II (pp. 179–205); PRC, II (pp. 174–200); *Leonardo e le vie d'aqua*, 1983; Pedretti, 1985; Harley/Woodward, 1987; Lippincott, 1996; Arasse, 1998 (pp. 210–217).

*Everyone acknowledged that this was true of Leonardo da Vinci, an artist of outstanding physical beauty who displayed infinite grace in everything he did and who cultivated his genius so brilliantly that all problems he studied he solved with ease.*

GIORGIO VASARI, 1568

256

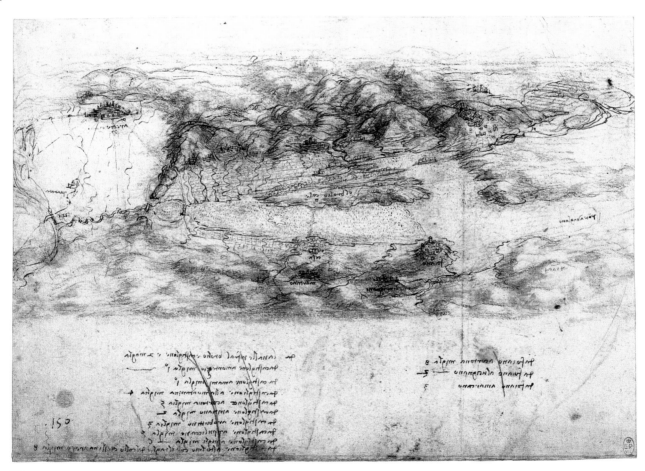

257

**256 Map of Northern Italy,**
**showing the West Coast**
**from the Mouth of the**
**Magra River to Toscanella**
**and Corneto,** *c. 1502/03*
*Pen and ink and watercolour,*
*317 x 449 mm*
*Windsor Castle, Royal Library*
*(RL 12277r)*

**257 Bird's-eye View of the**
**Region around Arezzo,**
*c. 1502*
*Pen and ink over black chalk,*
*209 x 281 mm*
*Windsor Castle, Royal Library*
*(RL 12682r)*

**▶ 258 Bird's-eye View of the**
**Landscape, showing the**
**Tuscan Cities of Arezzo,**
**Perugia, Chiusi and Siena,**
*c. 1502*
*Pen and ink and watercolour,*
*338 x 488 mm*
*Windsor Castle, Royal Library*
*(RL 12278r)*

258

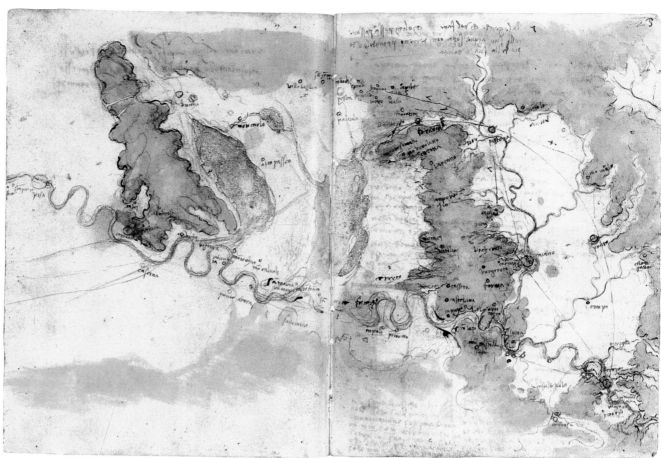

259

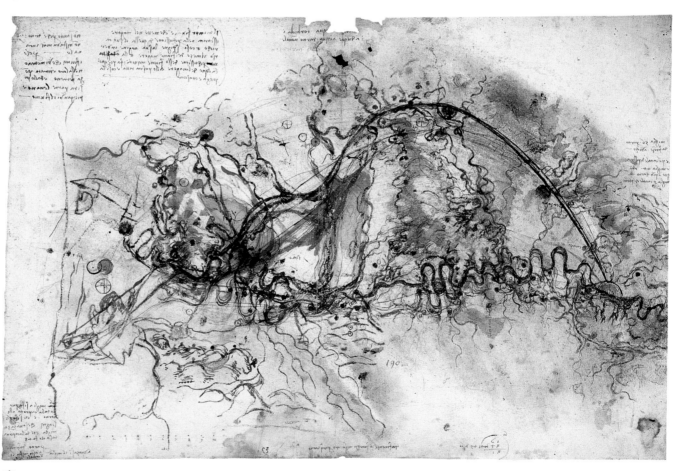

260

**259 Map showing a Part of
Tuscany around the Arno
Region,** *c.* **1503**
*Pen and ink and watercolour,*
*210 x 300 mm*
*Madrid, Biblioteca Nacional,*
*Codex Madrid II (MS 8936),*
*ff. 22v–23r*

**260 Map showing the
Proposed Course of the
Arno Canal,** *c.* **1503/04**
*Pen and ink over black chalk,*
*335 x 482 mm*
*Windsor Castle, Royal Library*
*(RL 12279r)*

261

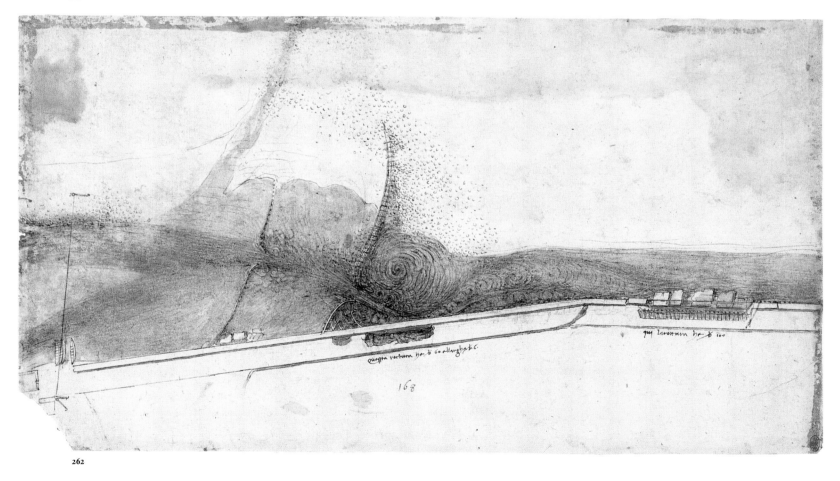

262

**261 Topographical Map of the Region to the Northwest of Florence, showing the Valleys of Lucca, Pistoia and Prato in the North and the Arno Valley in the South,** *c.* 1503/04
*Pen and ink over black chalk, 240 x 367 mm*
*Windsor Castle, Royal Library (RL 12685r)*

**262 Embankment and Breakwaters to Divert the Arno, a few Kilometres East of Florence,** *c.* 1504
*Pen and ink and watercolour, 236 x 416 mm*
*Windsor Castle, Royal Library (RL 12680r)*

▶ **263 Map showing a Part of Tuscany: Volterra in the Southeast, Pisa (beside the Arno) in the Northwest and some 100 km of Coastline,** *c.* 1503/04
*Pen and ink over black chalk and watercolour, 275 x 401 mm*
*Windsor Castle, Royal Library (RL 12683r)*

▶▶ **264 Cartographic View of the Pontine Marshes and the Coast North of Terracina,** *c.* 1514–1516
*Pen and ink and watercolour, 277 x 400 mm*
*Windsor Castle, Royal Library (RL 12684r)*

▶▶▶ **265 Map of Imola,** *c.* 1502
*Pen and ink and watercolour, 440 x 602 mm*
*Windsor Castle, Royal Library (RL 12284r)*

# 11 Architectural studies

Whole books have been written about Leonardo's activities as an architect, but there is still no convincing evidence that the artist ever constructed a single building. In the period before 1490, furthermore, Leonardo was at no point officially engaged as an architect, but was simply employed as a consultant on certain projects. The importance of Leonardo's architectural studies, accordingly, is primarily to be found in the fact that they take up architectural principles and systematically expand upon them in drawings.

This is all the more significant when we consider that Leonardo was a witness to the two biggest architectural feats of the late 15th century, namely the completion of the cupolas crowning Florence and Milan cathedrals. These were not just extraordinarily monumental but also technologically very ambitious projects, in both cases placing high demands on the competence of the architects in charge. Starting from the same challenge of erecting a dome over the crossing of a monumental church, Leonardo took up in his sketches the then topical discussion of the sacred building on a centralized ground plan. His architectural studies also include designs for a model city from his first Milanese period, projects for secular buildings such as palaces and villas from the years after 1500 and studies for fortresses. Many of Leonardo's drawings also include notes relating to urban planning, the various genres of architecture, ornament, structural engineering and the repairing of structural damage (RLW § 741–795).

Amongst Leonardo's earliest architectural studies are two drawings in which the artist explores the structural challenges posed by the still unfinished dome of Milan cathedral (Cat. 267 and 268). Following the death of the incumbent architect Guiniforte Solari (1429–1481), the cathedral authorities sought advice from a number of outside architects, including Leonardo, who during the period 1487–1488 supplied them with drawings and designs for an architectural model. The two sheets from the Codex Atlanticus show him considering the structural design of a double-skinned cupola whose relatively steep pitch takes up the Gothic character of the existing body of the cathedral, but which is simultaneously indebted to the design by Filippo Brunelleschi (1377–1446) for the dome of Florence cathedral. Indeed, the desire to tie in the formal principles of Gothic architecture with those of the Renaissance was one of Leonardo's fundamental concerns. Thus his first sketch-like designs for the cupola of Milan cathedral (Cat. 269) have much in common with the proposals put forward by Donato Bramante (c. 1443/44–1514) for the new St Peter's, whose construction commenced in 1506. The cupola rises above a drum whose proportions are reiterated in a portico topped with a gable. At the same time, however, the flying buttresses in Leonardo's sketches recall the older, Gothic traditions of northern Europe, as still current in Milan. In the end, however, both Leonardo's proposals and those of the other outside experts were rejected; the authorities opted for a crossing tower crowned with a pinnacle, as proposed by local Milanese architects, and thus for a solution that fell fully in line with the tradition of medieval Lombard architecture.

Over the following years, however, Leonardo continued to return to the idea of a monumental cupola resting on a drum, as realized by Brunelleschi in Florence, in his numerous studies for churches (Cat. 269, 271–277, 279, 281). Indeed, in virtually every single one of his drawings we find the drum-mounted cupola that characterizes Florence cathedral and that would become the leitmotif of the sacred architecture of the Renaissance and the Baroque.

Leonardo's drawings of centrally planned architecture, and in particular those from Manuscript B in the Institut de France (Cat. 270–272, 273–277, 279), not only illustrate possible theoretical solutions for the cupola of Milan cathedral, but also point to the importance of Leonardo's sketches for the visualization of architectural ideas. These are not finished drawings of ground plans and elevations, all drawn to scale, which could have been translated into real buildings, but are visionary variations on a compact spatial concept. There is a system and a persistence to the way in which Leonardo pursues this concept: a system in the way in which ground plan and perspective overall view are logically combined on the same sheet, and a persistence in the artistic development of a compact central space around which are laid out peripheral rooms in ever new variations. A number of these architectural designs are portrayed in a strangely block-like manner, as if hewn from solid material by a sculptor (Cat. 272, 273, 275, 276).

In his theoretical writings on architecture and in the notes accompanying his drawings, Leonardo occasionally refers to existing buildings, such as San Sepolcro in Milan (RLW § 756), above whose Romanesque crypt he then proceeds to develop an imaginary centralized building (Cat. 271). Other references to known churches are found in a design for a centrally planned building with seven radial chapels and an elongated narthex with rounded ends (Cat. 272). In his accompanying notes (RLW § 754), Leonardo stresses that churches of this kind should not have a bell-tower attached to the main building, but rather that any such *campanile* "must stand apart like that of the Cathedral and of San Giovanni [i.e.

*I would not like to neglect to repeat the words I heard King François I say about him: [...] he did not believe there could be anyone else on earth who knew as much as Leonardo, not just about sculpture, painting and architecture, but also insofar as he was a great philosopher.*

BENVENUTO CELLINI, 1558–1566

the Baptistery] at Florence". Leonardo was thus aiming at a spatial aesthetic whose formal compactness would not support interruption by the addition of a bell-tower.

Almost as visionary as Leonardo's studies for centrally planned churches, but at the same time oriented somewhat more closely to practical requirements, are Leonardo's designs for secular buildings and the redevelopment of Milan. There is a degree of modernism in his proposals for improving the standard of hygiene in a new town (Cat. 266/RLW § 741; Cat. 278/RLW § 746). Probably against the backdrop of the plague raging in Milan in 1484/85, the artist suggested creating high-level streets solely for use by pedestrians and separate from the low-level streets used by traffic and where the drains also ran. Leonardo also recommended that the buildings should be no higher than the width of the street. The concept of creating two levels or storeys, each designated to serve different purposes, also makes its way into his design for some stables (Cat. 280/RLW § 761/PRC, II, pp. 37–38).

Leonardo's architectural duties at the Milanese court naturally also extended to the design and construction of stage sets, as evidenced by numerous references in the sources and by a number of sketches, one of them showing a design for a performance of Baldassare Taccone's *Danaë* (Cat. 282). Other architectural sketches from this period appear to have got no further than the drawing board. These include a design for the façade of a church (Cat. 283), which can be dated to *c.* 1495–1497 (possibly later) and the ground plan for an urban residence, the so-called Casa Guiscardi (Cat. 284 and 285). This drawing is interesting because it offers an insight into the design practice of the day. At the top of the first sheet, the patron has written down what he wants

in his new house. Leonardo develops the floor plans of the individual storeys in line with these wishes and provides a brief commentary on the layout. In one of his accompanying notes, for example, he advises that the domestic quarters used by the servants should not be located too close to the owner's apartments.

Leonardo continued to devote himself to designs for secular buildings after 1500, too, for example for the villa of his friend and pupil Francesco Melzi (Cat. 286). Much grander in scale, however, were his plans for a château for the French king in Romorantin on the Saudre, a subsidiary of the Loire. Several sketches of ground plans relating to this project are still extant (Cat. 288), as well as a perspective view of the palace complex as a whole (Cat. 289). The ground plans probably relate to pavilions or antique temples (left) and to the challenges of building a château complex surrounded by water and with water even running through it (right). The accompanying text delves only briefly into issues of hydraulic engineering before wandering off in another direction in typical Leonardo fashion. Thus he reflects on how wooden houses can be transported and suggests sub-letting the rooms of the château to the local population when the court is absent, and considers the positioning of fountains and the use of dams, mills and sluices in the Loire region (RLW § 744, 747, 1075, 1077). The project for the château of Romorantin would ultimately also remain unfinished, since the climatic conditions prevailing in the region proved unsuitable.

We may conclude this chapter with a look at Leonardo's copious designs for fortresses, of which only a few are reproduced here (Cat. 290–292). The artist had already addressed this genre of architecture in his first Milanese period (Cat. 276), and designs for

fortresses would form a regular theme of his later studies, too. The dating of these drawings is particularly difficult, and in the case of some sheets has been placed between 1495 and 1513 (Cat. 290). The problems that Leonardo addresses in his studies are all very much the same: in view of the ever-increasing importance of artillery, existing fortifications had to be reinforced or new fortresses built so as to provide more effective protection. This included flattening ramparts and bastions and building round instead of square peel towers, since these shapes were better able to withstand direct artillery fire (Cat. 291). Leonardo also looked at designing effective moat systems to keep the enemy at bay (Cat. 276, 290, 292) and at developing means of warding off enemy fire and aligning one's own cannon and gun fire.

*Frank Zöllner*

**Literature:** Heydenreich, 1929, 1953 (pp. 86–93); Pedretti, 1972, 1980; Marani, 1984; Guillaume, 1987; *Leonardo da Vinci: Engineer and Architect*, 1987; Schofield, 1989, 1991; *Rinascimento*, 1994.

◄ **266 Architectural Studies for a City on Several Levels,** *c.* **1487–1490**
*Pen and ink, 233 x 165 mm*
*Paris, Bibliothèque de l'Institut de France, MS B 2173, fol. 16r*

*Clearly, it was because of his profound knowledge of painting that Leonardo started so many things without finishing them; for he was convinced that his hands, for all their skill, could never perfectly express the subtle and wonderful ideas of his imagination.*

GIORGIO VASARI, 1568

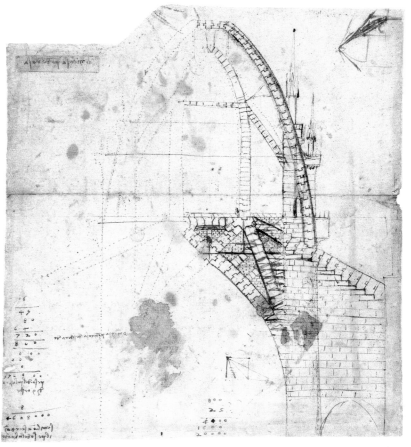

267

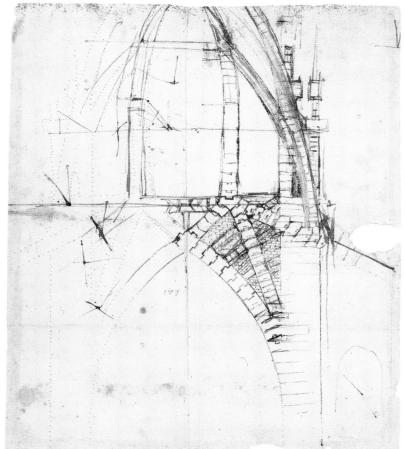

268

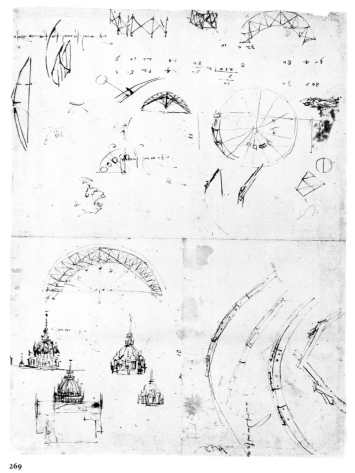

269

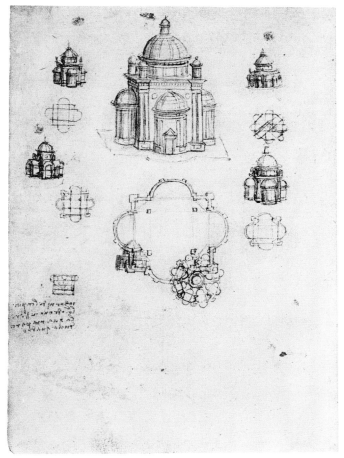

270

**267 Study for the Cupola of Milan Cathedral**, *c.* 1487–1490
*Pen and ink (pricked),*
*332 x 293 mm*
*Milan, Biblioteca Ambrosiana,*
*Codex Atlanticus, fol. 850r/310r-b*

**268 Study for the Cupola of Milan Cathedral**, *c.* 1487–1490
*Pen and ink (pricked),*
*282 x 237 mm*
*Milan, Biblioteca Ambrosiana,*
*Codex Atlanticus, fol. 851r/310v-b*

**269 Studies for the Crossing Cupola of Milan Cathedral and for Scaffolding for the Vault**, *c.* 1487–1490
*Pen and ink, 275 x 271 mm*
*Milan, Biblioteca Ambrosiana,*
*Codex Atlanticus, fol. 719/266r-a-b*

**270 Studies for a Building on a Centralized Plan**, *c.* 1487–1490
*Pen and ink, 233 x 163 mm*
*Paris, Bibliothèque de l'Institut de France, Codex Ashburnham 1875/1 (MS B 2184), fol. 3v*

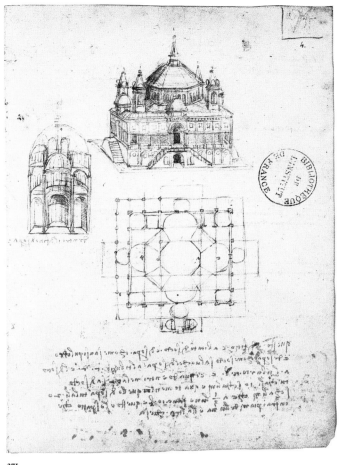

271

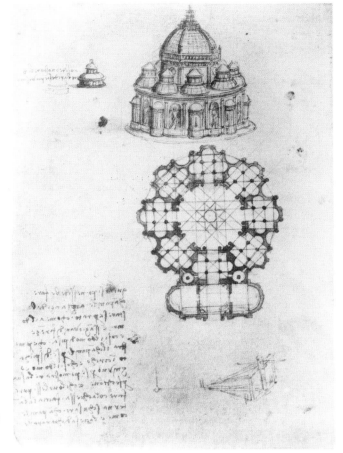

272

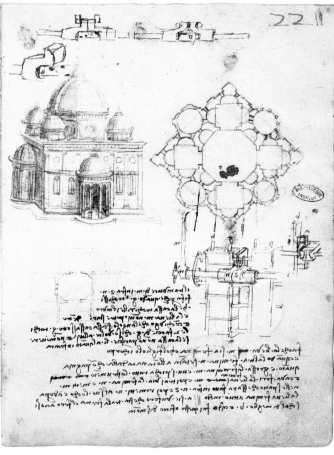

273

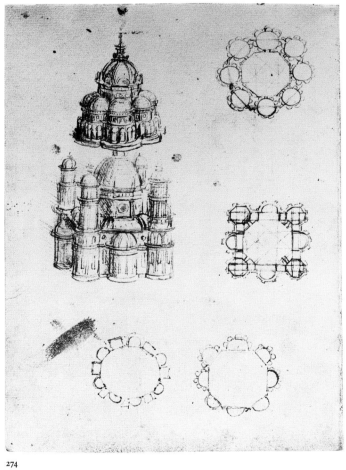

274

**271 Studies for a Building on a Centralized Plan,**
*c.* 1487–1490
*Pen and ink, 233 × 166 mm*
*Paris, Bibliothèque de l'Institut de France, Codex Ashburnham 1875/1 (MS B 2184), fol. 4r*

**272 Studies for a Building on a Centralized Plan,**
*c.* 1487–1490
*Pen and ink, 233 × 162 mm*
*Paris, Bibliothèque de l'Institut de France, Codex Ashburnham 1875/1 (MS B 2184), fol. 5v*

**273 Studies for a Building on a Centralized Plan,**
*c.* 1487–1490
*Pen and ink, 230 × 167 mm*
*Paris, Bibliothèque de l'Institut de France, MS B 2173, f. 22r*

**274 Studies for a Building on a Centralized Plan,**
*c.* 1487–1490
*Pen and ink, 230 × 166 mm*
*Paris, Bibliothèque de l'Institut de France, MS B 2173, fol. 25v*

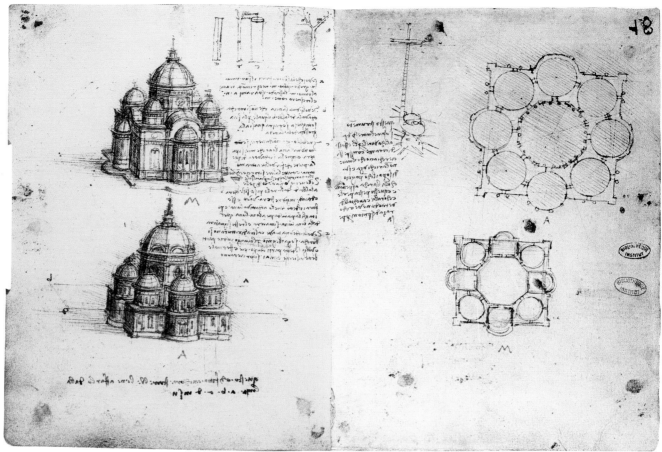

275

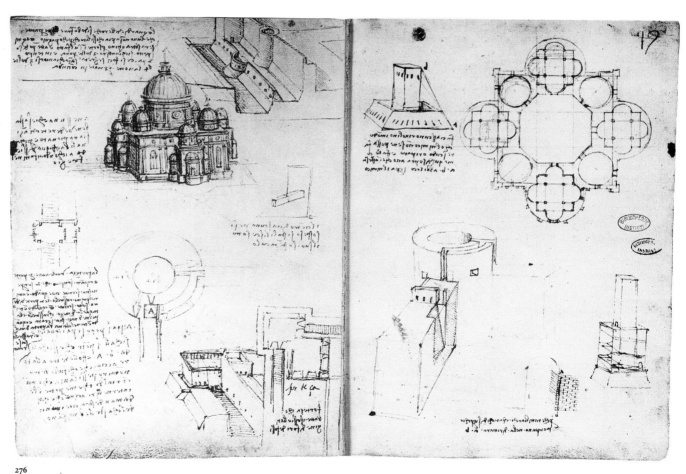

276

**275 Studies for a Building on a Centralized Plan,**
*c. 1487–1490*
*Pen and ink, fol. 17v:*
*232 x 165 mm and fol. 18r:*
*233 x 165 mm*
*Paris, Bibliothèque de l'Institut de*
*France, MS B 2173, ff. 17v–18r*

**276 Studies for a Building on a Centralized Plan and Sketches of a Fortress,**
*c. 1487–1490*
*Pen and ink, fol. 18v:*
*232 x 165 mm and fol. 19r:*
*232 x 165 mm*
*Paris, Bibliothèque de l'Institut de*
*France, MS B 2173, ff. 18v–19r*

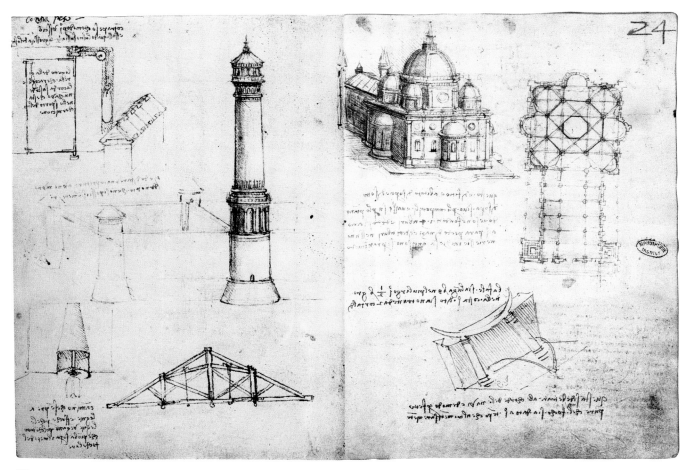

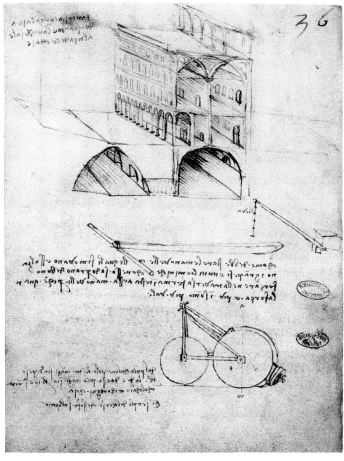

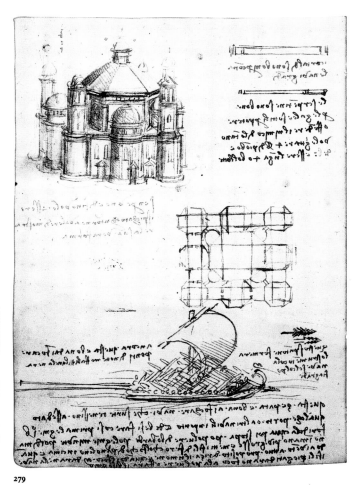

277

278

279

**277 Ground Plan and
Perspective Elevation of a
Centralized Building and
other Architectural Studies,**
*c. 1487–1490*
*Pen and ink, fol. 23v:*
*232 x 165 mm and fol. 24r:*
*230 x 166 mm*
*Paris, Bibliothèque de l'Institut de
France, MS B 2173, ff. 23v–24r*

**278 Architectural Studies,**
*c. 1487–1490*
*Pen and ink, 232 x 165 mm*
*Paris, Bibliothèque de l'Institut de
France, MS B 2173, f. 36r*

**279 Studies for a Building
on a Centralized Plan and
Sketch of a Ship,** *c. 1487–1490*
*Pen and ink, 233 x 165 mm*
*Paris, Bibliothèque de l'Institut de
France, MS B 2173, fol. 39v*

280

281

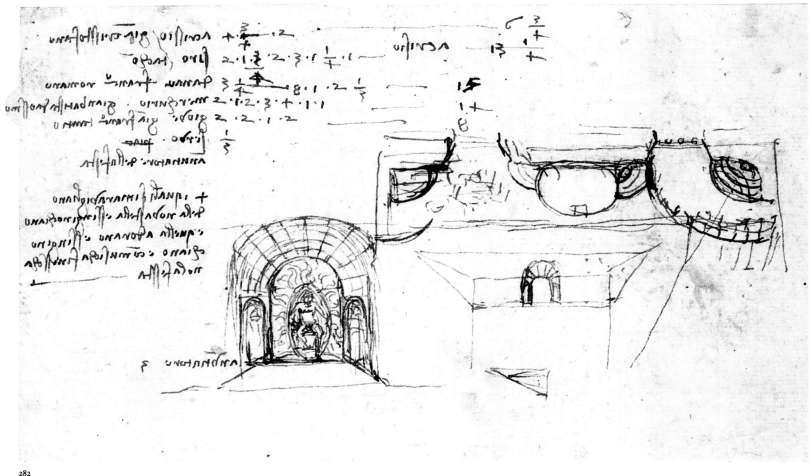

282

**280 Design for a Stables,**
*c. 1487–1490*
*Pen and ink, 233 x 165 mm*
*Paris, Bibliothèque de l'Institut de*
*France, MS B 2173, fol. 39r*

**281 Perspective Section**
**through a Centralized**
**Building and Design for a**
**Building on a Centralized**
**Plan,** *c. 1487–1490*
*Pen and ink, 280 x 215 mm*
*[detail above: 100 x 215 mm]*
*Milan, Biblioteca Ambrosiana,*
*Codex Atlanticus,*
*fol. 547v/205v–a*

**282 Studies for the Stage-**
**Set of** *Danaë* **by Baldassare**
**Taccone,** *c. 1496*
*Pen and ink, 202 x 133 mm*
*New York, The Metropolitan*
*Museum of Art, Rogers Fund, 1917*
*(17.142.2 recto)*

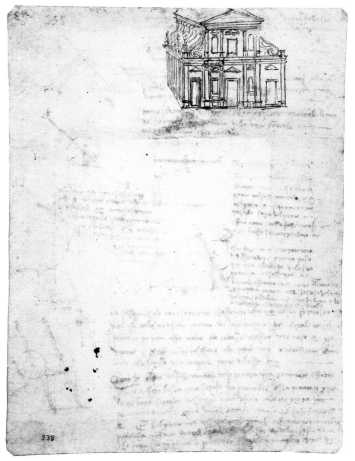

283

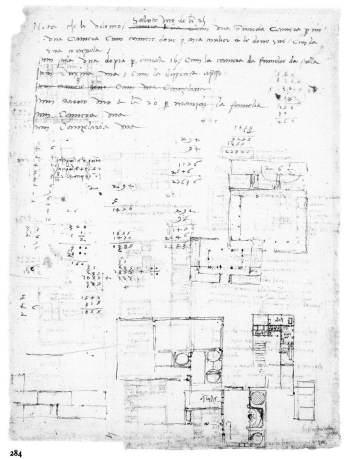

284

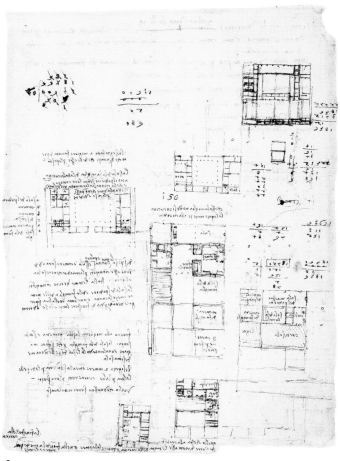

285

286

**283 Design for a Church Façade,** *c. 1495–1497*
*Pen and ink over metalpoint on yellowish prepared paper, 213 x 152 mm*
*Venice, Gallerie dell'Accademia, Inv. 238v*

**284 Architectural Designs for the Casa Guiscardi,** *c. 1497 or later (?)*
*Pen and ink, 284 x 204 mm*
*Milan, Biblioteca Ambrosiana, Codex Atlanticus, fol. 426r/158r-a*

**285 Architectural Designs for the Casa Guiscardi,** *c. 1497 or later (?)*
*Pen and ink, 284 x 204 mm*
*Milan, Biblioteca Ambrosiana, Codex Atlanticus, fol. 426v/158v-a*

**286 Various Architectural Studies and Anatomical Drawing of a Bird's Wing,** *c. 1513*
*Pen and ink, 274 x 201 mm*
*Windsor Castle, Royal Library (RL 19107v)*

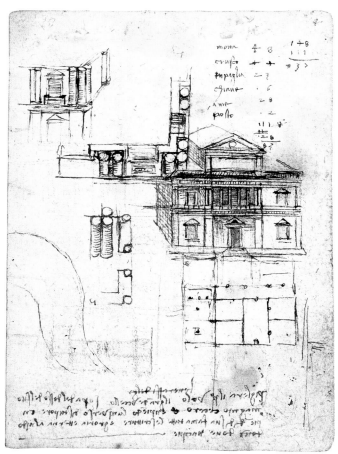

287

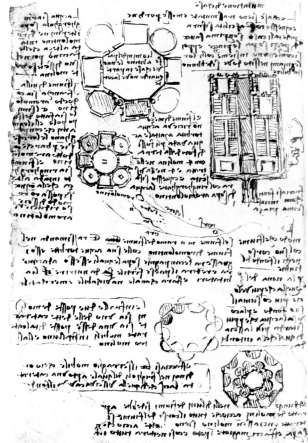

288

289

**287 Studies for the Villa Caprini**, *c.* 1506
*Pen and ink, 212 x 152 mm*
*Turin, Biblioteca Reale, Cod.*
*Var. 95 [Treatise on the Flight of Birds], fol. 19r*

**288 Design for a Palace and Park (Romorantin)**,
*c.* 1517/18
*Pen and ink, 190 x 125 mm*
*London, British Museum,*
*Codex Arundel, fol. 270v*

**289 Perspective View of a Palace (Romorantin)**, *c.* 1518
*Black chalk, 180 x 245 mm*
*Windsor Castle, Royal Library*
*(RL 12292v)*

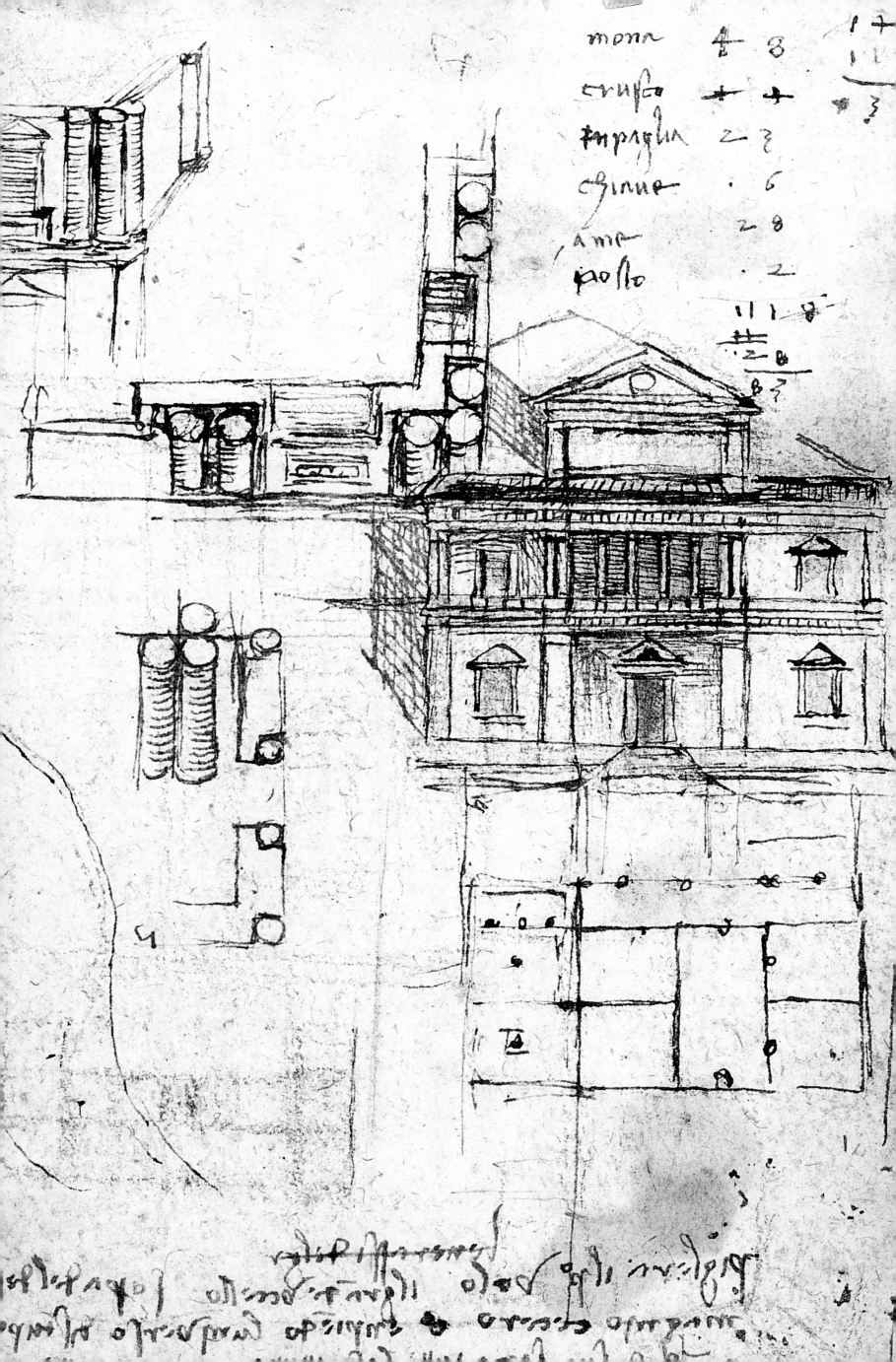

mona 4 8
crusto + +
travaglia 2 3
colonne . 6
ame 2 8
posso . 2

290

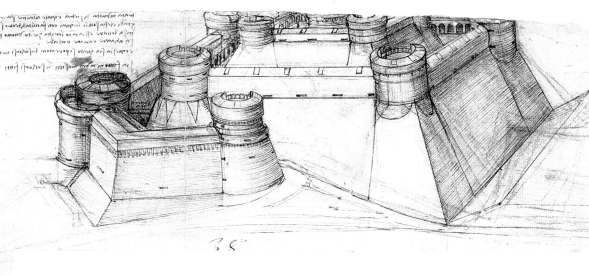

291

**290 Study for a Fortress on a Square Ground Plan,**
*c. 1500–1505 (?)*
*Pen and ink, 228 x 305 mm*
*Milan, Biblioteca Ambrosiana,*
*Codex Atlanticus, fol. 120v/43v-a*

**291** Leonardo (?) (Francesco di Giorgio Martini?)
**Study for a Fortress,**
*1504–1508 (?)*
*Pen and ink, 131–202 x 422 mm*
*Milan, Biblioteca Ambrosiana,*
*Codex Atlanticus, fol. 117/41v-b*

▶ **292 Study for a Fortress on a Polygonal Ground Plan with a Double Moat,**
*1504–1508 (?)*
*Pen and ink and Indian ink,*
*440 x 290 mm*
*Milan, Biblioteca Ambrosiana,*
*Codex Atlanticus, fol. 116v/41v-a*

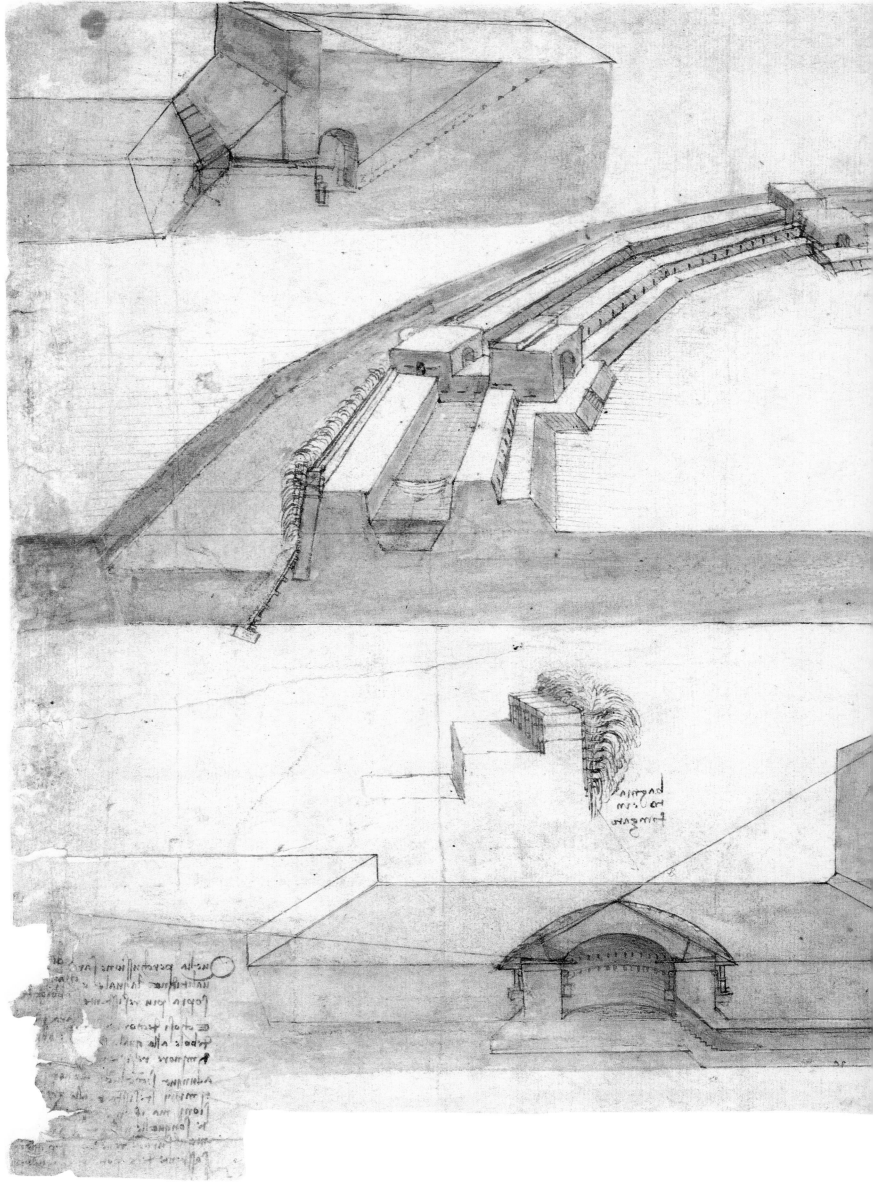

292

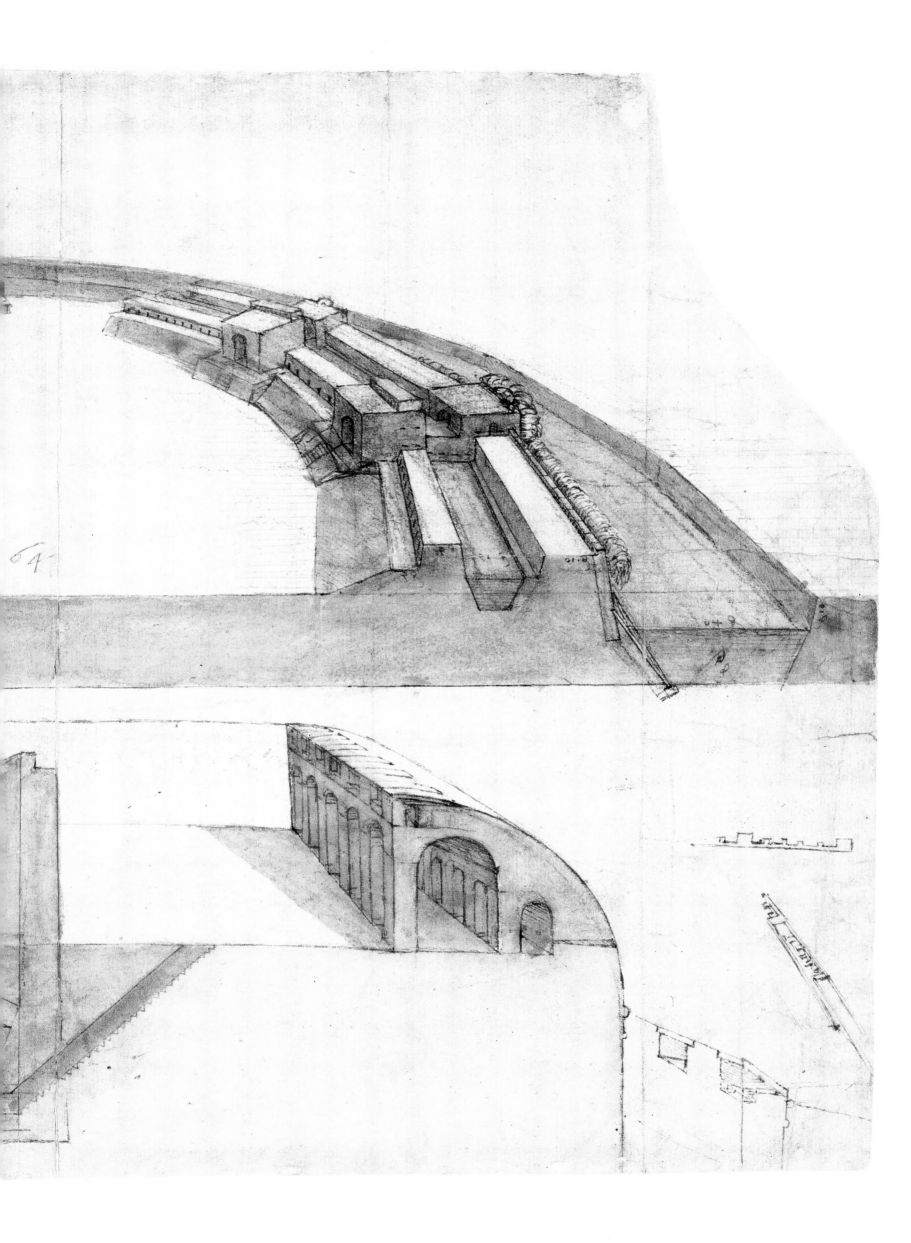

# 12 Engineering and machinery studies

The following three sections of this catalogue of drawings are devoted to Leonardo's studies of machines and their components. Although they thus enjoy a relatively large presence within this catalogue, Leonardo might still have considered them under-represented. Indeed, the Codex Atlanticus – so called because of its enormous size – was an album originally compiled in the 16th century and comprising over a thousand sheets of studies relating to engineering, machinery and science. Many of these sheets – which have since been removed from their binding – carry drawings on both sides. The majority of Leonardo's bound manuscripts, which contain not only writings but also large numbers of drawings, also deal with technical and scientific subjects. Altogether, these works today make up well over half of all the works on paper surviving from Leonardo's hand.

Whether this offers an accurate reflection of the original distribution of Leonardo's graphic œuvre, whether the artist indeed produced more scientific than artistic studies, are questions we can no longer answer with certainty, since it is enormously difficult to estimate the percentage of drawings lost. That Leonardo, at least in certain phases of his life, was just as keen to sell himself as an engineer as to recommend his services as an artist, can be deduced from the letter of introduction that he drafted in the 1480s to Ludovico il Moro, and which we will discuss in further detail in the next chapter.

There are nevertheless good reasons to follow the traditional, art-first-science-second weighting when presenting Leonardo's graphic œuvre. After all, he was known and appreciated in his own lifetime chiefly as an artist. This may be connected with the fact that his designs – or at least those still extant – for the large part take the form of cursory sketches, accompanied at times by brief explanations; while this barely affects our high opinion of Leonardo's artistic drawings, it has been greatly detrimental to our appreciation of his technical studies. For while the sketch-like qualities of a design can serve to heighten the effect of an artistic study, these same qualities in a technical drawing – where feasibility and precision play a major role – are sooner perceived as undesirable. Leonardo himself was well aware of this problem, as evidenced by the fact that by far his most meticulously drawn series of studies is devoted to machinery (Cat. 302–321). Apart from the drawing of the "Vitruvian Man" (Cat. 136), none of his artistic and only a few of his technical studies demonstrate a comparable degree of care and precision.

Thus disadvantaged from the outset, it is not surprising that Leonardo's technical and scientific studies should have received a more muted reception. Although Francesco Melzi attempted to put Leonardo's loose sheets into some kind of order soon after the latter's death, he was able to provide only a transcription of his master's hard-to-read mirror-writing in the case of Leonardo's notes on painting. No serious study of Leonardo's legacy would subsequently be attempted for several centuries. When art historians in the 19th century finally decided to take a

fresh look at Leonardo's studies on engineering and science, they found themselves presented with the enormous task of transcribing Leonardo's handwriting and making sense of his sometimes idiosyncratic use of language.

Although this task has since been completed, our understanding of Leonardo's scientific studies continues to be hampered by his unsystematic approach. As already discussed in the Introduction, Leonardo is frequently to be found working on quite different problems at the same time, and evidently found it difficult to draw hard and fast lines between his various fields of interest. This is evident in the very first drawing in this section (Cat. 294), which illustrates the lack of discipline typical of Leonardo's manner of working in the early part of his career. Apparently a fragment of a larger sheet, it is dotted with sketches and notes in an arbitrary fashion, whereby some of the words on the sheet are written vertically and even upside down. The study of the head in profile in the lower third shows a so-called puffer, a device that had already been sketched by a well-known engineer from the early 15th century, Mariano Taccola (1382–1458?): when the head, which is in fact made of metal and filled with water, is heated, a powerful jet of steam comes out of the mouth.

The next sheets in this section (Cat. 295, 297–299), which are devoted to hydraulics, are somewhat more disciplined. Here we find Leonardo sketching devices predominantly designed to raise water from one level to the next. Mechanisms such as the Archimedean screw can also be found in drawings by other engineers of the 15th century. Another sheet (Cat. 300), also from the early part of Leonardo's career, shows – in addition to further items of hydraulic equipment – devices for walking under and over water. Halfway down the left-hand side of the sheet Leonardo has sketched someone walking on water, and in the top right-hand corner he has drawn a diver wearing a sort of snorkel, concepts already envisaged by Taccola and Francesco di Giorgio Martini (1439–1501). Leonardo takes up the ideas of his contemporaries in two further drawings: Cat. 296 shows a revolving crane as probably used by Filippo Brunelleschi in the construction of the cupola of Florence cathedral (cf. Ch. 11), and Cat. 303 a hoist, complete with counterweight, to raise a bell, which is based on an almost identical hoist by Taccola (De machinis, fol. 42v). In stylistic terms, too, these sketches go little beyond those of Leonardo's predecessors and contemporaries – something that would change in his later studies.

In contrast to these early sketches, the drawings from the Codex Madrid I (Cat. 302–321), compiled in Milan in the 1490s, demonstrate an impressive precision and clarity, whereby the pleasing layout of text and image suggest that Leonardo may have produced this manuscript with a view to having it published. The majority of these studies relate to the transmission of motion, as for example on folio 45 recto (Cat. 321), which illustrates a volute gear designed to equalize the amount of power delivered by an un-

winding spring (a power that otherwise diminishes as the spring nears the end of its unwinding). The problem of power transmission is investigated in the drawings on folios 43 recto to 44 recto (Cat. 316, 318, 319). The lifting devices illustrated here, which again demonstrate a certain connection with drawings by Francesco di Giorgio Martini (*Opusculum de architectura*, fol. 7v), are designed for raising long and heavy masts and beams. Leonardo paid particular attention to reducing the friction between the wood and the apparatus, a problem he sought to solve with toothed guiderails, as separately illustrated in Cat. 319.

The Codex Madrid is distinguished not just by the care with which the drawings are executed, but also by its greater degree of systematic organization. Thus Leonardo devotes a sequence of sheets (Cat. 308–310, 312–315, 317) to one particular problem, namely the transmission of power via gears. Just as significant as the more systematic approach they reveal to their subject, however, is the fact that these studies rarely serve specific applications (in the field of hydraulics or lifting technology, for example), but explore solutions to more general principles, thereby arriving at components that could be employed in mechanisms of widely differing types. In this they are analogous to Leonardo's studies into hydraulics: in the early part of the artist's career, these centred on the invention of solutions to specific problems (Cat. 295, 297–299), while in his latter years they investigated broader questions, in particular the behaviour of currents (cf. also Cat. 241, 243–245).

The breadth of scope of Leonardo's later technical studies is clearly illustrated by the drawings grouped here as Cat. 322 to 335, most of which are taken from the Codex Atlanticus. The first two sheets (Cat. 322) portray excavators designed for large-scale earthworking and may have arisen in conjunction with plans to divert the Arno, a scheme on which Leonardo began work in 1503, but which ultimately foundered (cf. Ch. 10). In other projects Leonardo seems to be anticipating the spirit of industrialization, for example in devices for incising files, a design for a rolling mill (Cat. 324) and in equipment for use in textile processing (Cat. 326: spinning machine; Cat. 328: cloth-cutting machine; and Cat. 329: machines for manufacturing ropes). Particularly noteworthy, finally, is the sketch of a "Perspectograph" (Cat. 331), a device for artists that illustrated the principle of perspective projection – something later analysed in more depth by Albrecht Dürer. Although the basics of this principle had been known since the early 15th century, this is the first surviving sketch of a corresponding piece of equipment.

*Johannes Nathan*

**Literature:** Feldhaus, 1922; Zubov, 1968; Gibbs-Smith, 1978; Truesdell, 1982; *Leonardo: Engineer and Architect*, 1987; Cianchi, 1988; Kemp/Roberts, 1989; *Prima di Leonardo*, 1991; *Renaissance Engineers*, 1996.

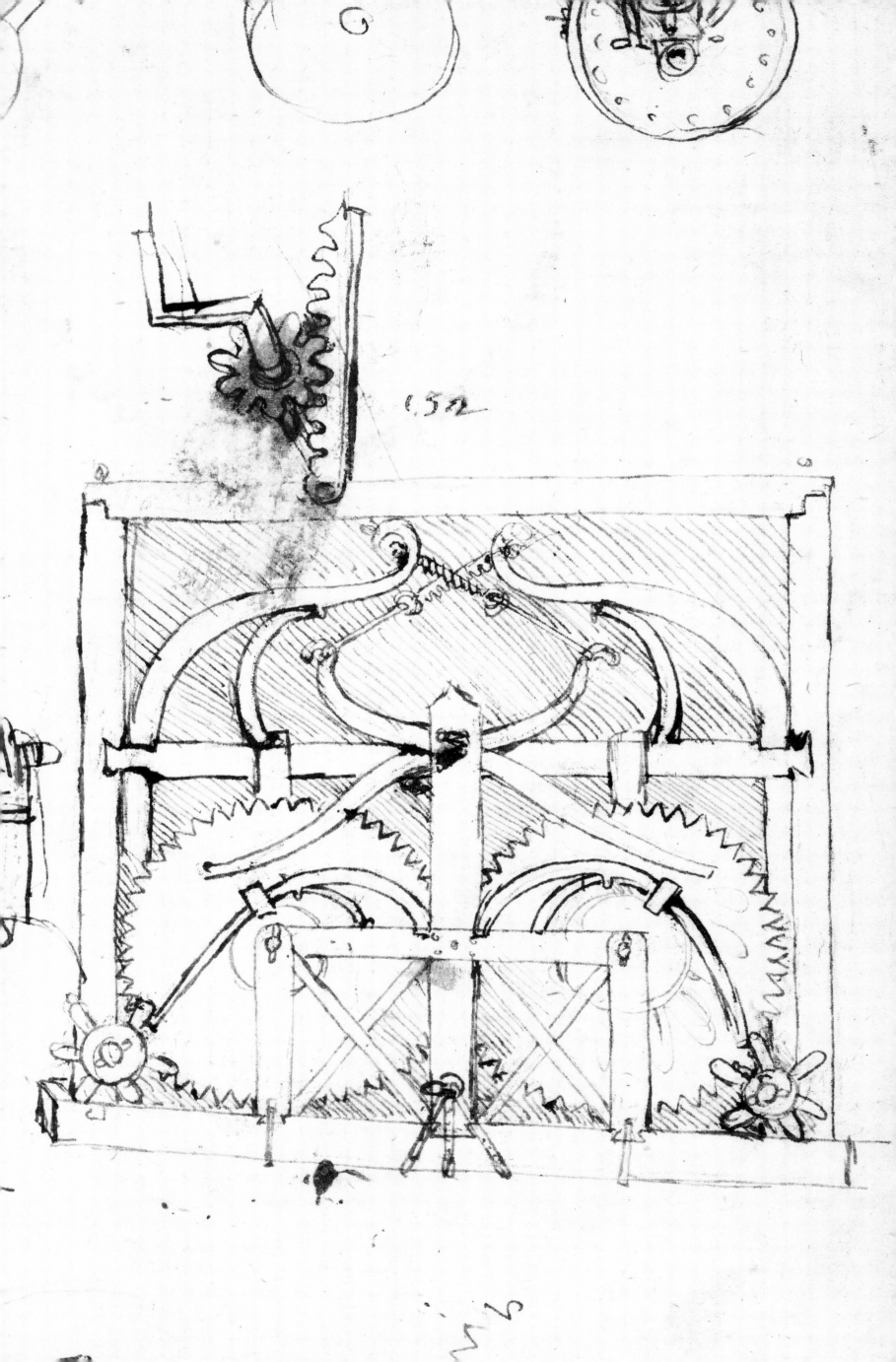

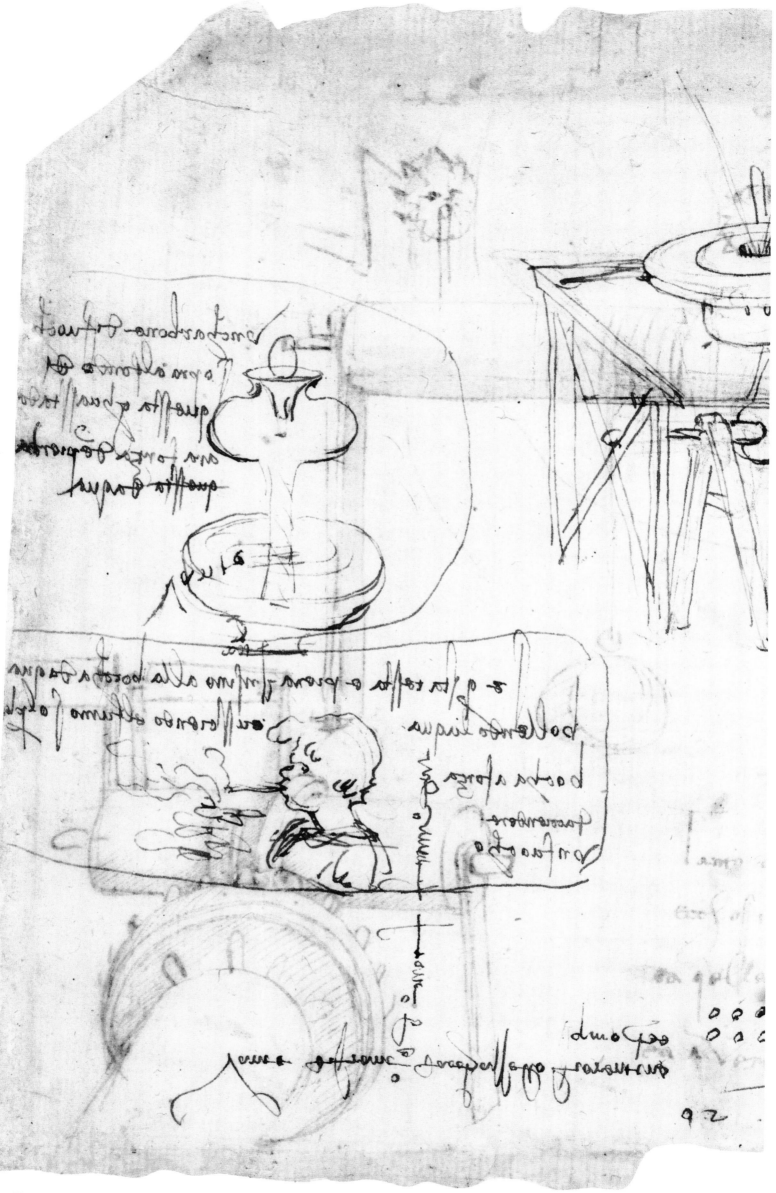

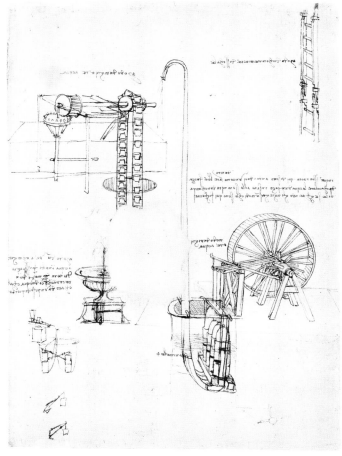

295

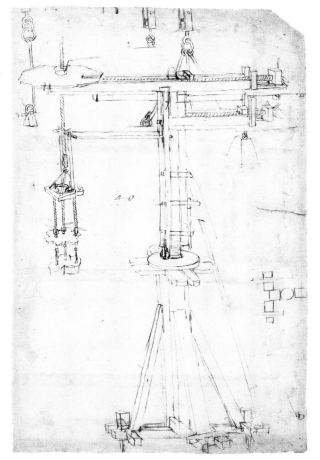

296

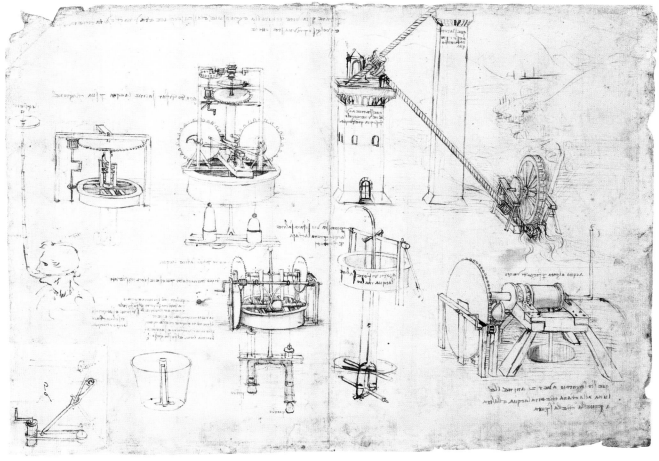

297

<< 293 Studies for an Auto-
mobile (Detial), 1478–1480 (?)
*Pen and ink over metalpoint,
265 x 167 mm
Milan, Biblioteca Ambrosiana,
Codex Atlanticus, fol. 812r/296v–a*

< 294 Studies for a Stream
Blower (Puffer) and a Drive
Mechanism for a Potter's
Wheel, 1478–1480 (?)
*Pen and ink,
203 x 286 mm
Milan, Biblioteca Ambrosiana,
Codex Atlanticus, fol. 1112r/400v–a*

295 Studies of Hydraulic
Devices, before 1483 (?)
*Pen and ink, 284 x 202 mm
Milan, Biblioteca Ambrosiana,
Codex Atlanticus, fol. 7r/386r–a*

296 Studies for a Revolving
Crane, before 1482
*Pen and ink, 315 x 200 mm
Milan, Biblioteca Ambrosiana,
Codex Atlanticus, fol. 965r/349r–a*

297 Hydraulic Devices
(Archimedean Screw) and
Other Studies, c. 1478–1480
*Pen and ink, 397 x 285 mm
Milan, Biblioteca Ambrosiana,
Codex Atlanticus, fol. 1069r/386r–b*

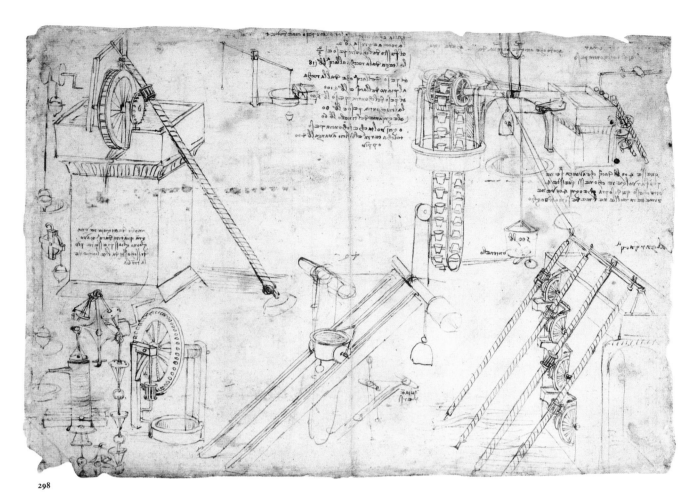

298

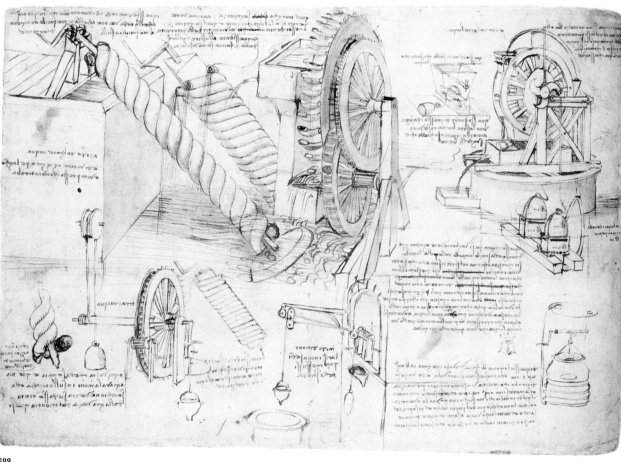

299

**298 Studies of Hydraulic
Devices, c. 1478–1480**
*Pen and ink, 397 x 285 mm
Milan, Biblioteca Ambrosiana,
Codex Atlanticus, fol. 1069v/386v-b*

**299 Hydraulic Devices
for Transporting Water,
c. 1480–1482 (?)**
*Pen and ink and Indian ink,
291 x 400 mm
Milan, Biblioteca Ambrosiana,
Codex Atlanticus, fol. 26v/7v-a*

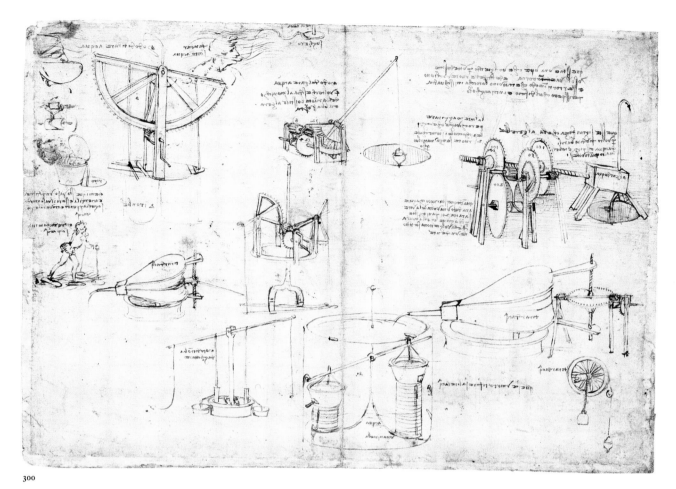

300

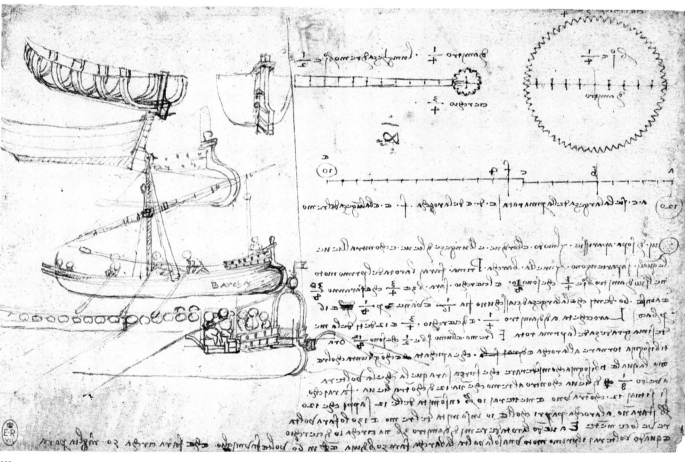

301

**300 Devices for Diving and
Other Studies,** *c. 1480–1482*
*Pen and ink, 291 x 400 mm*
*Milan, Biblioteca Ambrosiana,*
*Codex Atlanticus, fol. 26r/7r-a*

**301 Drawing of the Con-
struction and Functioning
of a Ship,** *c. 1485–1487*
*Pen and ink, 142 x 214 mm*
*Windsor Castle, Royal Library*
*(RL 12650r)*

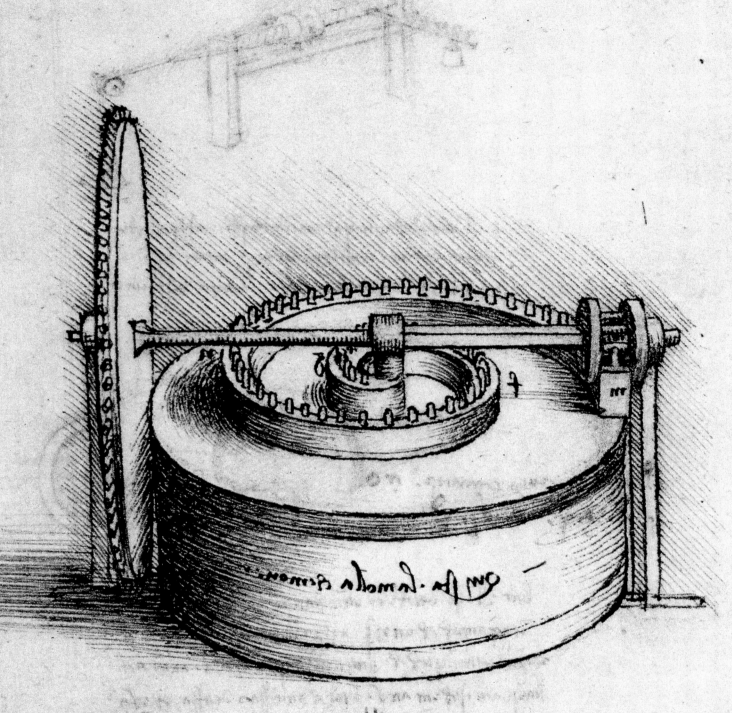

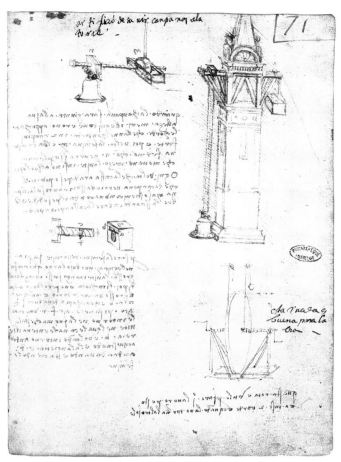

303

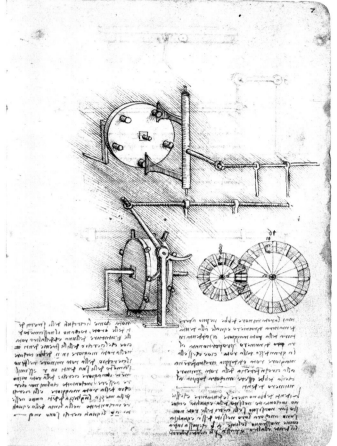

304

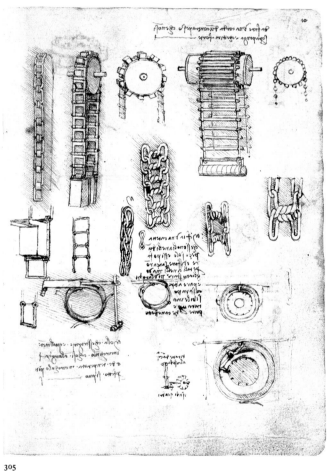

305

306

◄ **302 Study of the Mechanical Power of a Spring, 1493–1497**
*Pen and ink, 213 x 150 mm*
*Madrid, Biblioteca Nacional, Codex Madrid I, MS 8937, fol. 4r*

**303 Hoist for a Bell, c. 1487/88**
*Pen and ink, 231 x 165 mm*
*Paris, Bibliothèque de l'Institut de France, MS B 2173, fol. 71r*

**304 Studies of the Working of Cogwheels, 1493–1497**
*Pen and ink, 213 x 150 mm*
*Madrid, Biblioteca Nacional, Codex Madrid I, MS 8937, fol. 7r*

**305 Various Types of Metal Chain, 1493–1497**
*Pen and ink, 213 x 150 mm*
*Madrid, Biblioteca Nacional, Codex Madrid I, MS 8937, fol. 10r*

**306 Mechanism to Equalize the Power of an Unwinding Spring, 1493–1497**
*Pen and ink, 213 x 150 mm*
*Madrid, Biblioteca Nacional, Codex Madrid I, MS 8937, fol. 14r*

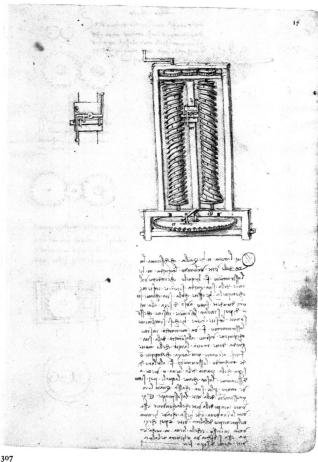

307

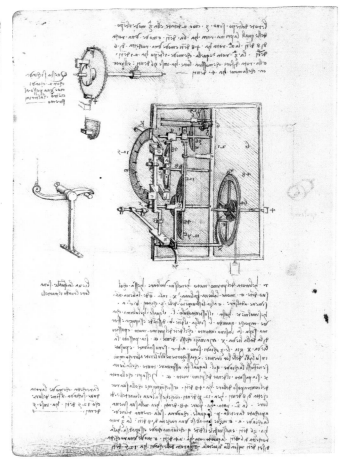

308

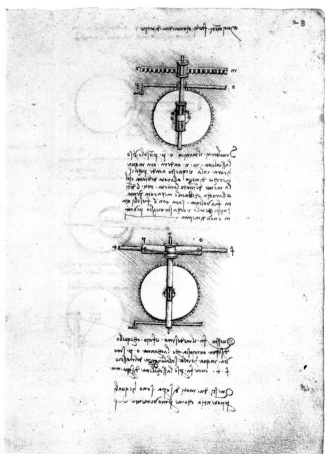

309

310

**307 Study of the Striking Mechanism of a Clock,**
**1493–1497**
*Pen and ink, 213 x 150 mm*
*Madrid, Biblioteca Nacional,*
*Codex Madrid I, MS 8937,*
*fol. 15r*

**308 Drawing of the Movement of a Clock,**
**1493–1497**
*Pen and ink, 213 x 150 mm*
*Madrid, Biblioteca Nacional,*
*Codex Madrid I, MS 8937,*
*fol. 27v*

**309 Mechanics of the Movement of a Toothed Rack, 1493–1497**
*Pen and ink, 213 x 150 mm*
*Madrid, Biblioteca Nacional,*
*Codex Madrid I, MS 8937,*
*fol. 28r*

**310 Drive Mechanism for Motion of Unequal Force,**
**1493–1497**
*Pen and ink, 213 x 150 mm*
*Madrid, Biblioteca Nacional,*
*Codex Madrid I, MS 8937,*
*fol. 28v*

**▶▶ 311 Study of the Diminishing Power of an Unwinding Spring,**
**1493–1497**
*Pen and ink, 213 x 150 mm*
*Madrid, Biblioteca Nacional,*
*Codex Madrid I, MS 8937,*
*fol. 16r*

**▶▶▶ 312 Studies of Power Transmission and for Lifting a Beam, 1493–1497**
*Pen and ink, 213 x 150 mm*
*Madrid, Biblioteca Nacional,*
*Codex Madrid I, MS 8937,*
*fol. 29r*

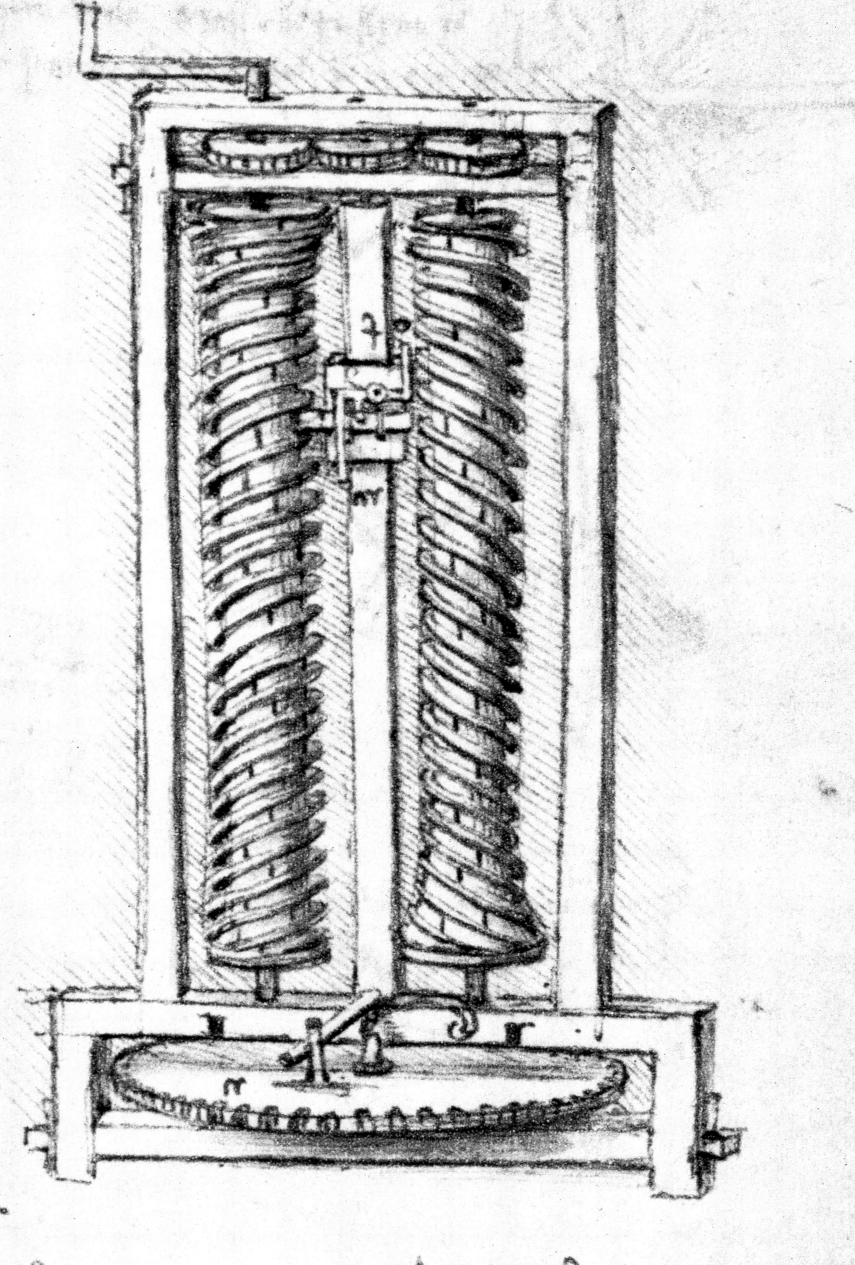

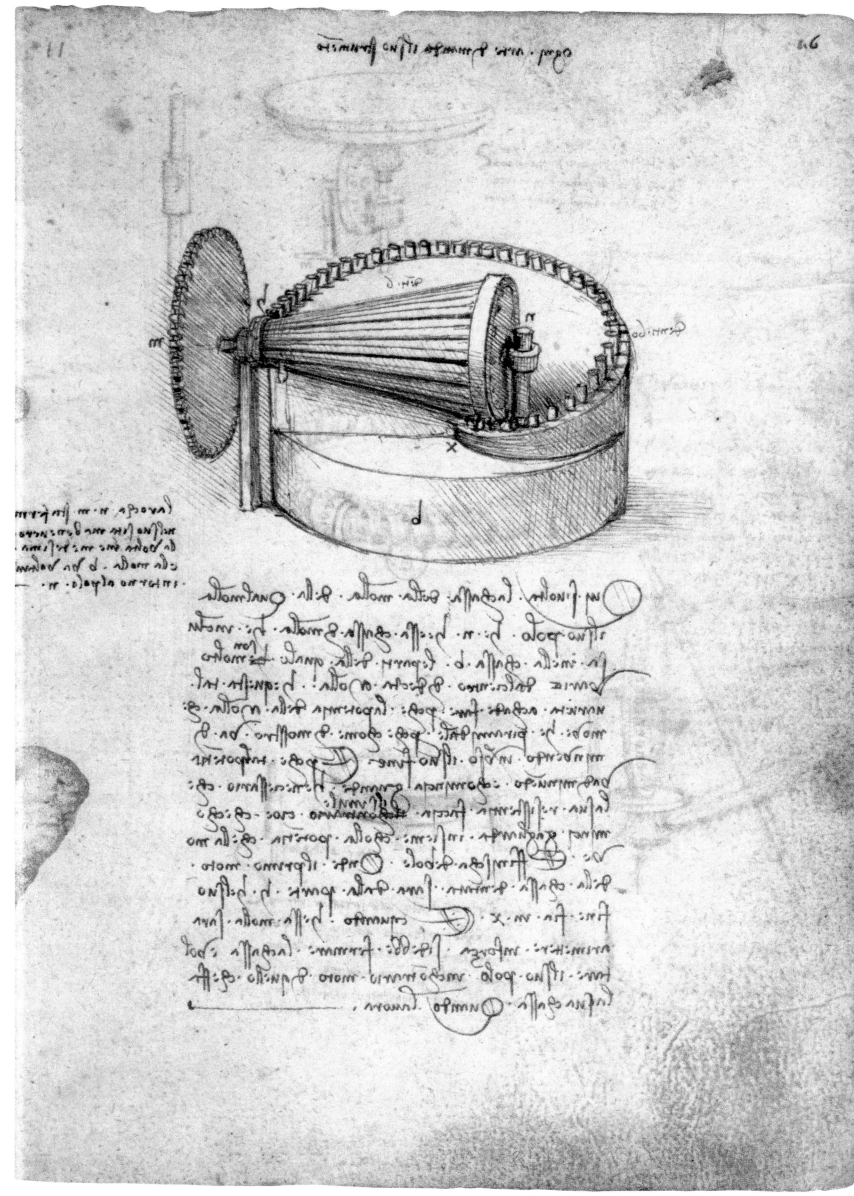

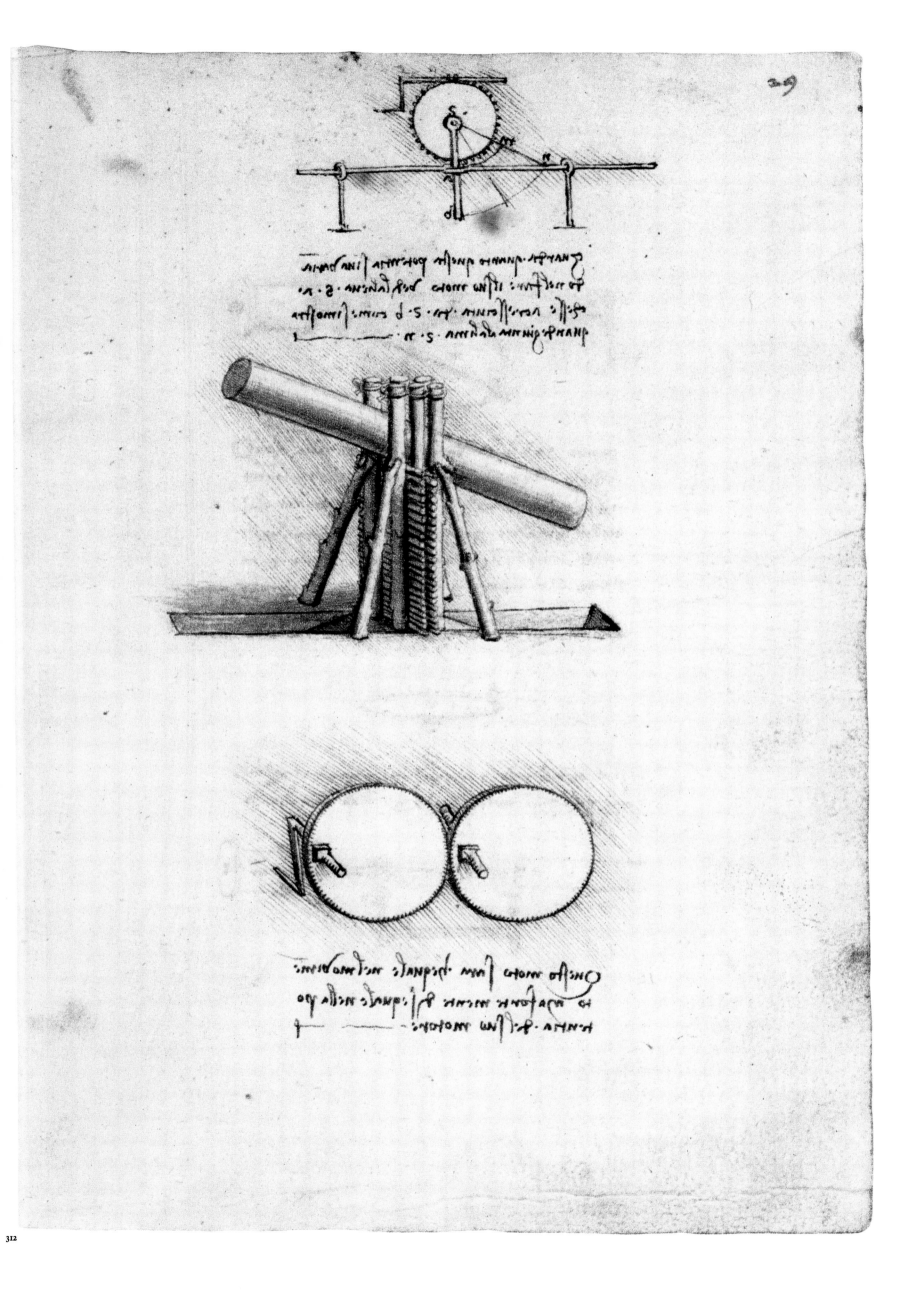

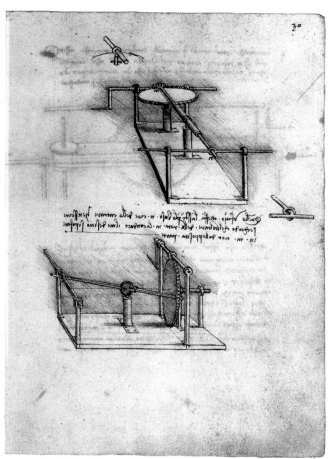

313

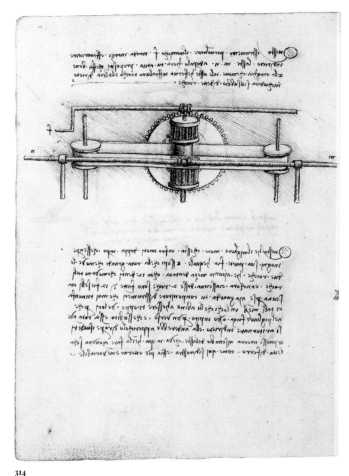

314

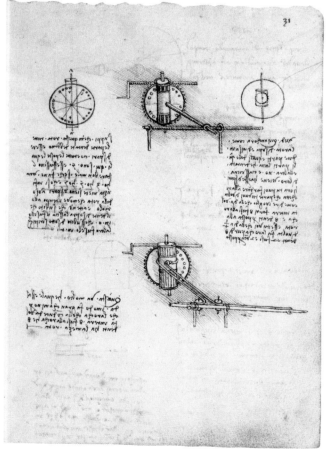

315

316

**313 Mechanical Device for the Transmission of Motion, 1493–1497**
*Pen and ink, 213 x 150 mm*
*Madrid, Biblioteca Nacional,*
*Codex Madrid I, MS 8937,*
*fol. 30r*

**314 Mechanism for Back-and-Forth Motion with Crank , 1493–1497**
*Pen and ink, 213 x 150 mm*
*Madrid, Biblioteca Nacional,*
*Codex Madrid I, MS 8937,*
*fol. 30v*

**315 Mechanisms for the Transmission of Power via Gears and Cranks, 1493–1497**
*Pen and ink, 213 x 150 mm*
*Madrid, Biblioteca Nacional,*
*Codex Madrid I, MS 8937,*
*fol. 31r*

**316 Device for Raising a Mast, 1493–1497**
*Pen and ink, 213 x 150 mm*
*Madrid, Biblioteca Nacional,*
*Codex Madrid I, MS 8937,*
*fol. 43r*

**▶ 317 Mechanism for Back-and-Forth Motion, 1493–1497**
*Pen and ink, 213 x 150 mm*
*Madrid, Biblioteca Nacional,*
*Codex Madrid I, MS 8937,*
*fol. 29v*

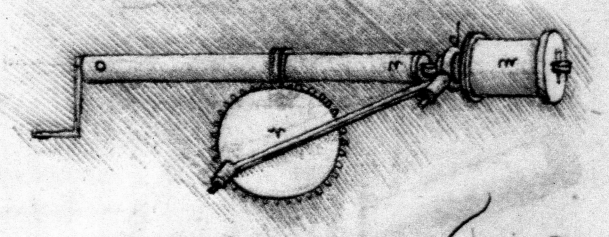

ivl mosse · maniutno · chinastumo · oguno · nacuno · spoul lui
opluariscio · onauilino · vollen · necocon · b · orsalilino · airvollen
loto · nesula · nlocoqono · m · oquiliones · nasalano · p ·
tiolanpdi · imilo · ollesulumo · manunmo · onuilucino · masulisoro
orsanpo · orvalsia · nquo · oslana · nva · onsequor · ollulo · m · m ·
nibiono · o · m · onpanpo · anuo · ndy · manuluso · opo · opusnilo

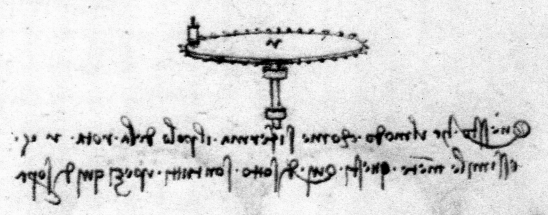

mello · ine · nlmoso · equona · llamua · nsuql · mnnolly · uspolu · nspola · della · vola · m · m ·
olliuilo · moia · onllu · onu · ollono · louml · lonuiu · vosul · del · dul · flodu

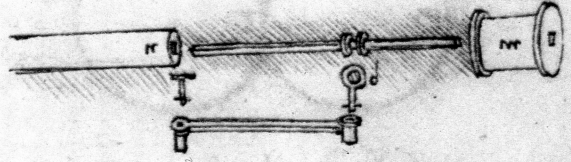

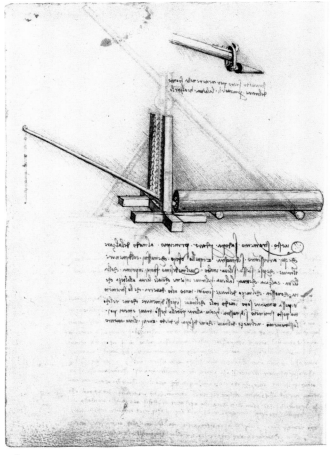

318

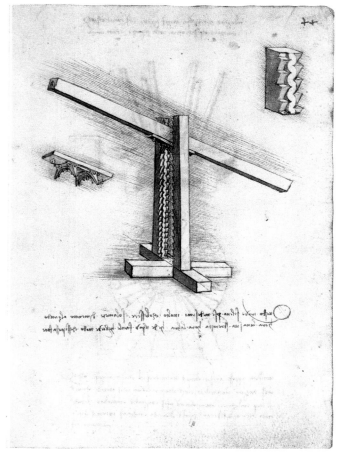

319

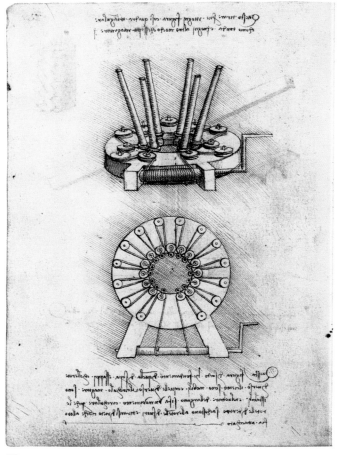

320

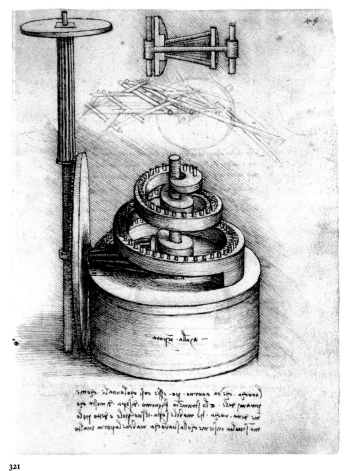

321

**318 Device for Raising a Beam, 1493–1497**
*Pen and ink, 213 x 150 mm*
*Madrid, Biblioteca Nacional,*
*Codex Madrid I, MS 8937,*
*fol. 43v*

**319 Hoist for a Beam, 1493–1497**
*Pen and ink, 213 x 150 mm*
*Madrid, Biblioteca Nacional,*
*Codex Madrid I, MS 8937,*
*fol. 44r*

**320 Hoist with Movable Rollers and Rope Winch, 1493–1497**
*Pen and ink, 213 x 150 mm*
*Madrid, Biblioteca Nacional,*
*Codex Madrid I, MS 8937,*
*fol. 44v*

**321 Tempered Spring with Volute Gear, 1493–1497**
*Pen and ink, 213 x 150 mm*
*Madrid, Biblioteca Nacional,*
*Codex Madrid I, MS 8937,*
*fol. 45r*

**▶▶ 322 Excavatot for Canal Construction (own design), c. 1503**
*Pen and ink and Indian ink,*
*280 x 400 mm*
*Milan, Biblioteca Ambrosiana,*
*Codex Atlanticus, fol. 4r/1v–b*

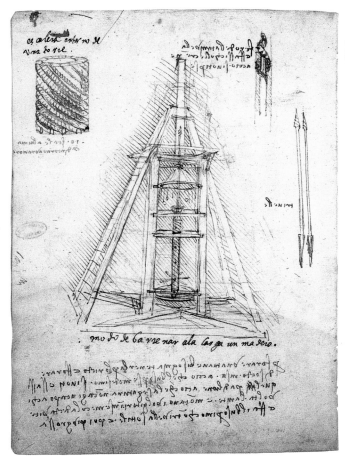

323

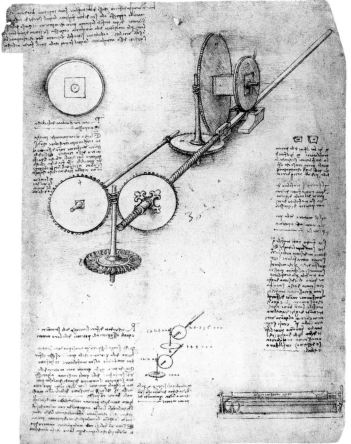

324

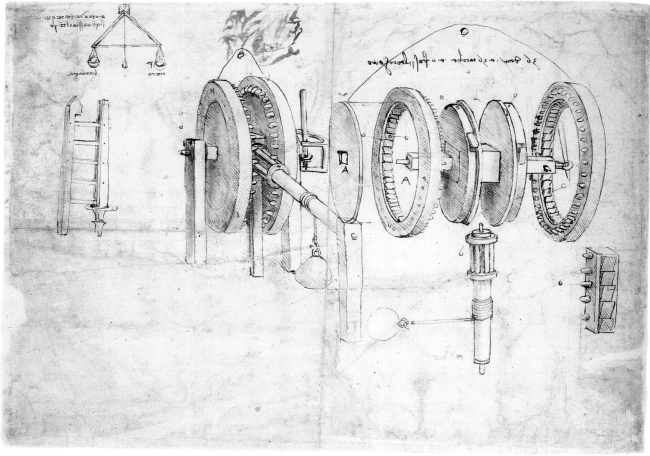

325

**323 Design for a Drill,**
*c.* **1487–1490**
*Pen and ink, 231 x 165 mm*
*Paris, Bibliothèque de l'Institut*
*de France, MS B 2173, fol. 47v*

**324 Sketch of a Rolling Mill,**
*c.* **1500–1510**
*Pen and ink, 300 x 225 mm*
*Milan, Biblioteca Ambrosiana,*
*Codex Atlanticus, fol. 10r/2r-a*

**325 Studies of Toothed Gears**
**and for a Hygrometer,** *c.* **1485**
*Pen and ink, 278 x 385 mm*
*Milan, Biblioteca Ambrosiana,*
*Codex Atlanticus, fol. 30v/8v-b*

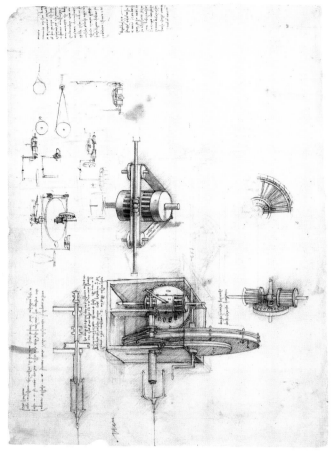

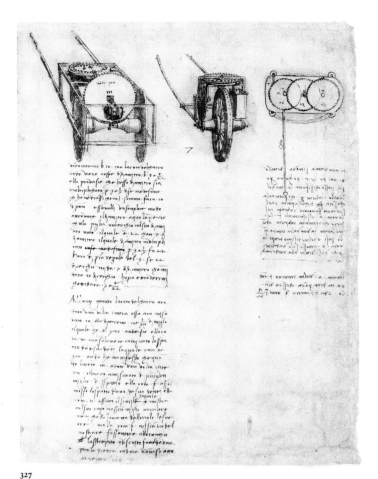

326

327

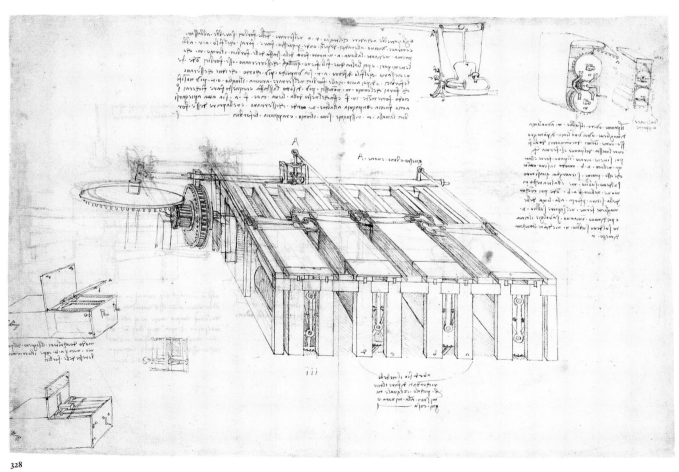

328

**326  Design for a Spinning Machine**, *c. 1497/98*
*Pen and ink, 414 x 287 mm*
*Milan, Biblioteca Ambrosiana,*
*Codex Atlanticus, fol. 1090v/393v-a*

**327  Study for an Odometer,**
**before 1500 (?)**
*Pen and ink, 265 x 195 mm*
*Milan, Biblioteca Ambrosiana,*
*Codex Atlanticus, fol. 1b-r/1r-b*

**328  Drawing of a Cloth-**
**cutting Machine,** *c. 1495 (?)*
*Pen and ink, 285 x 408 mm*
*Milan, Biblioteca Ambrosiana,*
*Codex Atlanticus, fol. 1105r/397-a*

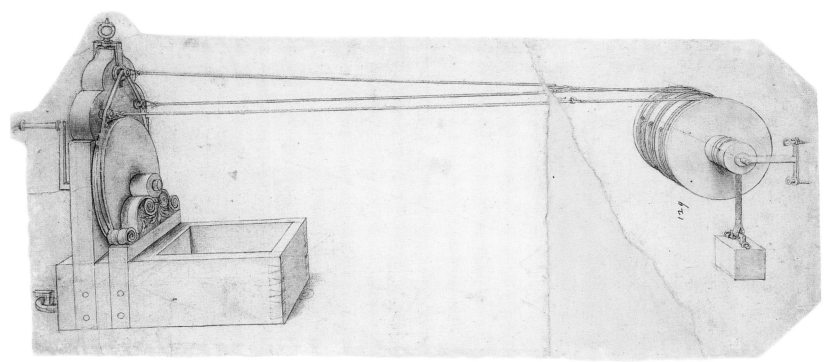

329

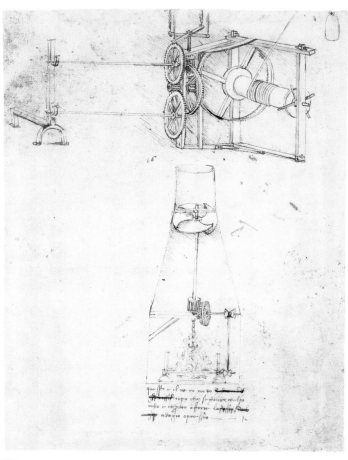

330

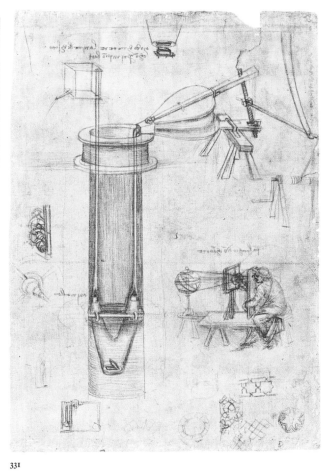

331

**329 Machine for Manu-
facturing Ropes**, *c.* 1513–1516
*Pen and ink,
169–158 x 385–375 mm
Milan, Biblioteca Ambrosiana,
Codex Atlanticus, fol. 13r/2v-b*

**330 Winch of a Goods Lift
and Mechanism for Turning
a Roasting Spit**, *c.* 1480 (?)
*Pen and ink, 255 x 191 mm
Milan, Biblioteca Ambrosiana,
Codex Atlanticus, fol. 21r/5v-a*

**331 Hydraulic Devices and
Study of a Figure in front of a
"Perspectograph"**, *c.* 1480–1482
*Metalpoint, pen and ink,
276 x 216 mm
Milan, Biblioteca Ambrosiana,
Codex Atlanticus,
fol. 5r/ex-Galbiati 1 bis r-a*

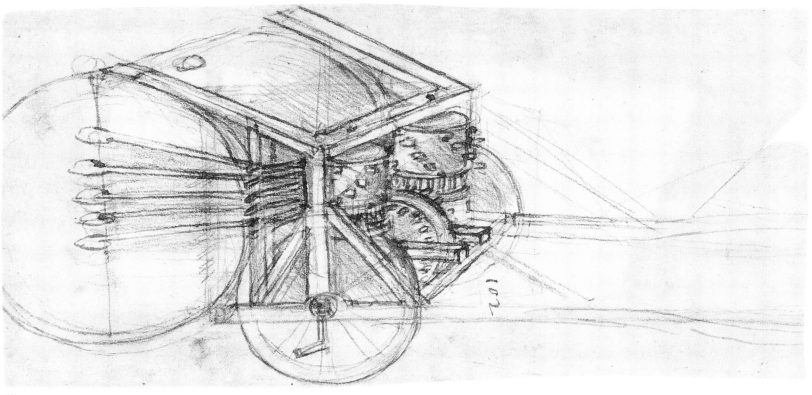

332

333

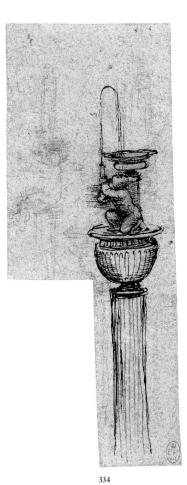

334

335

**332  A Mechanical Military
Drum,** *c.* **1493 (?)**
*Red chalk, 91 x 186 mm
Milan, Biblioteca Ambrosiana,
Codex Atlanticus,
fol. 837r/306v-a*

**333  Drawing of a Keyboard
Instrument (***viola organista***),**
*c.* **1494**
*Pen and ink, 238 x 96 mm
Milan, Biblioteca Ambrosiana,
Codex Atlanticus,
fol. 586r/218r-c*

**334  Fountain, consisting
of a Column topped with
a Stone Vase crowned by
a Naked Figure and Water
Basin,** *c.* **1513**
*Pen and ink over red chalk on blue
prepared paper, 172 x 63 mm
Windsor Castle, Royal Library
(RL 12691r)*

**335  Fountain, consisting
of an Column crowned by a
Naked Male Figure,** *c.* **1513**
*Pen and ink over red chalk on blue
prepared paper, 150 x 60 mm
Windsor Castle, Royal Library
(RL 12690r)*

# 13 Studies for military equipment

"My Most Illustrious Lord, having now sufficiently seen and considered the achievements of all those who count themselves masters and artificers of instruments of war, and having noted that the invention and performance of the said instruments is in no way different from that in common usage, I shall endeavour, while intending no discredit to anyone else, to make myself understood to Your Excellency for the purpose of unfolding to you my secrets, and thereafter offering them at your complete disposal, and when the time is right bringing into effective operation all those things which are in part briefly listed below" (MK § 612).

Astonishingly, in the opening lines of the letter that Leonardo composed to Ludovico Sforza, ruler of Milan, probably around 1482/83, he emphasizes not his abilities as an artist, but his inventiveness in the field of military engineering. In the letter, which Leonardo probably never sent, he sets out his plans, subdivided into no less than nine sections, for building portable bridges, special types of cannon and mortar, armoured vehicles and unusual catapults. He also claims to be able to drain the moats surrounding enemy fortresses or to cross them with other means. Only right at the end does he mention his skills in the fields of architecture, sculpture and painting. He evidently thought that the fairly limited experience in designing military equipment he had so far gained in Florence, here documented in a small number of sheets (Cat. 336, 337), was more likely to get him a job than his much greater talent as an artist. One of the reasons for this may have been the fact that Ludovico Sforza spent a vast amount of money on his army, leading Leonardo to hope for a well-paid job designing new war machines.

As is the case with Leonardo's drawings in general, many of his designs for military machines are self-explanatory and can be understood without the need for an accompanying text. This is true, for example, of two drawings showing various mechanisms designed to ward off an enemy assault and to repulse scaling ladders (Cat. 338 and 339). In the first of these two, a huge set of rotating blades is intended to prevent the enemy from scaling the walls, while in the second the ladders put up by the enemy are toppled backwards by a special framework. The way in which Leonardo intended his giant crossbow to work can also be understood largely without explanation (Cat. 348), as can the purpose of an enormous treadwheel, concealing within it four crossbows designed to be fired in succession as the wheel turns. Similarly intended to increase the speed and intensity of fire are Leonardo's multi-barrelled gun (Cat. 340), a wheel mounted with a total of 16 loaded crossbows (Cat. 347) and catapults designed to hurl several stones at once. (Cat. 341 and 342).

If the devices mentioned so far largely fall into the category of defensive equipment, Leonardo's mobile war machines seem to have been designed particularly for attack. Alongside a siege machine with a covered assault bridge (Cat. 337), these include above all his famous scythed chariots (Cat. 352) and similar horse-drawn vehicles equipped with catapults (Cat. 350). In the case of these war chariots, Leonardo was inspired by similar machines as illustrated in the treatise *De re militari* by Roberto Valturio (*c*. 1405/15–1475), which was published in Latin in 1472 and in Italian in 1483. Related designs, albeit somewhat less elegantly drawn, are also found in the writings by the Sienese engineers Francesco di Giorgio Martini and Mariano Taccola (cf. Ch. 12). Indeed, many of Leonardo's military machines reveal a kinship with corresponding designs by contemporary colleagues or with inventions documented by classical sources (above all Vegetius and Vitruvius).

Leonardo's "armoured car" (Cat. 337) also falls into an earlier tradition. For this vehicle to have the necessary stability and solidity, it would have to weigh an enormous amount, and would consequently require an equally enormous amount of force to move. Leonardo seems to have considered using horses or other draught animals (cf. Cat. 328), housed inside the armoured car, to provide this driving power. He eventually dropped this idea, however, on the grounds that the animals would be too frightened by the confined nature of the vehicle and the anticipated noise of battle. Leonardo finally came to the conclusion that manpower alone should be enough to move the armoured car quickly across the battlefield. In his notes, he expresses the view that armoured cars need to be accompanied by infantry – as, in modern warfare, they indeed are.

Leonardo lived in an era when military technology was being rethought. Warfare in the 15th century was changing, primarily as a result of the increasing use of artillery. Leonardo was clearly aware of this development, for he supplied instructions on casting, on mounting cannon and mortar (Cat. 344, 349, 358) and on building multi-barrelled guns (Cat. 340), and he also reflected upon a wide variety of problems relating to firearms and cannons in his Manuscript B (*c*. 1487–1490). This is evidenced by his designs for fortresses whose ramparts and towers are modified to better withstand the threat of heavy artillery fire (Cat. 291 and 292; cf. Ch. 11). The artist also turned his attention in several drawings to various kinds of gun and their aiming systems, looking for example at the way case-shot works and portraying the installation of a weapon of this type on a ship (Cat. 349). He also made a careful study of Archimedes' *architronito*, the so-called steam cannon. Here, water is poured through a valve into a heated cannon, and the steam that results produces excess pressure, which forces the ball out of the barrel at high speed. The use of "steam cannon" in a combat situation would hardly have been feasible, however. Leonardo comes some-what closer to contemporary reality in his enormous drawing of shrapnel mortars in action. Starting from the recognition that the ponderous artillery of the day was of only limited effectiveness against moving targets and scattered clusters of troops, he reflects on the effectiveness of shot that explodes over the heads of the enemy or on the ground and whose flying shrapnel subsequently sows death and destruction (Cat. 358/MS. B, 69r). The effect of mortar fire is also the subject of another sheet. In view of the unusual size and highly-finished nature of these two studies, it is possible that they were intended as presentation drawings with which Leonardo perhaps hoped to impress a patron.

In comparison with his reflections upon the use of cannon and mortar, Leonardo's drawings of catapults and other throwing devices seem somewhat anachronistic (Cat. 341, 343, 345, 346). In view of the technological advances being made throughout the 15th century, these machines are perhaps better seen as an expression of Leonardo's interest in portraying complicated devices – regardless of their practical use. The same may possibly be true of his studies for various side arms and shafted weapons (Cat. 353–357). There is a peculiar system and thoroughness to these drawings of heads for battle-axes, spears, arrows and halberds, whose suitability on the battlefield is not always obvious. The designs on these and other sheets owe their only limited practical value possibly to the fact that Leonardo's military "inventions" often arose outside the sphere of real war. Although the artist was employed as a military adviser to Cesare Borgia in Central Italy (1502–1503), by the Florentine government in the war against Pisa (1503–1504), for Iacopo Appiani in Piombino (1504) and possibly also for the Venetian Republic (1500), there is virtually no direct reflection of these engagements in his drawings of war machines. Perhaps Leonardo's military "inventions" were even more Utopian than has previously been suspected. A long way from reality in his own day, certainly, was his opinion as to the ideal purpose of his military designs: "To preserve Nature's chiefest boon, that is freedom, I can find means of offence and defence, when it is assailed by ambitious tyrants [...] and also I shall show how communities can maintain their good and just Lords " (RLW § 1204).

*Johannes Nathan/Frank Zöllner*

**Literature:** Feldhaus, 1922; Lücke, 1952 (pp. 631–666); McC, II (pp. 167–210); Solmi, 1976 (pp. 277–290); Gibbs-Smith, 1979; *Leonardo: Engineer and Architect*, 1987; Cianchi, 1988; Kemp/Roberts, 1989; *Prima di Leonardo*, 1991; *Renaissance Engineers*, 1996.

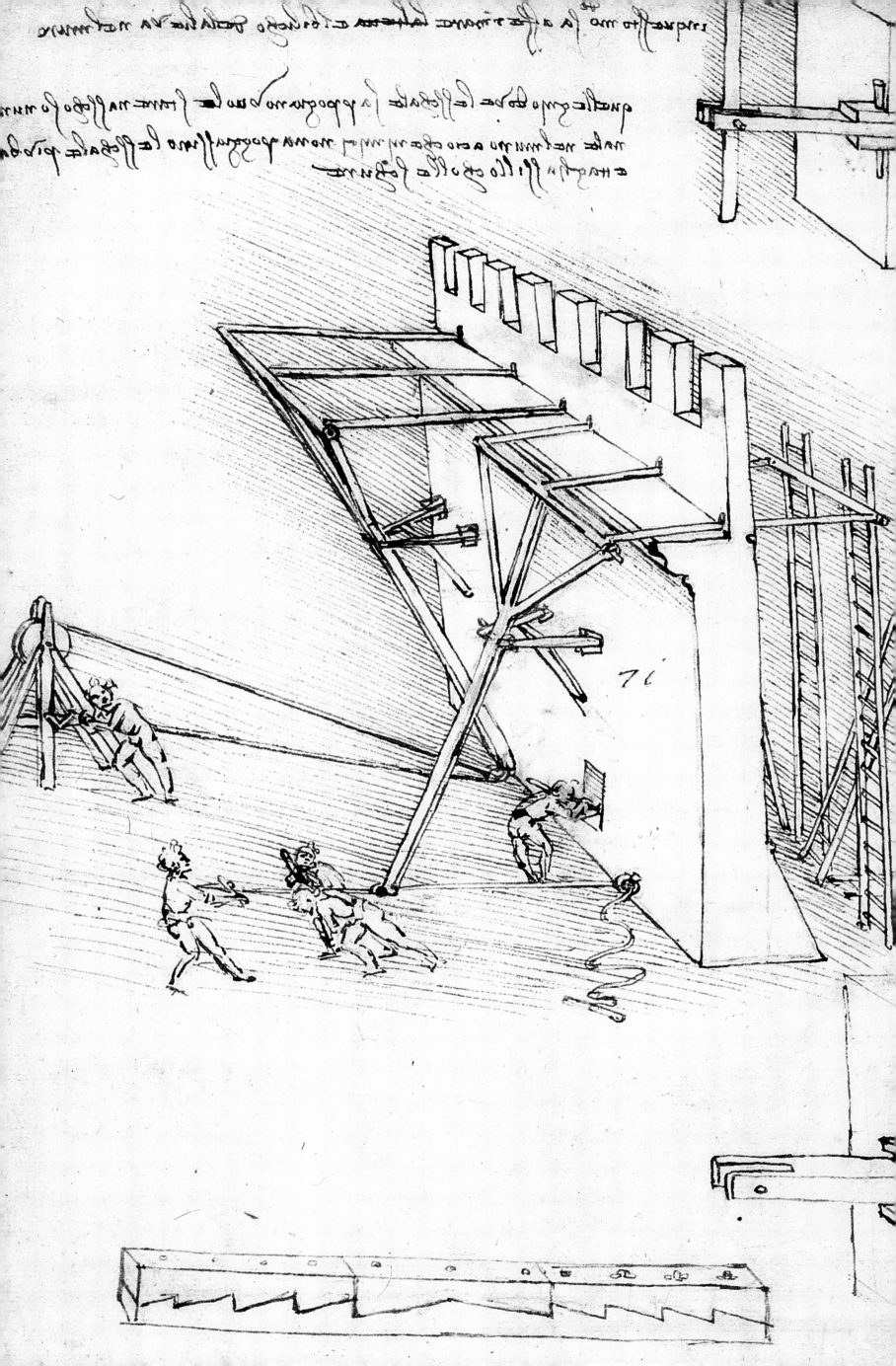

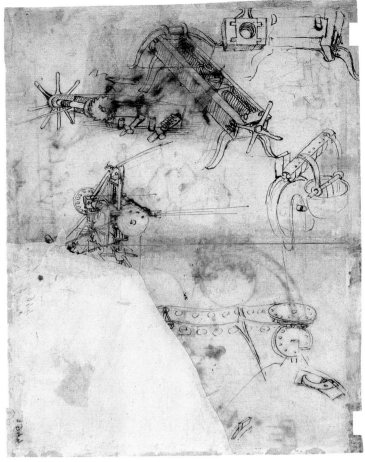

336

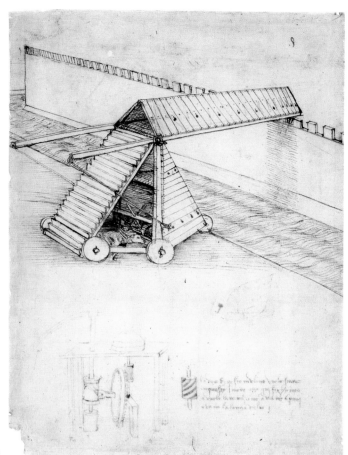

337

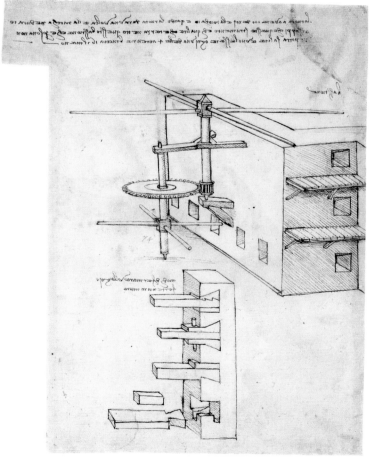

338

339

**336 Mechanism for Drawing Crossbows**, *c.* 1478
(verso of Cat. 104)
*Pen and ink, 206 x 266 mm
Florence, Galleria degli Uffizi,
Gabinetto dei Disegni e delle
Stampe, Inv. 446 Ev*

**337 Design for a Siege Machine with Covered Bridge**, *c.* 1480
*Pen and ink, 268 x 194 mm
Milan, Biblioteca Ambrosiana,
Codex Atlanticus, fol. 1084r/391v-a*

**338 Machine to Prevent Fortress Walls being Scaled**, *c.* 1480 (? before 1487)
*Pen and ink, 265 x 179–205 mm
Milan, Biblioteca Ambrosiana,
Codex Atlanticus, fol. 89r/32v-a*

**339 Mechanism for Repulsing Scaling Ladders**, *c.* 1480 (? before 1487)
*Pen and ink over chalk,
297 x 195 mm
Milan, Biblioteca Ambrosiana,
Codex Atlanticus, fol. 139r/49v-b*

▶ **340 Sheet of Studies with Multi-barrelled Guns**, *c.* 1482 (?)
*Pen and ink, 270 x 188 mm
Milan, Biblioteca Ambrosiana,
Codex Atlanticus, fol. 157r/56v-a*

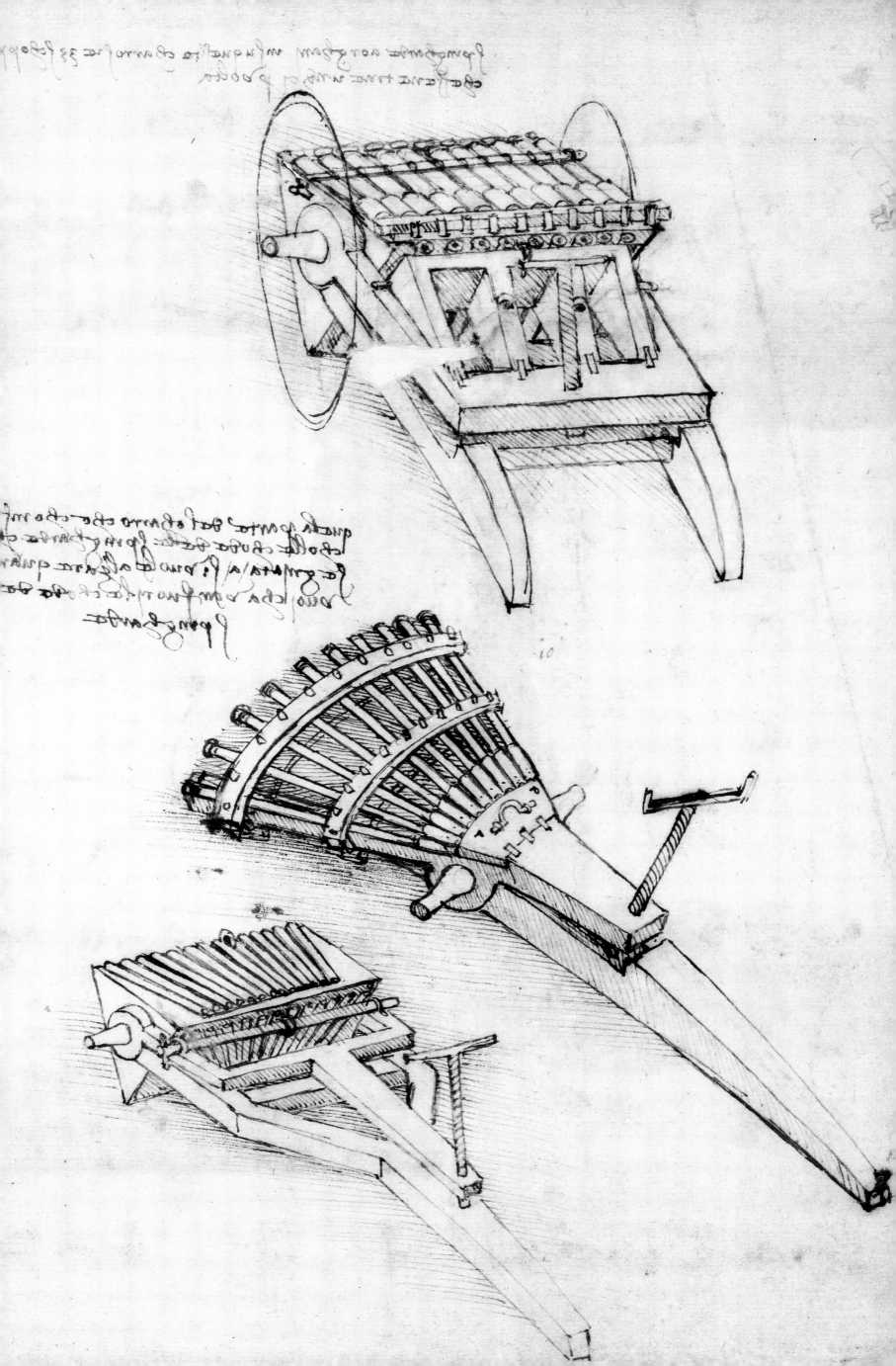

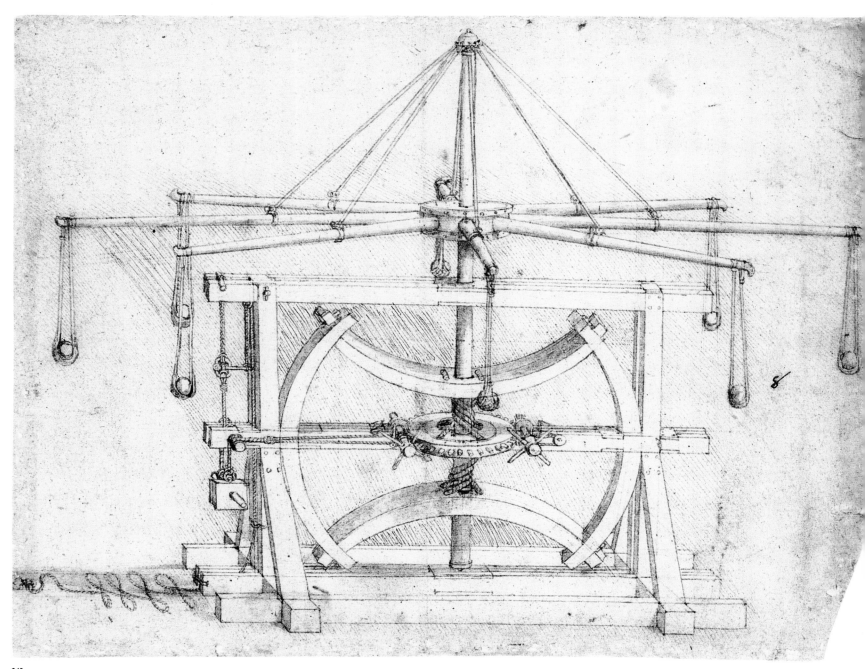

341

**341 Military Machine to
Catapult Stones,** *c. 1485*
*Pen and ink, 208 x 265 mm*
*Milan, Biblioteca Ambrosiana,*
*Codex Atlanticus, fol. 159b/57-b*

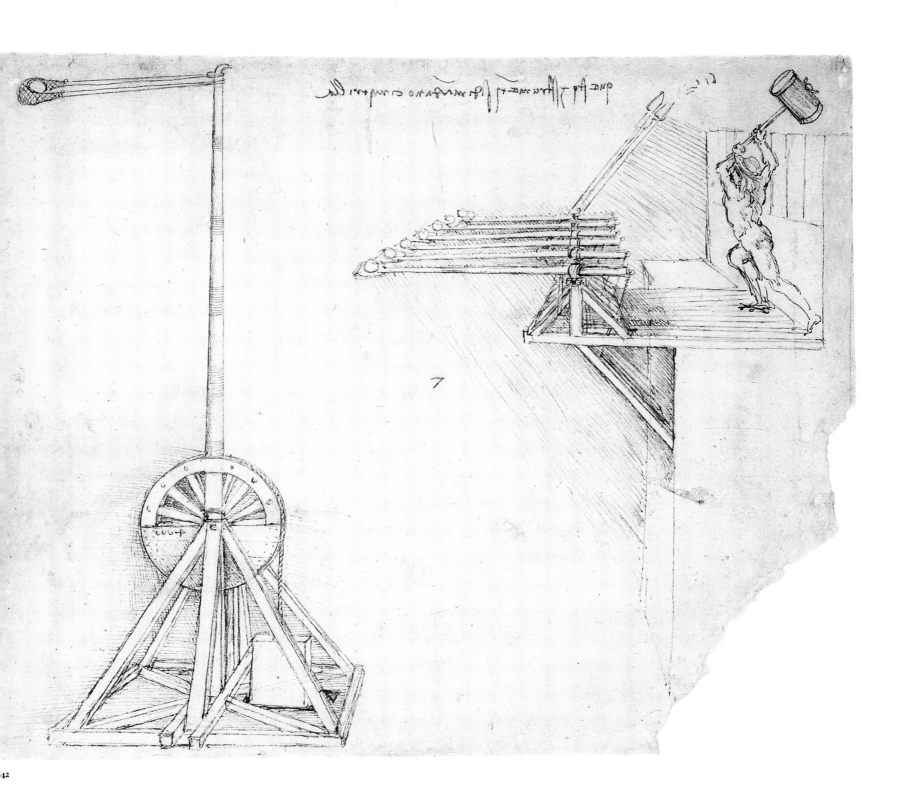

**342 Military Machine to
Catapult Stones,** *c. 1485*
*Pen and ink, 208 x 242 mm*
*Milan, Biblioteca Ambrosiana,*
*Codex Atlanticus, fol. 160a-r/57v-a*

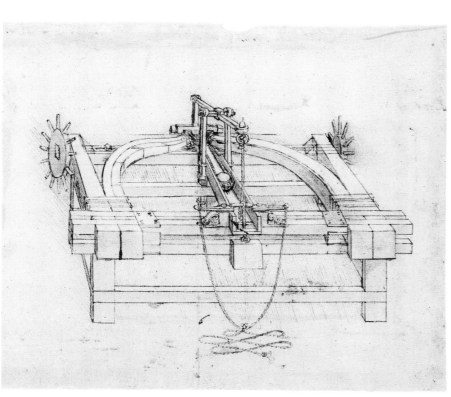

343

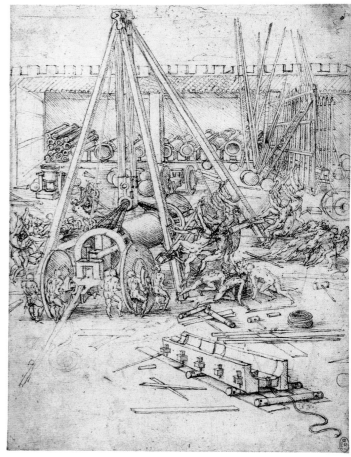

344

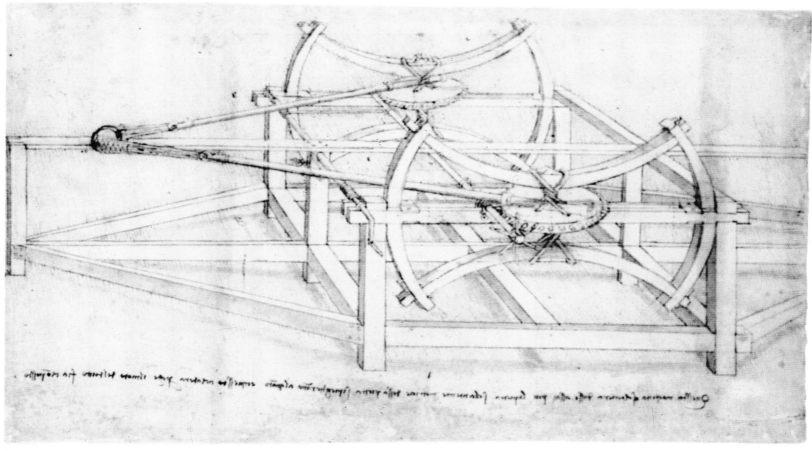

345

**343  Military Machine to
Catapult Stones,** *c.* **1485**
*Pen and ink, 179 x 243 mm*
*Milan, Biblioteca Ambrosiana,*
*Codex Atlanticus, fol. 160b-r/57v-b*

**344  Study with Hoist for
a Cannon in an Ordnance
Foundry,** *c.* **1487**
*Pen and ink on brownish prepared*
*paper, 250 x 183 mm*
*Windsor Castle, Royal Library*
*(RL 12647)*

**345  Machine for Hurling
Stones and Bombs,** *c.* **1485**
*Pen and ink, 172 x 305 mm*
*Milan, Biblioteca Ambrosiana,*
*Codex Atlanticus, fol. 145r/51v-b*

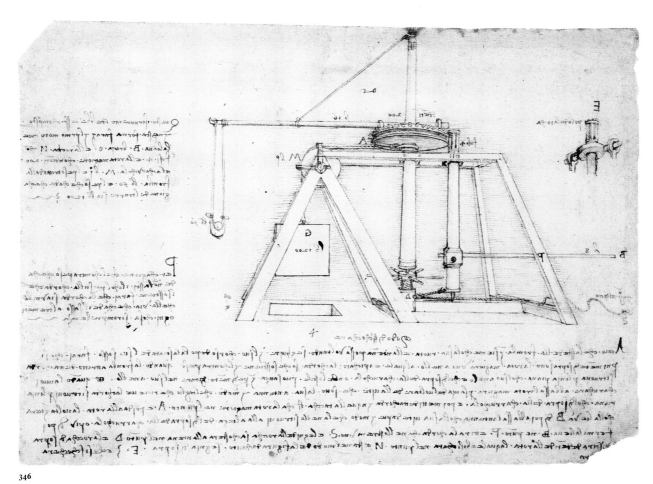

346

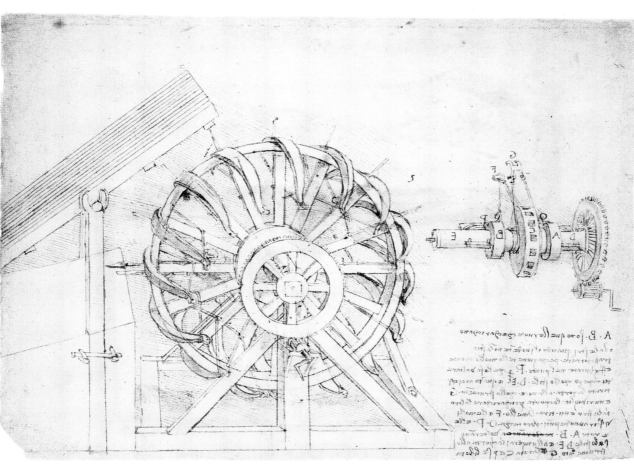

347

**346 Design for a Catapult,**
**c. 1485**
*Pen and ink, 220 x 300 mm*
*Milan, Biblioteca Ambrosiana,*
*Codex Atlanticus, fol. 182a-r/64v-a*

**347 Military Machine with**
**Sixteen Crossbows,** *c.* 1485
*Pen and ink, 220 x 300 mm*
*Milan, Biblioteca Ambrosiana,*
*Codex Atlanticus, fol. 182b-r/64v-b*

**▸ 348 Design for a Giant**
**Crossbow,** *c.* 1485
*Pen and ink, 203 x 275 mm*
*Milan, Biblioteca Ambrosiana, Codex*
*Atlanticus, fol. 149b-r/53v-b*

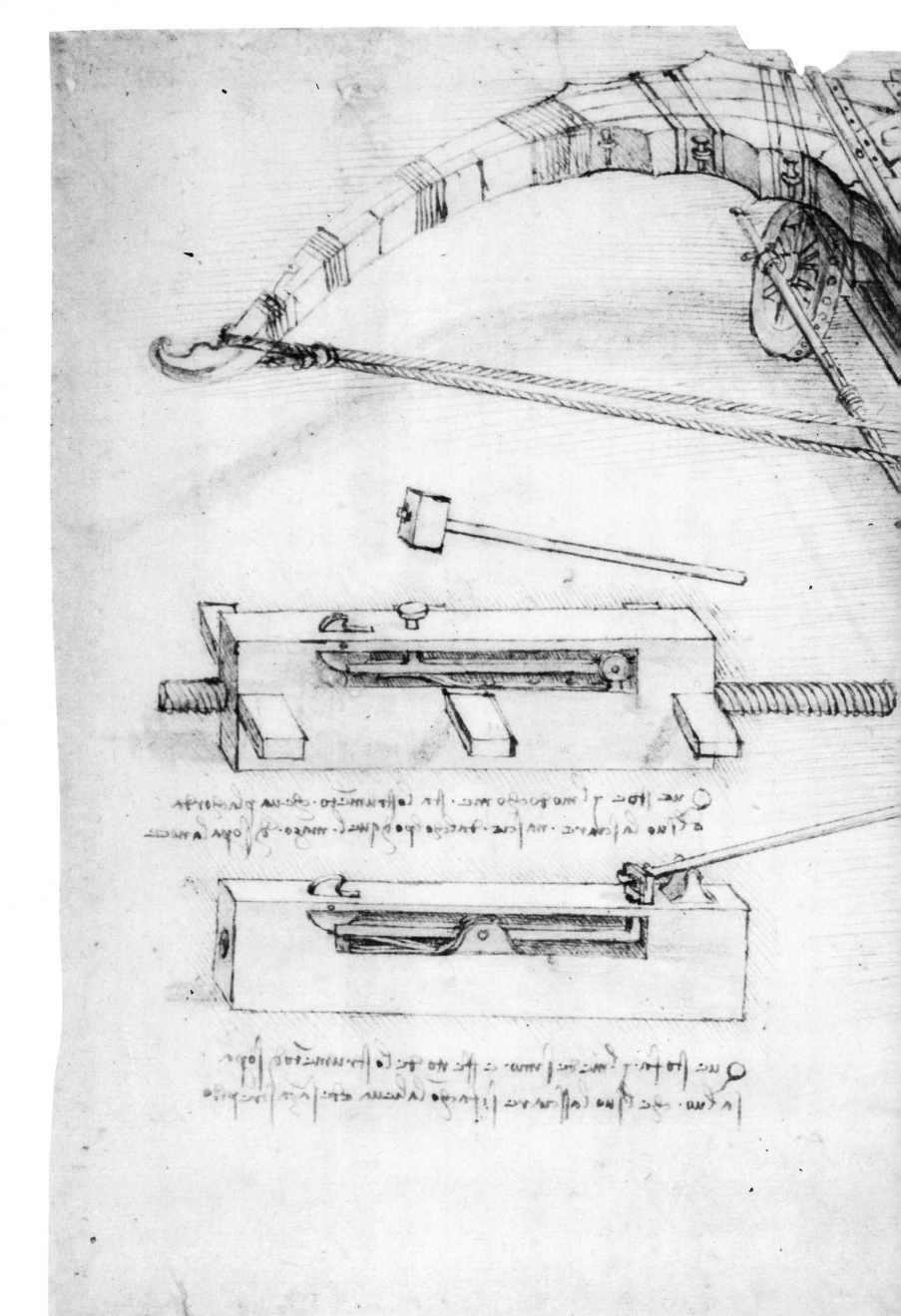

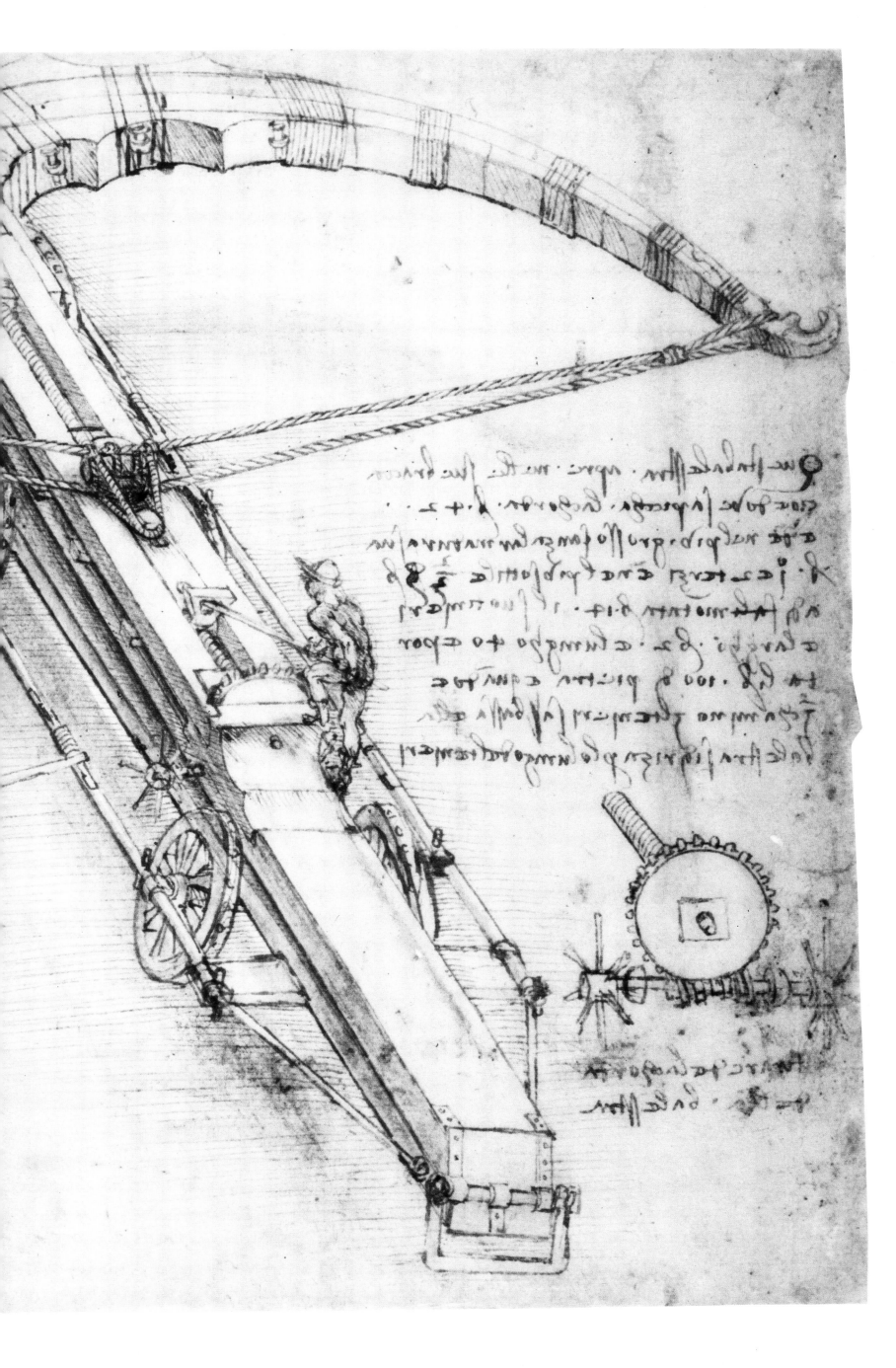

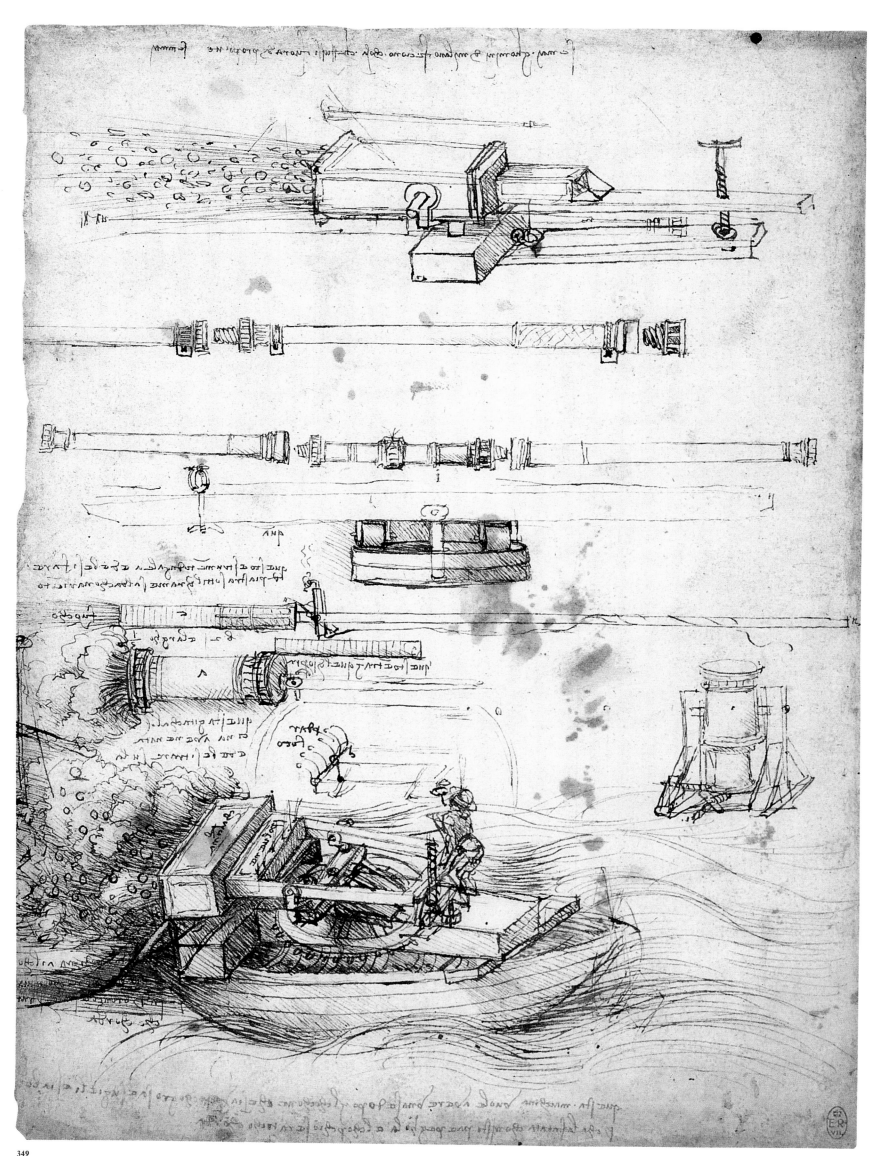

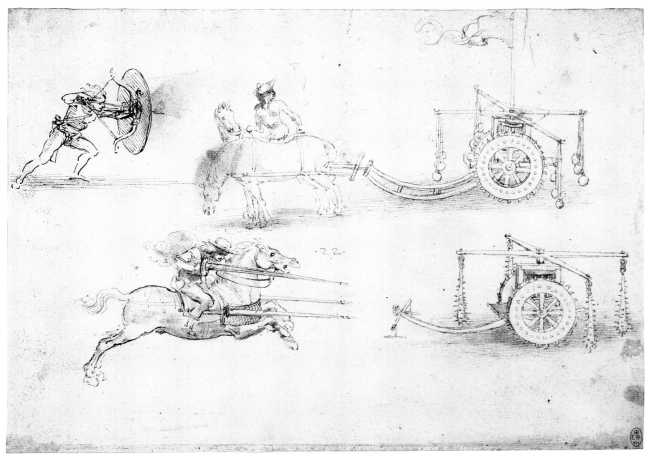

350

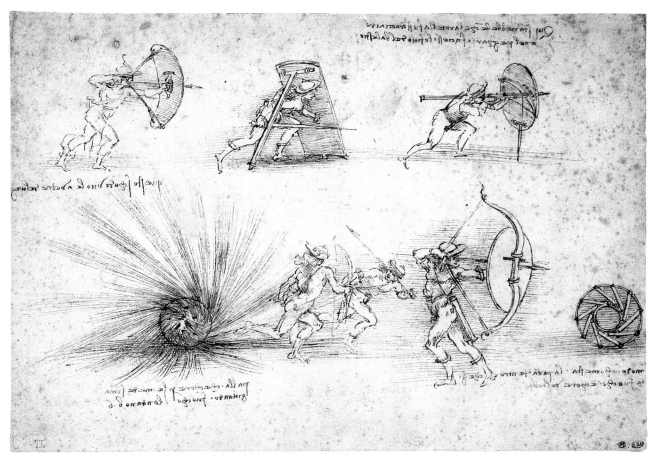

351

**349  Designs for Various Types of Cannon**, *c.* 1485
*Pen and ink, 282 x 205 mm*
*Windsor Castle, Royal Library*
*(RL 12652r)*

**350  Study with Battle Chariot, a Solder with Shield and a Horseman with Three Lances**, *c.* 1485–1488
*Pen and ink, 200 x 278 mm*
*Windsor Castle, Royal Library*
*(RL 12653r)*

**351  Study with Shields for Foot Soldiers and an Exploding Bomb**, *c.* 1485–1488
*Pen and ink, 200 x 273 mm*
*Paris, École nationale supérieure*
*des Beaux-Arts*

▶ **352  Design for a Scythed Chariot and Armoured Car (?)**, *c.* 1485–1488
*Pen and ink, 173 x 246 mm*
*London, British Museum*

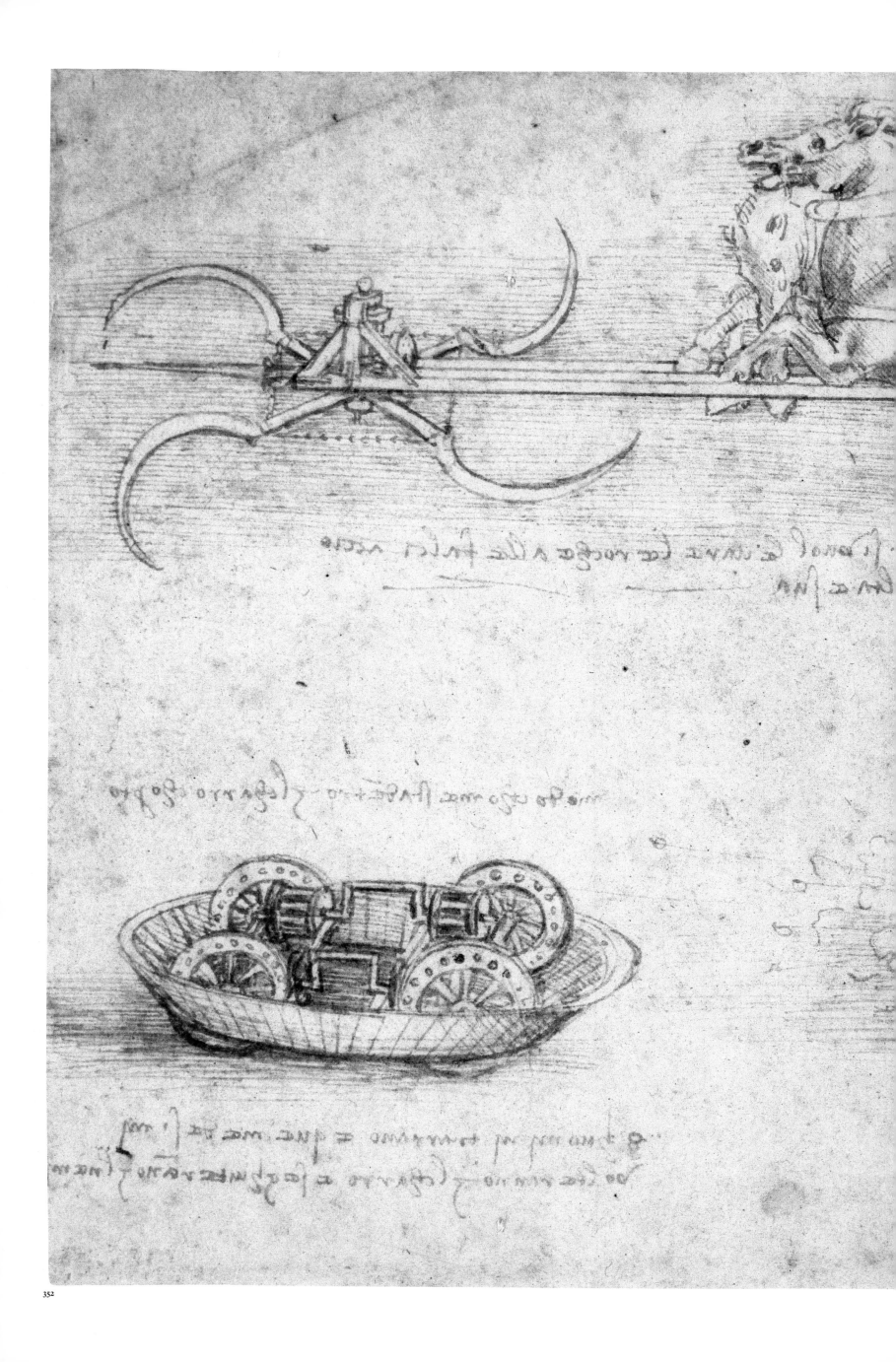

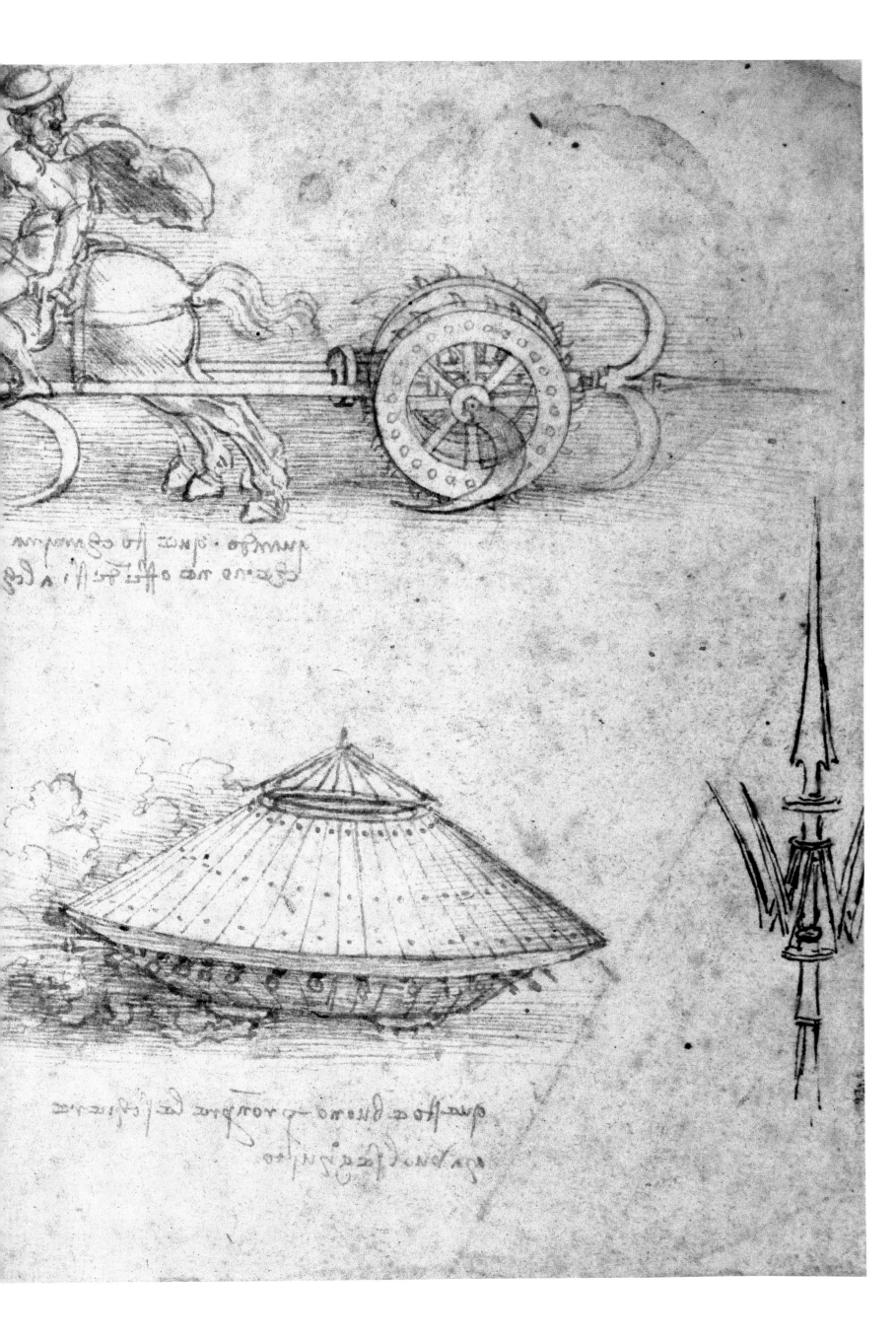

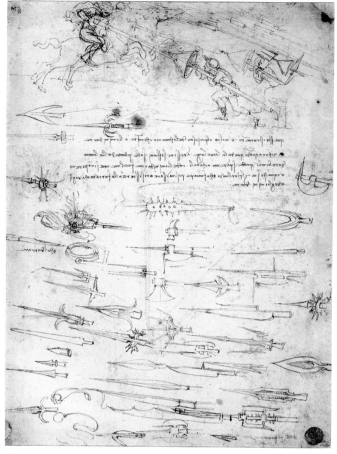

353

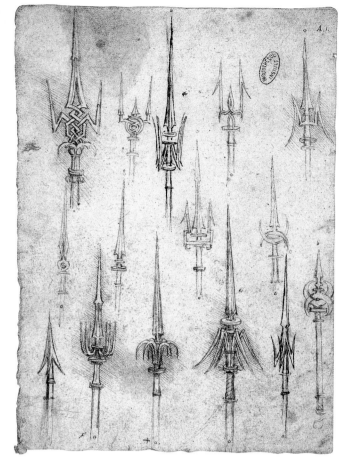

354

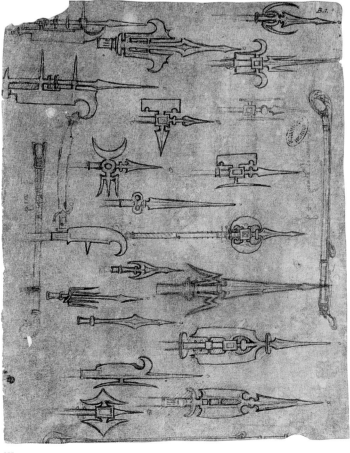

355

356

**353 Sheet of Studies of Foot Soldiers and Horsemen in Combat, and Halberds,**
*c.* **1485–1488**
*Pen and ink, 247 x 175 mm*
*Venice, Gallerie dell'Accademia*

**354 Study of Halberds,**
*c.* **1487–1490**
*Pen and ink, 210 x 144 mm*
*Paris, Bibliothèque de l'Institut de France, Codex Ashburnham 1875/1 (MS B 2184), fol. A.1*

**355 Study of Halberds,**
*c.* **1487–1490**
*Pen and ink, 210 x 160 mm*
*Paris, Bibliothèque de l'Institut de France, Codex Ashburnham 1875/1 (MS B 2184), fol. B.1*

**356 Study of Halberds,**
*c.* **1487–1490**
*Pen and ink, 215 x 155 mm*
*Paris, Bibliothèque de l'Institut de France, Codex Ashburnham 1875/1 (MS B 2184), fol. B.2*

**357 Study of Halberds,**
*c.* **1487–1490**
*Pen and ink, 212 x 146 mm*
*Paris, Bibliothèque de l'Institut de France, Codex Ashburnham 1875/1 (MS B 2184), fol. A.2*

357

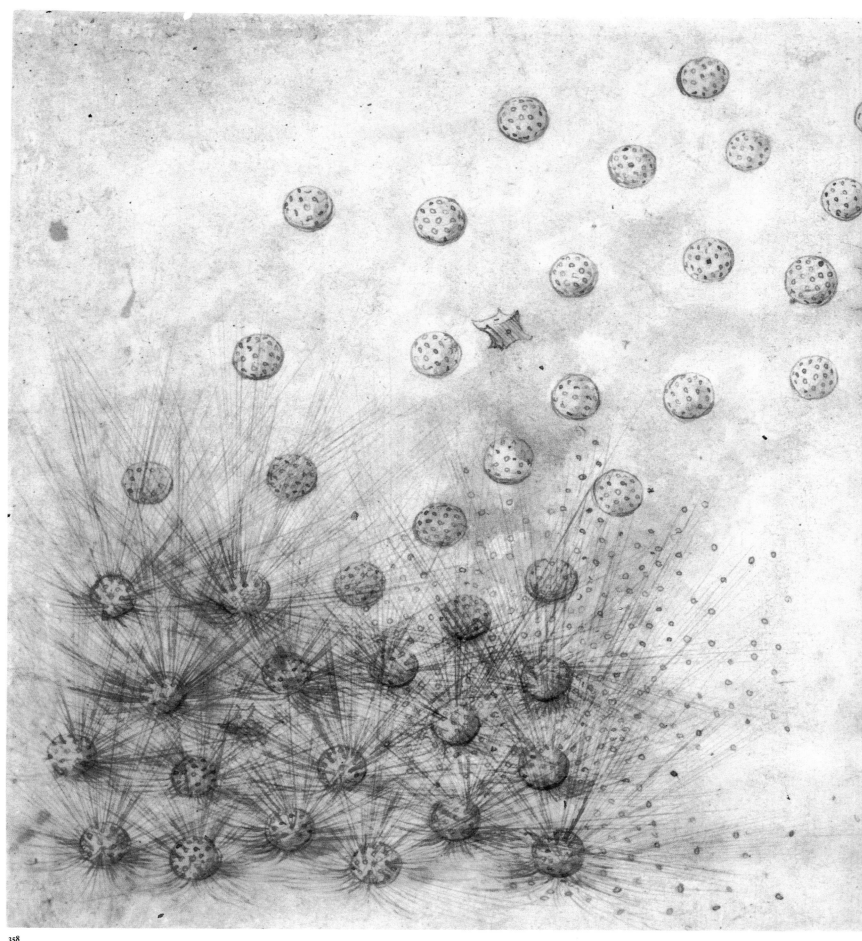

358

**358 Design for a Shrapnel
Mortar (Two Mortars with
Explosive Shells),** *c.* 1495–1499
*Pen and ink and Indian ink,*
*238 x 200 mm*
*Milan, Biblioteca Ambrosiana,*
*Codex Atlanticus, fol. 33r/9v-a*

# Bibliography


**1. ABBREVIATIONS**

**1.1. Anthologies of Leonardo's writings (see also 1.3.):**
McC: MacCurdy, 1977 (with page number)
McM: McMahon, 1956 (with paragraph number)
MK: Kemp/Walker, 1989 (with paragraph number)
PRC: Pedretti, 1977 (with page number)
RLW: Richter, 1970 (with paragraph number)
TPL: *Trattato di pittura/Das Buch von der Malerei*, ed. Ludwig, 1882, and ed. Pedretti/Vecce, 1995 (with number)

**1.2. Journals:**
AB: *The Art Bulletin*
AeH: *Artibus et Historiae*
AH: *Art History*
ALV: *Achademia Leonardi Vinci. Journal of Leonardo Studies*
AL: *Arte Lombarda*
BM: *The Burlington Magazine*
GBA: *Gazette des Beaux-Arts*
JWCI: *Journal of the Warburg and Courtauld Institutes*
MKIF: *Mitteilungen des Kunsthistorischen Institutes in Florence*
RV: *Raccolta Vinciana*
ZfKG: *Zeitschrift für Kunstgeschichte*

**1.3 Leonardo's writings (manuscripts):**
CA: Codex Atlanticus, Milan, Biblioteca Ambrosiana: *Leonardo da Vinci, Il codice atlantico della Biblioteca Ambrosiana a Milano*, ed. A. Marinoni, 24 vols, Florence 1974–1980
CL: Codex Leicester, Collection Bill Gates, Seattle: *The Codex Hammer* [i. e. the Codex Leicester], ed. C. Pedretti, Florence 1987 (see also Leonardo, 1999)
CM I–II: Codices Madrid I and II, Madrid, Biblioteca Nacional: *The Manuscripts of Leonardo da Vinci at the Biblioteca Nacional of Madrid*, ed. L. Reti, 5 vols, New York 1974
Codex Arundel, London, British Museum: *I manoscritti e i disegni di Leonardo da Vinci, il Codice Arundel 263*, 4 vols, Rome 1923–1930
Codex Forster, London, Victoria and Albert Museum: *Leonardo da Vinci, Il Codice Forster del Victoria and Albert Museum di Londra*, ed. A. Marinoni, 3 vols, Florence 1992
K/P: K.D. Keele/C. Pedretti, *Leonardo da Vinci. Corpus of the Anatomical Studies in the Collection of her Majesty the Queen at Windsor Castle*, 3 vols, London/New York 1978–1980
MSS A–I: Manuscripts A–I, Paris, Institut de France: Leonardo da Vinci, *I manoscritti del Institut de France*, ed. A. Marinoni, 12 vols, Florence 1986–1990
PDM: C. Pedretti (Hg.), *The Drawings and Miscellaneous Papers of Leonardo da Vinci in the Collection of her Majesty the Queen at Windsor Castle*, vol. 1: *Landscape, Plants and Water Studies*, London 1982, vol. 2: *Horses and Other Animals*, London 1987 (vol. 4: *Figure Studies*, and vol. 5: *Miscellaneous Papers*, in preparation)
RL: Royal Library, Windsor Castle: *The Drawings of Leonardo da Vinci in the Collection of Her Majesty the Queen at Windsor Castle*, ed. K. Clark/C. Pedretti, 3 vols, London 1968–1969 (first published 1935) [new edition: K. Keele/C. Pedretti, 1979–1980, Bibliography 2.1. – See also Pedretti/Roberts, 1984 Bibliography 3]

**2. SOURCES**
**2.1. Leonardo**
A. Chastel (ed.), *Leonardo da Vinci, Sämtliche Gemälde und die Schriften zur Malerei*, Munich 1990
K. Keele/C. Pedretti, *Leonardo da Vinci. Corpus of the Anatomical Studies in the Collection of Her Majesty the Queen at Windsor Castle*, 3 vols, London/New York 1978–1980
M. Kemp/M. Walker, *Leonardo on Painting*, New Haven/London 1989
*Leonardo da Vinci, Das Buch von der Malerei*, ed. H. Ludwig, 3 vols, Vienna 1882
Leonardo da Vinci. Der Codex Leicester, exh. cat., Munich/Berlin 1999/2000 [facsimile and German translation by M. Schneider]
Leonardo da Vinci, Libro di pittura, ed. C. Pedretti and C. Vecce, 2 vols, Florence 1995.
Leonardo da Vinci, *Der Vögel Flug. Sul volo degli uccelli*, ed. and trans. M. Schneider, Munich/Paris/London 2000
T. Lücke (ed.), *Leonardo da Vinci. Tagebücher und Aufzeichnungen*, 2nd edn, Leipzig 1952
H. Lüdecke, *Leonardo da Vinci im Spiegel seiner Zeit*, 2nd edn, Berlin 1953
E. MacCurdy (ed.), *The Notebooks of Leonardo da Vinci*, 2 vols, London 1977 (first published 1938)
A. McMahon (ed.), *Leonardo da Vinci. Treatise on Painting* (Codex Urbinas latinus 1270), 2 vols, Princeton 1956
J.P. Richter (ed.), The Literary Works of Leonardo da Vinci, 2 vols, 3rd edn, Oxford 1970 (first published 1883)

**2.2. Other sources (not Leonardo)**
Francesco Albertini, *Memoriale di molte statue e picture sono nell'inclyta ciptà di Fiorentia [...]*, Rome 1510 (reprint Letchworth 1909)
Anonimo Gaddiano, see Frey, 1892
Anonimo Morelliano, see Frimmel, 1888
de Beatis, see Pastor, 1905
L. Beltrami, *Documenti e memorie riguardanti la vita e le opere di Leonardo da Vinci*, Milan 1919
F. Benedettucci (ed.), *Il libro di Antonio Billi* [1506–1515/1527–1531], Anzio 1991
Billi, see Benedettucci, 1991
Giovanni Gaetano Bottari/Stefano Ticozzi, *Raccolta di lettere sulla pittura, scultura ed architettura*, 10 vols, Milan 1822–1825 (reprint Hildesheim 1976)
Neri di Gino Capponi, "Commentarii", in: Ludovico A. Muratori, *Rerum italicarum scriptores*, Milan 1731 (reprint 1981), XVIII, col. 1155–1220
Vincenzo Cartari, *Immagini delli Dei de gl'antichi*, Venice 1647
F. Casolini (ed.), *I Fioretti di San Francesco*, Milan 1926
Cennino Cennini, *Il libro dell'arte*, ed. F. Brunello, Vicenza 1998
Cesare Cesariano, *Di Lucio Vitruvio Pollione de Architectura* [...], Como 1521
Père Dan, *Le Trésor des merveilles de Fontainebleau*, Paris 1642
*Decor puellarum*, Venice 1461
Fioretti di San Francesco, see Casolini, 1926
K. Frey (ed.), *Il Codice Magliabechiano* [*c.* 1537 to 1547], Berlin 1892 (reprint Farnborough 1969)
T. Frimmel (ed.), *Der Anonimo Morelliano (Marcantonio Michiel's Notizia d'opere del disegno)*, Vienna 1888
Fulgentius Metaphoralis, see Liebeschütz, 1926
Giovanni Battista Gelli, "Vite d'artisti", in: *Archivio storico*, 17, 1896, pp. 33–62
C.E. Gilbert, *Italian Art 1400–1500. Sources and Documents*, Evanston 1980
Paolo Giovio, "Leonardi Vincii vita", in: P. Barocchi (ed.), *Scritti d'arte del Cinquecento* (La letteratura italiana. Storia e testi, XXXII), 3 vols, Milan/Naples 1971–1877, I, pp. 7–9 [also in Vecce, 1998, pp. 355–357, and Villata, 1999, no. 337]
Hieronymus, *Ausgewählte Briefe*, translated from the Latin by L. Schade, Munich 1936 (Bibliothek der Kirchenväter, 2nd series, XVI)
Serviliano Latuada, *Descrizione di Milano*, Milan 1738 (reprint Milan 1997)
H. Liebeschütz, *Fulgentius Metaphoralis*, Leipzig/Berlin 1926 (Studien der Bibliothek Warburg, IV)
Gian Paolo Lomazzo, *Scritti sulle arti*, ed. R.P. Ciardi, 2 vols, Florence 1973–1974
Luca Pacioli, *Summa de arithmetica, geometria, proportioni et proportionalita*, Venice 1494
Luca Pacioli, *Divina proportione. Die Lehre vom Goldenen Schnitt [1509]*, ed. and trans. C. Winterberg, Vienna 1889
L. v. Pastor, *Die Reise des Kardinals Luigi d'Aragona durch Deutschland, die Niederlande, Frankreich und Oberitalien, 1517–1518, beschrieben von Antonio de Beatis*, Freiburg 1905
Francesco Petrarca, *Opere*, Florence 1975
Pliny the Elder, *Naturkunde/Naturalis historiae*, ed. and trans. R. König, Munich 1977
G. Poggi (ed.), *Leonardo da Vinci. La vita di Giorgio Vasari nuovamente commentata*, Florence 1919
Giuseppe Richa, *Notizie istoriche delle chiese fiorentine*, 10 vols, Florence 1754–1762 (reprint Rome 1972)
Michelangelo Salvi, *Historie di Pistoia e fazioni d'Italie*, 3 vols, Rome 1656–1662
Giovanni Simonetta, *De gestis Francisci Sphortiae*, Milan 1483 (also in: *Rerum italicarum scriptores*, vol. 21, 1732)
G. Sironi, *Nuovi documenti riguardanti la Vergine delle Rocce di Leonardo da Vinci*, Florence 1981
Lorenzo Spirito, *L'altro Marte*, Venice 1489
Carlo Torre, *Il ritratto di Milano*, Milan 1674
Giorgio Vasari, *Le vite de' più eccellenti architetti, pittori, et scultori italiani [1550]*, ed. L. Bellosi and A. Rossi, Turin 1986
Giorgio Vasari, *Le vite de' più eccellenti pittori scultori ed architettori [1568]*, ed. G. Milanesi, 9 vols, Florence 1906
Giorgio Vasari, *Lives of the Artists*, trans. G. Bull, Harmondsworth 1965
Vasari, see also Poggi, 1919
E. Villata, *Leonardo da Vinci. I documenti e le testimonianze contemporanee*, Milan 1999
Gasparo Visconti, *I canzonieri per Beatrice d'Este e per Bianca Maria Sforza*, ed. P. Bongrani, Milan 1979
Jacobus da Voragine, *The Golden Legend*, trans. W.G. Ryan, 2 vols, Princeton 1993

**3. SECONDARY LITERATURE**
F. Ames-Lewis, "Drapery 'Pattern' Drawings in Ghirlandaio's Workshop and Ghirlandaio's Early Apprenticeship", in: AB, 63, 1981, pp. 49-62 (Ames-Lewis, 1981a)
F. Ames-Lewis, *Drawing in Early Renaissance Italy*, New Haven/London 1981
F. Ames-Lewis/J. Wright, *Drawing in the Italian Renaissance Workshop*, London 1983
D. Arasse, *Leonardo da Vinci. The Rhythm of the World*, New York 1998 (first published Paris 1997)
C.C. Bambach, *Drawing and Painting in the Italian Renaissance Workshop. Theory and Practice*, 1300–1600, Cambridge (Mass.) 1999
M. Baratta, "Contributi alla storia della cartografia d'Italia III. La carta della Toscana di Leonardo da Vinci", in: *Memorie geografiche*, 5, 1911, pp. 5–76
B. Berenson, *The Drawings of the Florentine Painters*, Chicago 1938
G. Berra, *La storia dei canoni proporzionali del corpo umano e gli sviluppi in area lombarda alla fine del Cinquecento*, in: RV, 25, 1993, pp. 159–310
A. Beyer/W. Prinz (eds.), *Die Kunst und das Studium der Natur vom 14. zum 16. Jahrhundert*, Weinheim 1987
S. Braunfels-Esche, *Leonardo da Vinci. Das anatomische Werk*, Stuttgart 1961
V.L. Bush, "Leonardo's Sforza Monument and Cinquecento Sculpture", in: AL, 50, 1978, pp. 47–68
F. Caroli, Leonardo. *Studi di fisiognomica*, Milan 1991
G. Castelfranco, *Studi vinciani*, Rome 1966
M. Cianchi, *Die Maschinen Leonardo da Vincis*, Florence 1988
K. Clark/C. Pedretti, *The Drawings of Leonardo da Vinci in the Collection of Her Majesty the Queen at Windsor Castle*, 3 vols, London 1968–1969 (first published 1935)
B. Degenhart, "Eine Gruppe von Gewandstudien des jungen Fra Bartolomeo", in: *Münchner Jahrbuch der bildenden Kunst*, 11, 1934, pp. 222–231
S.Y. Edgerton, Jr., "The Renaissance Development of the Scientific Illustration", in: *Science and the Arts in the Renaissance*, ed. J.W. Shirley and F.D. Hoeniger, Washington, DC, etc. 1985, pp. 168–197
W.A. Emboden, *Leonardo da Vinci on Plants and Gardens*, Portland 1987
F. Fehrenbach, *Licht und Wasser. Zur Dynamik naturphilosophischer Leitbilder im Werk Leonardo da Vincis*, Tübingen 1997
F.M. Feldhaus, *Leonardo der Techniker und Erfinder*, Jena 1922
J. Gantner, *Leonardos Visionen von der Sintflut und vom Untergang der Welt*, Berne 1958
C. Gibbs-Smith, *The Inventions of Leonardo da Vinci*, Oxford 1978
E.H. Gombrich, "Leonardo's Method of Working out Compositions", in: Gombrich, *Norm and Form*, Oxford 1966, pp. 58–63 (first published in French in 1954)
E.H. Gombrich, "The Form of Movement in Water and Air", in: Gombrich, 1976, pp. 39–56
E.H. Gombrich, *The Heritage of Apelles*, London 1976 (Gombrich 1976a)
E.H. Gombrich, "Ideal and Type in Italian Renaissance Painting", in: Gombrich, *New Light on Old Masters*, Oxford 1986, pp. 89–124
J. Guillaume, "Leonardo and Architecture", in: *Leonardo. Engineer and Architect*, 1987, pp. 207–286
L.H. Heydenreich, *Die Sakralbau-Studien Leonardo da Vinci's*, Leipzig 1929
L.H. Heydenreich, "La Sainte-Anne de Léonard de Vinci", in: GBA, 10, 1933, pp. 205–219 (also in Heydenreich, 1988, pp. 13–22)
*Il disegno fiorentino del tempo di Lorenzo il Magnifico*, exh. cat., Florence 1992
K.D. Keele, *Leonardo da Vinci's Elements of the Science of Man*, New York/London etc. 1983
M. Kemp, *Leonardo da Vinci. The Marvellous Works of Nature and Man*, London 1981
M. Kemp/J. Roberts (eds), *Leonardo da Vinci*, exh. cat., London 1989
M.W. Kwakkelstein, *Leonardo da Vinci as a Physiognomist. Theory and Drawing Practice*, Leiden 1994
D. Laurenza, *"De figura umana". Fisiognomica, anatomia e arte in Leonardo*, Florence 2001
*Leonardo da Vinci. Die Gewandstudien*, exh. cat., Munich/Paris/London 1989
*Leonardo da Vinci. Engineer and Architect*, exh. cat., Montreal 1987
*Leonardo da Vinci. Natur und Landschaft. Naturstudien aus der Königlichen Bibliothek in Windsor Castle*, exh. cat., Stuttgart/Zurich 1983
*Leonardo da Vinci's Sforza Monument Horse. The Art and the Engineering*, ed. D. Cole Ahl, London 1995
*Leonardo e le vie d'aqua*, exh. cat., Florence 1983
*Leonardo & Venezia*, exh. cat., Milan 1992
K. Lippincott, "The Art of Cartography in Fifteenth-Century Florence", in: *Lorenzo the Magnificent. Culture and Politics*, ed. M. Mallet and N. Mann, London 1996, pp. 131–149.
P.C. Marani, *L'architettura fortificata negli studi di Leonardo da Vinci*, Florence 1984
J. Meder, *Die Handzeichnung*, Vienna 1919
B. Morley, "The Plant Illustrations of Leonardo da Vinci", in: BM, 121, 1979, pp. 553–560
J. Nathan, "Some Drawing Practices of Leonardo da Vinci: New Light on the Saint Anne", in: MKIF, 36, 1992, pp. 85–102
J. Nathan, *The Working Methods of Leonardo da Vinci and Their Relation to Previous Artistic Practice*, PhD thesis, London (Courtauld Institute of Art) 1995 (forthcoming)
J. Nathan, "Kunst und Naturbetrachtung. Funktionale Bildformeln im Werk Leonardos", in: F. Fehrenbach (ed.), *Leonardo da Vinci*, Munich 2002 (forthcoming)
C.D. O'Malley/J.B. de C.M. Saunders, *Leonardo da Vinci on the Human Body*, New York 1952
E. Panofsky, "Die Entwicklung der Proportionslehre als Abbild der Stilentwicklung", in: *Monatshefte für Kunstwissenschaft*, 14, 1921, pp. 188–219
C. Pedretti, *Studi vinciani*, Geneva 1957
C. Pedretti, *Leonardo da Vinci on Painting. A Lost Book (Libro A)*, London 1965 (first published 1964)
C. Pedretti, *Leonardo da Vinci. The Royal Palace at Romorantin*, Cambridge (Mass.) 1972
C. Pedretti/J. Roberts (ed.), *Leonardo da Vinci. Drawings of Horses and Other Animals from the Royal Library at Windsor Castle*, New York 1984
A. Perrig, "Leonardo: Die Anatomie der Erde", in: *Jahrbuch der Hamburger Kunstsammlungen*, 25, 1980, pp. 51–80
A.E. Popham, *The Drawings of Leonardo da Vinci With a New Introductory Essay by M. Kemp*, London 1994 (first published 1946)
*Prima di Leonardo. Cultura delle macchine a Siena nel Rinascimento*, ed. P. Galluzzi, Milan 1991
*Renaissance Engineers from Brunelleschi to Leonardo da Vinci*, exh. cat., ed. P. Galluzzi, Florence 1996
*Rinascimento da Brunelleschi a Michelangelo. La Rappresentazione dell'architettura*, exh. cat., Milan 1994
R. Schofield, "Amadeo, Bramante and Leonardo and the 'tiburio' of Milan Cathedral", in: ALV, 2, 1989, pp. 68–100
R. Schofield, "Leonardo's Milanese Architecture: Career, Sources and Graphic Techniques", in: ALV, 4, 1991, pp. 111–157
E. Solmi, *Scritti Vinciani* (Le fonti dei manoscritti di Leonardo da Vinci e altri studi), Florence 1976 (first published 1908–1911)
G.-B de Toni, *Le piante e gli animali in Leonardo da Vinci*, Bologna 1922
C.A. Truesdell, "Fundamental Mechanics in the Madrid Codices", in: *Leonardo e l'età della ragione*, 1982, pp. 309–324
M. Wiemers, *Bildform und Werkgenese. Studien zur zeichnerischen Bildvorbereitung in der italienischen Malerei zwischen 1450 und 1490*, Munich/Berlin 1996
F. Zöllner, *Vitruvs Proportionsfigur*, Worms 1987
V.P. Zubov, *Leonardo da Vinci*, Cambridge (Mass.) 1968 (first published in Russian in 1962)

# Credits

ENDPAPERS:
**Torso of a Man in Profile, the Head Squared for Proportion, and Two Horsemen (Detail), c. 1490 and c. 1504**
*Pen and ink and red chalk over metalpoint, 280 x 222 mm*
*Venice, Gallerie dell'Accademia, Inv. 236r*

PAGE 2:
**Anatomical Study of the Layers of the Brain and Scalp, c. 1490-1493**
*Pen, two shades of brown ink and red chalk, 203 x 152 mm*
*Windsor Castle, Royal Library (RL 12603r)*

To stay informed about upcoming TASCHEN titles, please request our magazine at www.taschen.com or write to TASCHEN America, 6671 Sunset Boulevard, Suite 1508, USA-Los Angeles, CA 90028, Fax: +1-323-463.4442. We will be happy to send you a free copy of our magazine which is filled with information about all of our books.

© 2004 TASCHEN GmbH
Hohenzollernring 53, D–50672 Köln
**www.taschen.com**

Project management: Petra Lamers-Schütze, Cologne
Editorial coordination: Juliane Steinbrecher, Cologne
Translation: Karen Williams, Whitley Chapel
Design: Claudia Frey & Angelika Taschen, Cologne
Production: Martina Ciborowius, Cologne

ISBN 0–681–16586–3
Printed in China

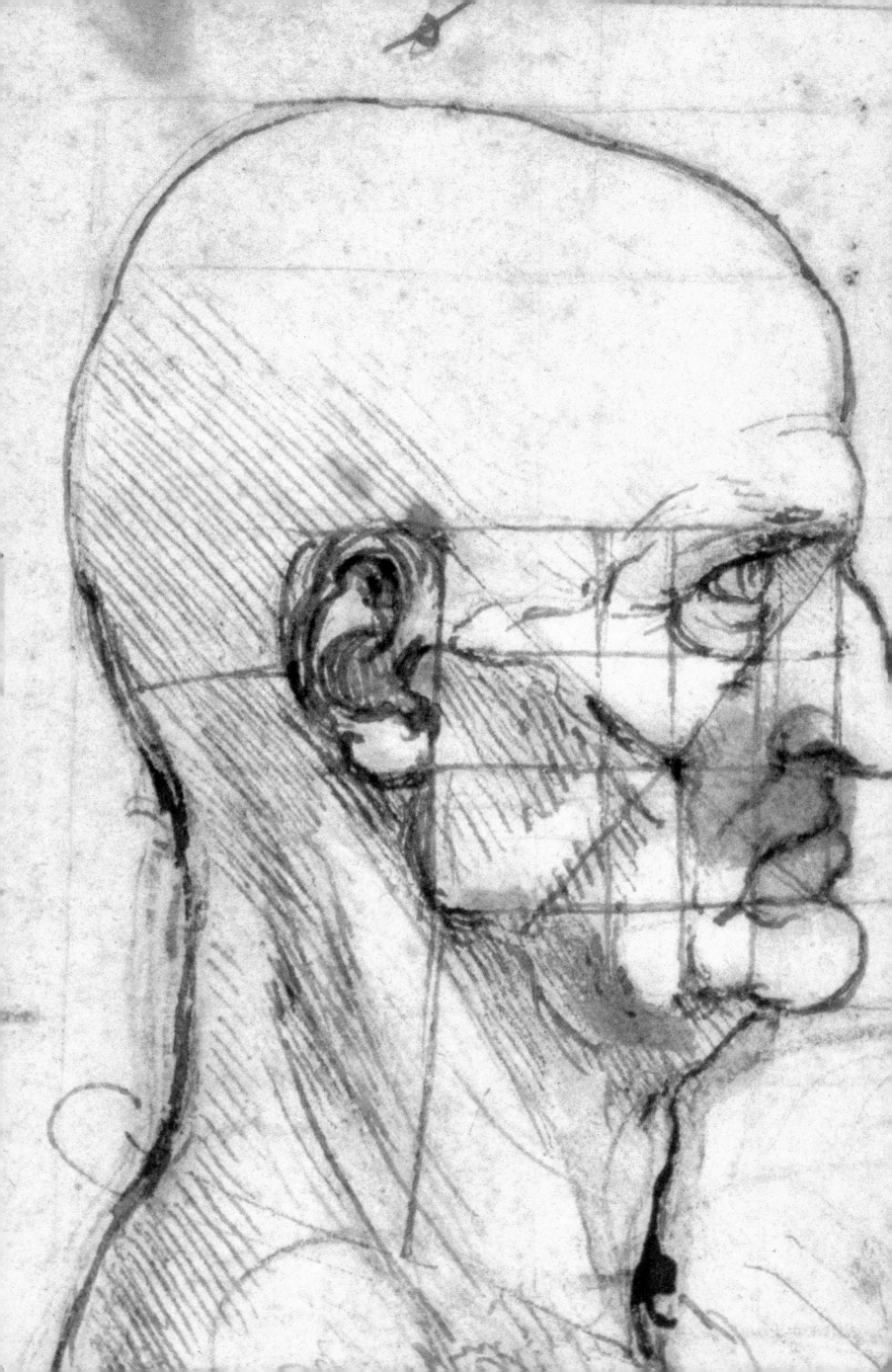